The Bureau

The Bureau

My Thirty Years in Hoover's FBI

William C. Sullivan

with **Bill Brown**

W · W · Norton & Company · New York · London

First Edition

The text of this book is typeset in photocomposition Caledonia, with Bembo and Clarendon Bold display. Manufacturing is by The Maple-Vail Book Manufacturing Group.

DESIGNER: MARJORIE J. FLOCK

Library of Congress Cataloging in Publication Data
Sullivan, William C
    The Bureau.
    Includes index.
        1. United States.   Federal Bureau of Investigation.
    2. Hoover, John Edgar, 1895–1972.   I. Brown, Bill,
    1930–   II. Title.
    HV8138.S93   1979   353.007'4   79-15416

ISBN 0-393-01236-0

1 2 3 4 5 6 7 8 9 0

*To the special agents
in the field
who are the backbone of the Bureau*

Contents

Introduction

I FIRST MET Bill Sullivan in the summer of 1968 when I was doing the preliminary research for a television documentary about the Vietcong. One important angle of the story seemed to be the extent to which antiwar activists had contact with Communist nations. We were being told by the Johnson administration that much of the militancy connected with the demonstrations was inspired by Communists inside and outside of the United States. I wanted to know if antiwar factions were trained by or received funds from the North Vietnamese, or maybe the Russians. I telephoned FBI headquarters in Washington and arranged for an appointment with their Crime Records Division, which, we all knew, functioned as a kind of press liaison office.

Although no one at the FBI knew me, an appointment was set for me to meet with a top official, the assistant director of the Intelligence Division, someone named William C. Sullivan. I fully expected to hear a bureaucratic litany about how many of those against the war were inspired by and even paid by Communists.

Sullivan was a short neat man who spoke logically and clearly. The total impression was that of a James Cagney type with a New England accent thrown in. What he said threw me off balance. It wasn't what I expected an FBI official to tell a stranger. Sullivan said, "There are only a tiny handful of antiwar people who have had contact with Communist nations. As far as American Communists are concerned, forget it. They are no longer important. Most of the young people who are against the war are simply that—young people who are patriotic but who are totally committed to seeing that the United States gets out of the war in Vietnam."

During the next few years Bill Sullivan and I met often. Each time, Sullivan would praise the FBI agents in the field and damn Hoover for his emphasis on public relations and his lack of judgment.

When Hoover forced Sullivan out of the bureau, in 1971, Sullivan was bitter but determined to play some role in the reorganization of the department which he had served for thirty years. I was convinced that he never wanted to become the director of the FBI: what he wanted was to make sure that a Hoover with such unwarranted political power would never again head the organization.

A few years after he left the bureau, Sullivan began talking to me about a book he wanted to write about his life in the FBI—a book, he said, that would set the record straight and give the public an opportunity to know exactly what it was like from the inside. He asked me to help.

During the next two years I met with Sullivan on dozens of occasions, either at his home in New Hampshire or near his birthplace in Bolton, Massachusetts. He was an energetic and rapid talker with a remarkable memory. What especially stands out from those sessions was that whenever he was quoting Hoover, which was often, he would speak in a loud, cold, and very disagreeable voice.

By July of 1977 I had compiled everything Bill wanted to say about the FBI and we were ready to put the book into final form. But on November 9, 1977, I saw a wire service report that he had been killed in a hunting accident in the woods near his home in New Hampshire. That report was followed by a bulletin from TASS, the Soviet press agency, doubting the accidental nature of his death and suggesting that because of all he knew he was the victim of an FBI/CIA plot. I flew up to Bill's home for the funeral and spoke with the local authorities as well as his family. I was convinced, as were they, that his tragic death was indeed accidental.

What follows is Bill Sullivan's book—every word is his, taken from conversations with him and from his texts. It is Sullivan's own story of his thirty years in Hoover's FBI.

BILL BROWN

New York City
March 1979

The Bureau

ONE

The End and the Beginning

SEPTEMBER 30, 1971—*it was our last meeting. Hoover was shouting.*

"I've never received such a letter since I've been the director of the FBI, and nobody has ever spoken to me like this before."

"If someone had spoken to you like this before," I answered, "I wouldn't have to be speaking to you like this now. I should have told you these things a long time ago."

Staring down at my memorandum before him on his desk, Hoover said, "I've been giving this controversy between us a good deal of prayer."

The old fraud! Involking prayer. That was a first for him. Several days later, thinking back on the meeting, I realized that I should have said, "Mr. Hoover, let's both kneel down right here, right now, and pray together."

What I did tell him was that he ruled the bureau by fear and that men along in years who had served faithfully in the FBI lived in dread of him. I added that I no longer intended to be intimidated. I told him everything I'd been wanting to tell him since I was a new agent.

When I finished, he grew red and began to sputter and stammer. Finally he shouted, "It's very clear that you have no faith in my leadership."

"Yes," I replied. "Nothing could be more clear than that."

"You no longer have any faith in my administration."

I agreed again. "Right. I think you'd be doing the country a great service if you retired."

"Well, I don't intend to," he shot back, his eyes still on my letter.

"Senator Green stayed on in the Senate till he was ninety years of age."

Hoover paused to let that sink in. Finally, for the first time he looked up and our eyes met.

"I've taken this up with Attorney General Mitchell and he agrees with me that it is you who should be forced out. I've discussed this matter with President Nixon and he also agrees."

I walked out.

The next morning I couldn't get into my office. The locks had been changed. My name had been removed from the door.

After thirty years in the FBI, I was out.

● ● ●

You are hereby offered an appointment as a Special Agent in the Federal Bureau of Investigation, United States Department of Justice, in Grade CAFO, with a Salary at the rate of $3,200 per annum.

The letter was signed by J. Edgar Hoover, director of the Federal Bureau of Investigation. I received it on 3 July 1941 and read it with mixed emotions. In fact, when two college friends who had joined the FBI first suggested I apply, the application stayed in my desk for weeks while I weighed the pros and cons.

Although it would be half a year before the Japanese bombed Pearl Harbor, even in mid-1941 it was obvious that America's participation in the war in Europe was merely a matter of time. I was eager to join the armed forces, and I had already filed an application with army intelligence requesting foreign duty.

I was working for the Internal Revenue Service in Boston then, and when I did decide to take the FBI exam, my boss told me he would not approve my transfer. I took my problem to the top IRS man in Boston, who agreed to authorize my release—but only because I was going to the FBI. He never would have let me go to any other branch of government, he assured me, and then started telling stories of brave agents and dangerous criminals, of the exciting and worthwhile life I would soon be leading. In the years that followed, from the early 1940s through the late 1960s, wherever I went in this country, I met thousands of men and women in every profession who shared this starry-eyed impression of the FBI. From the beginning, I was intrigued by the FBI's public relations operation, and by the time I held senior FBI staff positions I realized that J. Edgar Hoover had created a public relations miracle.

Once I had passed the preliminary exam and gained my release from the IRS (I had not heard from army intelligence), the only obstacle still to be overcome was of my own making: Did I really want to join the FBI? I knew nothing about law enforcement. I wasn't even very interested in learning.

My only ambition was to join the faculty of a small New England college. I had been an English teacher in my hometown of Bolton, Massachusetts, before I went to work for the Internal Revenue Service. My roots were in Bolton, a town of only about four hundred people, where I grew up on the land my parents farmed for fifty years. I wanted to settle in Bolton or a town very much like it. I took the job in Boston only because it gave me the opportunity to take courses toward my graduate degree while allowing me to work at the same time. But I knew I'd have to forget about my teaching career if I went to work as a special agent. Working for the FBI would be a full-time job.

In my confusion, I turned to one of the two agents who had been responsible for my application, bombarded him with questions, and finally presented him with a questionnaire I had devised. If FBI officials had seen that questionnaire with its pages of doubts and criticism I would never have been hired. But my friend kept my questions to himself, and though I remained ambivalent about the bureau, his answers convinced me to try for the job. On 4 August 1941, I was one of fifty men who reported to the Department of Justice to train as a special agent. I knew this was to be no ordinary job. I felt that the fifty of us were on the threshold of the unknown.

First there were the details common to every new job: forms to be filled out, documents to be signed, a tour of the office. On the tour, I grew curious about a group of young women I noticed reading and clipping newspapers, and I stopped to ask one of them what they were doing.

"Clipping articles critical of the director of the bureau," she answered. And she went on to tell me that every field office in the country ran its own clipping service. The articles were sent to Hoover in Washington.

As I took a closer look at my classmates, I started to notice a certain sameness about the fifty of us. Although we came from every part of the country and from every type of background, there were no Jews, blacks, or Hispanics in the class. I was later to learn that this was Hoover's policy.

My agent friend had warned me that one or two men in my class would probably be acting as spies for the higher-ups in the bureau, and he told me how to spot them. Senior FBI men sought out as candidates for the spying trainees who had joined the bureau as clerks right out of high school at the impressionable age of eighteen or so. These men were ambitious (many would go on to earn degrees in law or accounting at night), and even as trainees fiercely loyal to the FBI. It is more unusual now, though still possible, to find that kind of blind allegiance in men who joined the bureau with a college or law degree. Many years later, I learned that Soviet intelligence operated the same way. It put its real trust only in those American Communists who had been trained and disciplined in a Soviet school, like the Lenin School in Moscow.

In direct contrast were men like me, "men from the outside." We were older than the average trainee. Many of us had held responsible positions and gained considerable experience prior to becoming agents. We were more independent and self-reliant, and less apt to be intimidated by power-hungry bureaucrats. At the beginning, some of us even questioned FBI policy, but we quickly learned that such an attitude was a sure road to early retirement.

The pressure on a trainee to conform was unremitting. Internal spies were a constant threat to free expression. Horror stories made the rounds, stories of special agents who were "dismissed with prejudice" after violating FBI rules, never again able to find work in any branch of government. Class enthusiasm remained high, however, in spite of the fear and suspicion that were all around.

We were a spirited group, capable, industrious, and ready to put ourselves to the test as special agents of the FBI. We had been lawyers, professors, government employees, businessmen, professional athletes, law enforcement officers, engineers, insurance adjusters, reporters, and teachers. "The overall quality of this class," said one instructor, "demonstrates the superiority of the FBI's recruitment program." Who were we to disagree?

Only one man out of hundreds, we were told repeatedly by our instructors, could survive the rigorous screening and testing to be offered an appointment as special agent. We were an "elite group," "the cream of the crop." Agents of the bureau were "a substantial cut above" all other federal employees, just as the bureau itself was clearly head and shoulders above all other federal agencies. During the late 1940s Hoover had the bureau furnish material for a magazine article written by an executive of the General Foods Corporation, Thomas McDade, an ex-FBI agent. It was entitled "The Most Carefully Selected Men in the World."

Hoover thought of the FBI only in superlatives, and his feeling that everything about the bureau was "the best" filtered down to our instructors. One of them explained to our class that the FBI motto, WE NEVER CLOSE A CASE, was better than the Canadian Mounties' WE ALWAYS GET OUR MAN. It was difficult to understand why, since never closing a case meant never solving it, but no one wanted to contradict our serious and hard-working instructors.

Our training took three months. Classes were held from nine in the morning until nine at night, five days a week at the Department of Justice in Washington and the nearby marine base in Quantico, Virginia. We also met for additional classes on Saturday and Sunday afternoons.

I was impressed by one of my instructors in particular, Jepeth Rogers. He looked and acted just as I'd expected—intelligent, perceptive, and knowledgeable. He lectured with poise and patience, and was willing to stop at any time to answer a question.

It was difficult, however, for the bureau to come up with knowledgeable instructors in the new (to the FBI) field of national defense. Dealing with Nazism, fascism, communism, and espionage were not at all the same as catching bank robbers and kidnappers. Agents who had spent years working on criminal cases had to master new and complex methods of investigation almost overnight, and not all of them were equal to the task. Great credit, therefore, should be given to the FBI instructors who spent many long and difficult hours of their own time preparing for this new work. Two in particular stand out: Edward P. Morgan, now a successful lawyer in Washington, D.C., and Kenneth McIntire, now retired.

Morgan was a dynamic instructor, but because he was a moderate liberal Hoover didn't trust him. Morgan finally quit, so Hoover had Morgan's name removed from the FBI mailing list and had it placed instead on the dreaded "no contact" list. Ironically, in 1976 Morgan was hired to defend active and former FBI agents who were facing criminal charges brought against them by the Department of Justice.

McIntire missed his calling. He should have been a professor of political science. Like Morgan, he was well read and articulate, and I found him to be surprisingly objective. But McIntire was eventually asked to request early retirement—Hoover found his point of view "too objective."

Our instructors announced one day that Mr. Hoover was coming to speak to our class and we were quickly coached on how to act in his presence. Just prior to his arrival, fifteen or twenty agents positioned themselves on either side of the hall and stood silently at attention as he passed between them, inspiring in us a sense of awe, wonder, anticipation. We were completely silent, absolutely attentive. He spoke rapidly, positively, and briefly. His topic was the difficulty of the FBI screening process, a theme that the classes never tired of hearing. But it didn't matter what he said—his presence alone was enough to persuade us that he was a great and unique man.

He didn't convince us all, however, and one of my classmates in particular, a man who had been a successful lawyer before joining the FBI, became increasingly critical of the bureau, its leadership, and the training program. Bearing in mind what my friend had told me about internal spies, I was careful not to encourage him or to express any of my own doubts. One day at lunch he looked seriously at me and said, "Damn it, Sullivan, I know you must have some thoughts about the training. Well, if you won't say anything, I will. This organization puts too much emphasis on propaganda and not enough emphasis on investigation. I'm going to quit and join the army. When the war comes, I'll be ready!"

I urged him to reconsider, to go out and work at his first assigned field office for at least a month or two. I was sure the emphasis in a working field office would be on law enforcement, not discipline or public relations. But he had less faith than I did and went home a few days later.

One of the most exciting parts of our training was the firearms program. After class, the instructors, all expert marksmen, would tell us of bloody gunfights with such dangerous criminals as Ma Barker and Alvin Karpis, and of such FBI hero agents as Walter Walsh, who brought down his assailant despite being shot below the heart, and Charles Winstead, who killed John Dillinger. It was men like Walsh and Winstead who helped build the legend of the FBI. We younger men of the 1940s benefited from the bureau's reputation though we had yet to contribute anything to it ourselves.

While firearms training is a highly serious business with the element of danger always present, our instructors did have their light-hearted moments. One instructor, a man in his late fifties who was known for his sense of humor and his ability to break up the most serious trainee with laughter, became the victim of an elaborate practical joke that involved our class. When we arrived at Quantico to begin the program, one of my fellow trainees was warned "in great confidence" that a certain firearms instructor would try to make the class laugh as a test of our serious intent. Any trainee who laughed would receive demerits on his permanent FBI record.

The story of this new, devilish scheme to weed out inferior trainees, though told in confidence, spread like wildfire. It is some measure of how paranoid "The Most Carefully Selected Men in the World" had become since starting our training with the FBI that we believed the improbable story to a man. When the firearms instructor we had been warned about told our class his first joke (which was really funny), we were ready for him—not one trainee laughed. When he tried again, with an equally funny joke but with a little less confidence, no one even smiled. After class, we walked out feeling as if we had beaten the FBI at its own game and reaffirmed our manhood.

Visibly disturbed, the instructor went to his colleagues for advice. Led by the same instructor who had made up the story, they convinced him that he had lost touch with the younger generation. But the jokers didn't stop there. Distraught, the victim wrote a letter to Hoover requesting reassignment, which the others pretended to mail. While the hapless instructor waited for a reply, they sat back, watched, and let him wonder why Hoover hadn't acted on his request. As paranoid as the next man, he finally concluded that Hoover must be angry with him. After a week had passed, on the brink of a nervous collapse, he finally decided to ask Hoover's secretary what was wrong. It was then that his colleagues let him in on the joke.

At the end of three months, we took exams in six major subjects like federal criminal law and investigative techniques, and nine minor subjects from courtroom techniques and firearms to crime scene search and public speaking. No courses were given in burglary or opening mail, though today some members of Congress make considerable political headway by suggesting the opposite.

The passing grade was eighty-five, but since we never saw the test papers after we handed them in, we had to take the bureau's word for it that we passed or failed. I got the feeling that the FBI's own men—the spies—always passed, just as a trainee with the "wrong attitude" toward the bureau would always fail.

The FBI has a way of disposing of its own undesirables. I saw Hoover send out more than one inspection squad to get the goods on an agent who had offended the director in some way—from insubordination to driving a dusty car. At one time, Hoover had a fetish for clean, shiny cars. An agent I worked with down near the Mexican border used to laugh and say, "Bill, don't worry about your investigations. Be damn sure you wash your car every day you come to work though, or you'll be in real trouble."

After exams, waiting to see whether I had passed, wondering what my first field assignment would be, I thought hard about the FBI and my future in law enforcement. What I had learned about the FBI during training did little to overcome the doubts I had always felt about it. Did I really belong there? When I wrote a letter to my wife expressing my confusion, she wrote back advising me to get out of it while I still could.

The elitism of the FBI, the stress on blind obedience and rigid discipline made me feel out of place. But the work could be exciting and genuinely meaningful. Any large organization, I rationalized, demands loyalty from its employees. And the strict selection process and vigorous training helped to eliminate fledgling agents who wouldn't be able to withstand the pressures of working at a field office. The training, the things I had learned in class, opened new vistas for me. I decided to try it for a while.

On 26 September 1941, I received my first assignment, to the field office in Milwaukee, Wisconsin. I was intrigued. I had never traveled far from Bolton, and the chance to see the Midwest was very inviting. Like my classmates, I looked forward to the chance to put my newfound knowledge to the test. It was with a mixture of enthusiasm, curiosity, and doubt that I packed for the trip. Who knows? I might even like it.

In December of 1941, two months after I arrived in Milwaukee, I found myself sitting in a small room in the same building that housed the Communist party headquarters. I was wearing earphones and recording in longhand what was going on in their meeting. We had a "bug," a microphone, planted in their meeting room, but there were no tape recorders back then.

During that particular meeting, the Communists had just received news that Pearl Harbor had been bombed by the Japanese. I remember that they shouted with jubilation and began talking feverishly, quieting when their leader Josephine Nordstrand began talking in her measured, quite distinct way. I was taking it all down. She said, "This is the greatest opportunity we've ever had. At long last we're in the war. The Japs did what we weren't able to do, get America into the war. Now our job is to penetrate all the patriotic organizations. By doing that, we're going to gain the respectability we've never had. Let's be more patriotic than the most patriotic non-Communist." Not once during that meeting did anyone express any feelings about the many Americans who died at Pearl Harbor.

With its large German population, Milwaukee was a great assignment, a new agent's dream. When I arrived, I found everyone in the office up to his neck in national security cases. They were so busy tracking down Bund members, Nazi spies, and Communists that they were more than willing to share the overload with a new recruit.

The special agent in charge (SAC) of the Milwaukee office, tall and wiry Harry T. O'Conner, was a natural leader and administrator. Intelligent and knowledgeable, he was in full command of his office and his men. Everyone from the clerical help to the agents appreciated the opportunity to work and learn under him. (It was the FBI's real loss when Mr. O'Conner resigned to become a corporate executive. One of the unfortunate things about the bureau is that too many talented men like O'Conner resign.)

O'Conner's assistant was a seasoned Bureau veteran. One day, as I walked past his office, he called me in. "I like to get to know some of the new agents personally," he told me. Looking me straight in the eye, he added, "You are one of the very few new agents I would like to get to know on a man-to-man basis."

This both pleased and surprised me, especially since this man had never shown any interest in me before—up to that point he had been formal, almost austere. "We older men have a private poker game every Saturday night," he continued, "and we'd like you to join us this weekend, but don't mention the game to the men who aren't invited."

As flattered as I was, I had to say no to the invitation. I didn't know how to play poker! No one in my family played cards, I explained, and I'd never had a chance to learn how. He was stunned. He finally walked away, shaking his head. I was to learn later that these hard-to-get poker invitations were dangled before all new agents, one at a time. The ones who accepted usually lost money. Had it not been for my ignorance of card playing, I would have gone the way of the rest.

At the outbreak of war, there were an estimated one million Germans, Italians, and Japanese in the country who were classified as "alien enemies." We were told that these people were "dangerous to the peace and safety of the United States," and we went after them with everything we had, including hidden microphones, telephone taps, and physical surveillance. We weren't taught these techniques during our training program, we learned them on the job from more experienced agents. Every one of us believed that tapping phones and opening mail was official government policy, necessary to national security. It is doubtful that we would have carried out our orders, however, had we known that years later politicians would accuse us of violating the law and performing criminal acts. (In light of what has gone on in the last few years, a man would have to be either stupid or self-destructive to look for work in the intelligence community.)

The declaration of war brought to the surface much suspicion among and about the German population of Milwaukee, the overwhelming majority of whom were entirely loyal to the United States. In one case, I was sent out to one of Milwaukee's most exclusive neighborhoods to interview a man who had grown suspicious of his German-American next-door neighbor. For eleven days he had kept track of the smoke coming out of his neighbor's chimney in a very strange manner—"in well regulated puffs, three puffs at a time," followed by eight minutes of no smoke at all, ending with "two puffs, then four, rising and disappearing." He was convinced that his neighbor was a Nazi spy, signaling to his contact.

Not every lead was so obviously false, and during the first weeks of December 1941 the Milwaukee FBI office took fifty-six enemy aliens into custody for a closer look. The entire group was hauled to the House of Corrections. While they were being processed, I noticed one man in the group who seemed to be waving at me. I went over to him and he asked if we could walk a few steps away from the others to talk privately. He seemed very nervous, which was not surprising under the circumstances. When we were alone, he whispered that although he was a German alien, he was also Jewish and had left Germany to escape the Nazis. I told him to go home. As I walked him to the door, I asked why he had chosen me to talk to. "I thought you looked more sympathetic than the others," he replied. I never knew his name and never saw the man again.

It was FBI policy in the early 1940s to move new agents from field office to field office as often as possible in their first year. This enabled new agents like myself to meet many people, to learn that there was more than one way to live. It broadened our horizons.

Soon I received orders to complete work on my current cases

and report to El Paso, Texas. As I left Milwaukee on 11 January 1942, I pondered the change. It would be a sharp transition, nothing like snowy Wisconsin with its woods, farmlands, and country towns that reminded me of Bolton.

In El Paso I was shown to my desk by Tom Meyers, the assistant special agent in charge, and while I was unpacking and organizing, I heard someone come up behind me.

"Why in hell are you carrying so much junk?" a deep voice said. "In five years," it continued, "you'll need a fleet of pack mules to carry the rubbish you'll have collected." I turned around to see a man who seemed to be looking through me rather than at me.

"This isn't junk," I argued, somewhat intimidated, "these are bureau manuals, documents, and letters of instruction."

"It's still junk," he replied. "Headquarters showers all that useless paper on every new agent as if they were throwing confetti at a bride. Throw it away," he advised, "just keep the manuals." Then he stuck out his hand and said, "I'm Bryce, special agent in charge." His handshake was so strong it might have been painful had not years of working on my family farm given me enough strength to withstand the pressure. With just the slightest trace of a smile, which vanished as quickly as it had appeared, Bryce started going through my possessions, discarding most of them. Then he left the room without another word.

The day went by without anyone giving me further instructions, so I busied myself getting acquainted with the other agents and studying my remaining manuals. I also read about El Paso, a fascinating town on the Mexican border with a violent history.

On the morning of my second day in El Paso, Bryce called me into his office. I had learned that Bryce killed eight men while he was on the Oklahoma City police force. He spoke quietly, clearly, forcefully, and in a manner which did not encourage disagreement. I was careful to give him none. My first case, Bryce told me, would be a brief special assignment to Phoenix, Arizona. I had heard about special assignments during training, and they sounded mysterious, adventurous, even a bit dangerous. I was surprised that a very new agent would be selected for such exciting work.

My assignment would take about three days, Bryce said. I was to travel to Phoenix, pick up an extra staff car, and drive it back to El Paso. Very exciting.

When I returned, car intact, there was a message on my desk to see SAC Bryce at once. I wondered whether he had another special assignment. He did, but of a different nature.

The El Paso office, Bryce explained, covered a lot of territory, including New Mexico. I was one of many agents in El Paso, but one man, Charles B. Winstead, was working the entire state of New Mexico alone. Though Winstead, the man who'd killed John Dillinger, was a tough and experienced agent no one man could carry that much responsibility. I left that evening to assist Winstead in Albuquerque, taking the night train, and arrived at 6:30 the next morning. Although I was sure Mr. Winstead would not yet be at work, I decided to go directly to the office, which was in the Federal Building.

En route to the office from the station, I thought of all the terrible things I'd heard about Charles Winstead in my one day in El Paso. Once the other agents heard about my assignment, they couldn't tell me enough about my new boss—he was sour, disagreeable, eccentric, impossible to work for or with. He disliked new agents, college graduates, and anyone from the East Coast. If forced to work with a new agent, Winstead always assigned that agent to work on the "old chestnuts," undesirable and sometimes unsolvable cases that had been around for years.

The office door, to my astonishment, was open. The light was on and a small, slender man wearing a large sombrero which only partially covered a heavy thatch of gray hair was banging away with two fingers at an ancient typewriter. Typing faster with two fingers than I could with ten, he looked up as I walked in, but continued to type without saying a word. For what seemed a very long time, but must have been just thirty or forty seconds, I stood in front of his battered desk, hat in one hand, briefcase in the other, waiting for him to stop typing.

He didn't stop. More ill at ease with every second, I reached down to take out my FBI manuals by way of introduction. At this point he stopped typing and pulled the paper from the machine with such force that I thought it surely had to tear. He leaned back in his chair, put his boots up on the desk, and stared. I couldn't help staring myself since I had never seen such boots before—they were like something out of Zane Grey. A phrase from FBI training flashed through my mind: "A special agent of the FBI is always a gentleman." Courtesy, good manners, and proper dress were required at all times. Never put your feet on the desk, we were told; never wear boots, be conservative in your dress. This man was violating important rules.

"My name is Charlie Winstead," he finally said, "and I reckon you're the new agent Bryce sent. Hell, you'll be no help. It'll take all my time just telling you what to do. The training they give the new agents in Washington just confuses them. What I need is a seasoned, experienced man who knows how to catch a fugitive and arrest him without dragging along a squad of police officers and deputy sheriffs. What did you say your name is?"

By the time Winstead stopped talking, I was ready to get right back on the train to El Paso. When I told him my name, he exploded.

"Goddamn it," he shouted, "am I to be saddled with another Sullivan? A year ago they sent me an Irishman from the East. He had a fist fight with every man he arrested, and when there was no one to arrest, he started hitting policemen. He didn't last long."

Winstead stared continuously at me and I said nothing. Finally, he barked, "Boy, what did they tell you about me in El Paso?" I was to learn that "boy" was Winstead's favorite term of disrespect. I didn't want to make him angrier by repeating the harsh comments I'd heard in El Paso, but I certainly didn't want to lie to him either.

"Mr. Winstead," I started to say, but he interrupted me at once.

"Don't call me 'mister,' boy, that's not my name. My name is Charlie, Charlie Winstead."

It got worse by the minute. "Charlie," I started again, feeling more like a fool than ever, "they told me you were an experienced investigator burdened with an overload of cases." Vague, yet truthful. I thought it would work.

"Boy, that's a goddamned lie," Winstead replied. "I know what they told you," he said, and he proceeded to repeat the opinion of the El Paso agents almost word for word.

Somehow I mustered the courage to speak again. "If you already knew what they said, why did you ask?"

"I just wanted to find out how you'd handle the question," he said. "Your answer didn't win any prizes." He kept staring at me and kept talking. "What those agents told you is true, and you'd better not forget it if you want to work with me. I'm old, mean, disagreeable, overworked, and tired. I'm a cynic about life both in and out of the FBI. This isn't the same country I fought for in the First World War. Boy, do you know how bad it is?"

I just kept quiet and kept listening. "When I investigate a man and prove he's a criminal," Winstead continued, "if he doesn't already work for the government, they'll hire him. If he already has a government job, once they hear he's a crook they'll promote him. The criminals in Congress only feel comfortable with other criminals."

He shook his head sadly and told me to unpack. As he was already using the only file cabinet in the office, I arranged all my things on top of a table. As bad a picture of Winstead as the agents in El Paso had painted, I felt they had been guilty of gross understatement. Feeling a need to get away from him, to be alone for a while, I told Charlie I was going out for some breakfast. "Boy," he said in an unpleasant tone of voice, "I have my breakfast at 5:30 every morning. We're not going out until later. Then I'll show you around and introduce you to some people in town who'll be able to help you out when you're working on a case. It won't hurt you to wait until lunch. You're in the FBI now, not nursery school."

It was a busy morning, meeting policemen, town and county officials, lawyers, doctors, newspapermen, and some of our informants and special contacts. At noon, Charlie told me that he went to the same place for lunch every day but it was up to me to find my own restaurant, eat lunch, and meet him in a hotel lobby in half an hour.

Terrified of being late, I was there in twenty minutes. Charlie showed up five minutes later looking mildly annoyed at finding me waiting, but he didn't say anything. The rest of the afternoon was just like the morning, meeting people, people, and more people. Out of all those I met that day, the only unpleasant one was Charles B. Winstead. When we finally got back to the office, he assigned me to thirty or so minor criminal and security cases. I looked through the list quickly, trying to spot the "old chestnuts" I'd been warned about. They were there in abundance.

"I've been instructed to work with you for the first month," he told me before leaving me to study my "new" cases, "so that you can't get us both in trouble. After a month, you're on your own. Trouble or no trouble, I won't be your babysitter."

That night, alone in my tiny room at the Elks Club (at eighteen dollars a month, though, I wasn't complaining), I made an extra-long and detailed entry in the diary I had been keeping since I joined the FBI. Then I took a solitary walk in the cool, dry air of Albuquerque under the biggest, most star-filled sky I had ever seen.

The next few weeks with Charlie Winstead taught me what it meant to be unwanted. During my third week in El Paso, a teletype message arrived from FBI headquarters. A dangerous fugitive had been located living a few miles outside of Las Vegas, Nevada. The SOG, or "Seat of Government," as Hoover called the FBI headquarters, furnished a description of the fugitive and gave directions to his isolated cabin. The man was armed and dangerous, the teletype stated; two men were needed to locate him and make the arrest.

Charlie looked up after reading the message. "Boy," he said, "this is a two-man job, so I'll call Jack Nichols, a state trooper, to go along. You can come and watch if you want."

Despite my hurt pride at not being considered man enough to make the arrest, and despite Winstead's implication of "Two's company, three's a crowd," I went along. After all, this was the kind of adventure I had in mind when I'd joined the FBI. When we arrived at the hideout, though, it was empty. We searched the area all night and at dawn Charlie took us to one of his special restaurants for breakfast. It turned out to be a tiny, one-room shack with one old man who served as cook, waiter, dishwasher, and, very occasionally, sweeper. Charlie sat on a battered stool at my left and the state trooper sat at my right.

Charlie barked out an order for coffee. The trooper, who had a deep bass voice, ordered coffee too. When the old man looked at me, I asked for Postum, which I was raised on. The minute I said it, I was sorry. Charlie looked at me in shock, the trooper in disgust, the old man in wonderment. He had never heard of Postum. I ordered hot water.

As soon as we were back outside, Charlie turned on me. "Boy," he said angrily, "where in hell did you learn to drink Postum?" In New England, I told him, where I grew up. "Well," he said, "you're in the Southwest now, and here men drink coffee. Don't embarrass me in a public place again by ordering Postum." Until the day I left New Mexico I drank coffee, black and strong.

About a week after our unsuccessful trip to Las Vegas, Charlie got another two-man assignment and this time when Charlie couldn't find anyone else, he turned to me and said, "You drive."

Once we were on our way, Charlie didn't speak at all. At one point I had to stop the car for three or four minutes while a large herd of cattle crossed the road. Sitting there, watching the cattle, made me think of our farm and of how much I missed New England. The Southwest was awesome, but it was alien land. Overwhelmed by homesickness, I momentarily forgot my fear of Charles B. Winstead and commented on the state of the herd and estimated their number.

When the last cow had crossed, the silence was resumed. But after a few minutes, Charlie startled me by speaking. "Boy," he said, "what do you know about cattle? You're a big city boy from the East, aren't you?"

"I was born and raised on a farm," I told him. "I walked six miles to get to school every day. There was no public transportation to or in Bolton. We had no telephone, no mail service, and no electricity. I worked around cattle and horses all my life, and I think I made a big mistake leaving the farm."

"Worked around cattle and horses all your life . . ." Charlie repeated in wonder, "I'll be damned. You never know what headquarters will send out next. Just as well, I guess," he continued philosophically. The subject never came up again, but his attitude toward me changed overnight.

During the months ahead, Winstead became the willing teacher, I the appreciative student. The more I worked with him the more I came to appreciate his sharp, quick intelligence, the variety of his experiences, and the scope of his thoughts. He had not gone to college; in fact, his formal education was almost nonexistent. He was self-educated and he had done a good job. He was so well read that he stood out in sharp contrast to most men with college and graduate degrees, those who stopped learning when they left school.

Charlie had a naturally probing mind, a mind which could absorb, retain, and use information. He was not an easy man to know, but he was well worth knowing. We talked about everything: how to arrest a difficult suspect ("Never wrestle with any of these thugs," Charlie advised, "just hit him on the side of the head with the barrel of your gun—it's that easy").

But mostly we talked about the FBI. I asked Charlie what the bureau was like when he entered in 1926. "Small, disorganized, and inefficient," he told me. When Winstead worked as a special agent in Los Angeles, he had been assigned to over a hundred cases. The majority of these cases were far too complex for one man to handle, and when he looked over the case list more closely, he found that many of the cases had been dismissed long ago by the U.S. attorney. True to the FBI motto WE NEVER CLOSE A CASE, the Los Angeles field office listed these cases as open and unsolved.

"Sullivan," he advised, "if you want to earn your salary, do right by the taxpayer and help the local, county, and state police officers and ask for their help in return. Just don't tell headquarters in Washington. They don't believe in helping the police, or in sharing credit with them either. This shortsighted, petty policy has hurt and will continue to hurt the bureau. It's a lone-wolf attitude," Charlie concluded, "and it's unprofessional, inefficient—and it costs the taxpayers a bundle to boot."

I asked Charlie how much training he received on entering the FBI. "None at all," he answered. "I entered the FBI on July 27, 1926, took my oath of office that day, and left that night for my first assignment in Oklahoma City," he told me. Charlie had been tracking and capturing murderers and bank robbers in East Texas when the call came from Washington instructing him to report to Chicago to join the "Dillinger Squad."

A few months after Charlie started working on the case, one of Dillinger's women friends, Anna Sage, decided to turn informer. She told an agent that she planned to see a movie at the Biograph Theater later that evening. The agents didn't want to get the wrong man, so she promised to wear a red dress to signal Dillinger's presence. On the evening of 22 July 1934, Charles B. Winstead was waiting in the

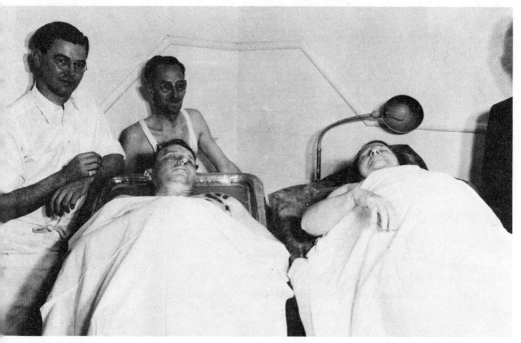

Kate "Ma" Barker and her son Fred after their deaths at the hands of FBI agents at Ocklawa, Florida, on 17 January 1935. *Wide World Photos*

lobby when the movie ended, looking through the crowd for a woman wearing a red dress.

When he finally spotted her, she was just one of two women with Dillinger. As they passed, Charlie moved in behind them. The other woman, Polly Hamilton, saw him and said something to Dillinger, and in a split second Dillinger pushed the girls away, wheeled around, and drew his gun.

He was fast, but not fast enough. Charlie shot Dillinger three times. When the first two shots hit him under the heart, Dillinger reeled and pitched forward. When the third hit him in the head, he spun like a top and fell dead. Dillinger had a forty-five-caliber automatic pistol in his hand, but he died before he could pull the trigger. Other agents were in on the ambush, but it was Winstead's bullets that killed Dillinger.

The two women ran. For her part in the shooting the woman in red was paid ten thousand dollars, a bargain when you consider the

The Biograph Theater in Chicago, where Dillinger was killed.

John Dillinger in the morgue after he was killed by Special Agent Charles Winstead.

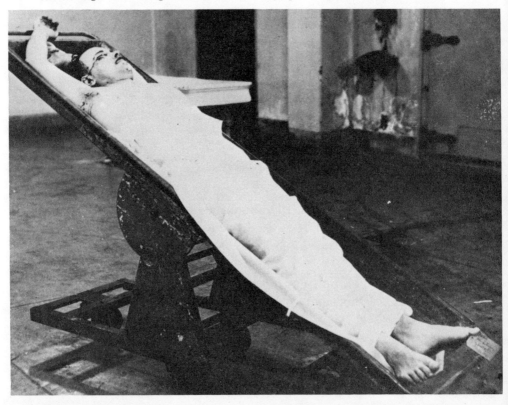

salaries of the agents who had been working full time on the case. For his participation, Charlie Winstead received a letter from Hoover congratulating him on his "fearless and courageous action."

John Dillinger was not the only infamous hoodlum who met his match in Charlie Winstead. Charlie was in on the investigation of "Baby Face" Nelson, Ma Barker and some of her larcenous offspring, and the capture of Alvin Karpis. Charlie said it was the shots from his 30–06 rifle which brought down Ma Barker herself. But Winstead told me he always regretted having had to kill a woman.

When the time finally arrived for me to leave Albuquerque and move on to my next field office (I had been assigned to work in Philadelphia), I hated leaving the Southwest and I hated leaving Charlie. I was pleased to know that Charlie regretted my departure as much as he had resented my arrival. We had become and stayed close friends over the years.

Some months after Charlie died of cancer in 1974, I learned that he had willed the 357 Magnum pistol he always carried, his Stetson sombrero, and his boots, saddles, and rope to me.

"Never initiate a meeting with Hoover for any reason," Charlie once told me, because if the director was less than impressed for any reason, "your career would end on that very day. If Hoover ever calls you in," he went on, "dress like a dandy, carry a notebook, and write in it furiously whenever Hoover opens his mouth. You can throw the notes away afterward if you like. And flatter him," Charlie added, "everyone at headquarters knows Hoover is an egomaniac, and they all flatter him constantly. If you don't, you'll be noticed."

In 1942, just before I left Albuquerque, in a dispute with Hoover Winstead told him to "go to hell," and a little later, after sixteen years in the FBI, he resigned to take a captain's commission in army intelligence.

In a letter I got from Winstead on 15 December 1942, he wrote:

Dear Bill:

I was rather shocked at the Bureau's stand over perfectly proper statements made by me in a private conversation, concerning Communism, with and while trying to develop that little newspaper reporter into a Confidential

Informant. I contradicted her statement that "Russia is fighting our battles," and she reported me to Mr. Hoover.*

He wrote that I should know I could not divorce myself in a private conversation from my official position for so "terribly embarrassing" the Bureau. I was being transferred to Oklahoma City.

I knew better than anybody that after doing my little bit from 1917 to 1920 to save the world for Democracy, and so many of the boys doing it again now, I wasn't going as far as Oklahoma City as a penalty for exercising my rights of free speech.

Anyhow, after more than 16 years with the Bureau with its inhibitions, insecurity, whims and ability for becoming embarrassed and astounded, the Army seems very attractive.

* At that time the United States was supplying the Soviet Union with weapons and other equipment to fight the Nazis. Although Hoover was anti-Soviet, he was not about to let one of his agents publicly refute U.S. policy.

TWO

Roosevelt, Truman, and Ike

J EDGAR HOOVER didn't like President Franklin D. Roosevelt. Hoover didn't trust liberals and FDR had surrounded himself with other liberals. Hoover hated Henry Wallace, Roosevelt's secretary of agriculture. He hated Harry Hopkins, administrator of some of the most important programs of the New Deal, and most of the rest of the president's staff was also unacceptable to the director. Hoover's attitude toward the administration was filtered down and made known at every level of the bureau, down to the lowest trainees like myself, and by the time I finished my training and took my first assignment as an FBI agent in 1941, it was clear to me that Hoover was passively anti-Roosevelt only because he couldn't be actively anti-Roosevelt. Whenever it was possible to throw in a barb, Hoover threw it.

On my last afternoon as an agent in Albuquerque, New Mexico, Charlie Winstead and I rode out into the mountains together on horseback. It was a good, long ride, and we brought along provisions for supper. As the sun was setting, we picked out a nice spot and started a fire. Over a dinner of steak and coffee, Charlie started talking about the infighting, the personality conflicts, and the politics of survival at the bureau. Naturally, our conversation soon turned to J. Edgar Hoover.

Hoover had always used the bureau for his own political purposes, Charlie said, and in 1936 Hoover got the idea that he should run for president against FDR. In the early 1930s, after a number of well-publicized FBI victories against colorful criminals like "Baby Face" Nelson, "Pretty Boy" Floyd, John Dillinger, and Ma Barker, Hoover believed he had become a major national figure. He thought that if he had the support of the entire law enforcement community—

federal, state, city, and county—he could run as a Republican and turn Roosevelt and his crew of liberals out of office. What he wanted to assess was whether he could win the election for president of the United States.

In early 1936, Hoover sent out some of his most trusted veteran agents, including Charlie, most of them southerners (Winstead was from Sherman, Texas) on a top-secret mission to test the political waters in the South and the Southwest where the director thought his support was strongest. Charlie was told to approach local chiefs of police or sheriffs on some minor matter, then redirect the conversation to the subject of J. Edgar Hoover. "He's a great man," Charlie would say, just as he'd been told to, "and he's done an awful lot for law enforcement on every level in this country. Many people think we'd be better off if Hoover were president." Then he would wait for the reaction.

Much to Hoover's surprise, response to his presidential ambitions was overwhelmingly negative. Not only did the local police not want him to be chief executive, many didn't even want him to continue as director. When Hoover learned the results of his informal poll, he never again mentioned running for president.

But he continued to have political ambitions beyond the FBI and he continued to dislike Roosevelt. In 1939, FDR empowered the bureau to investigate security affairs as well as criminal cases. This meant that Hoover would have virtually unlimited opportunities to get his name in the papers. It was the best present any president could have given him, but it didn't alter the way Hoover felt toward FDR, just the way he acted toward him. He started playing up to him, telling him little tidbits of gossip about high-ranking public officials whenever he could (which, incidentally, Roosevelt loved to hear).

Even after 1945, when I had been promoted to FBI headquarters in Washington as a supervisor, I could never understand Hoover's attitude when it came to Roosevelt. The FBI achieved its greatest growth during the Roosevelt years, from the 1930s when the president gave the bureau more and more jurisdiction to go after criminals like "Baby Face" and "Pretty Boy," to the 1940s when the bureau became involved in national security and intelligence.

Hoover's attitude never changed, though. He never passed up a chance to make a snide remark when FDR's name was mentioned, and he never failed to express his feelings about the president in internal memos handwritten by the director with his familiar blue pen. Later in my career, in 1945 when I was assigned to the Research Division, I'd see these blue ink remarks about Roosevelt. One said, "He has an emperor's complex."

Hoover disliked Mrs. Roosevelt even more than he did her husband. Hoover once told me why he had never married. He said, "Because God had made a woman like Eleanor Roosevelt." He also lacerated her in his memos for supporting blacks, and he said in one memo that she was "in love with a Negro," and gave her hell in another for giving the commencement address at Gibbs Junior College, a school for blacks. Hoover thought there was unrest developing among black Americans. There wasn't any at that time, but whenever a black would speak out he attributed it to Mrs. Roosevelt. Another Hoover memo, referring to a black educator's speech, noted, "If she wasn't sympathizing with them and encouraging them, they wouldn't be speaking out like this!"

Prior to World War II, Roosevelt had the bureau investigate people and organizations that were opposed to his Lend-Lease program. He turned to Hoover to see if he could get anything on these critics of help to England. In doing so, Roosevelt unfortunately established the precedent of using the FBI as the president's personal political tool. Roosevelt also had the bureau look into Harry Hopkins and Henry Wallace (nothing ever came of these inquiries). One strange request from Roosevelt had to do with Supreme Court Justice Frank Murphy. It seemed that everywhere Murphy went he carried a violin case. The White House requested that we find out what was in the case. One day he had a luncheon meeting at the Carlton Hotel in Washington and had the damned thing with him there in the lobby. When Murphy went to the men's room, leaving the case behind, it gave the agents who had him under surveillance their first opportunity to check it out. They moved in fast, opened the case, and found a tennis racket.

When Roosevelt died and Truman became president, the word went out to the entire bureau that anyone related to, friendly with, or personally known by the new president should step forward to become Hoover's personal emissary to the White House. Hoover hoped to develop a personal relationship with Truman, a relationship which would allow him to thumb his nose at Truman's attorney general. He would use this ploy again and again, after each new president was elected. It sometimes worked, but not when John F. Kennedy named his brother to head the Justice Department and not when Hoover's man approached Harry Truman.

Hoover selected Marion Chiles III, an agent from Missouri whose father had been a boyhood chum of the president's, to carry his message. Truman had known the young man since he was a baby, and he suited the director's purposes perfectly. (Chiles told me he didn't want to get involved, but he knew his job at the bureau depended on it, so he went over to the White House.)

After a few preliminary remarks, Truman asked the agent why he was there. "With a message from Mr. Hoover," Chiles said. "Mr. Hoover wants you to know that he and the FBI are at your personal disposal and will help you in any way you ask." Truman looked at his old friend's son, smiled, and remarked on Mr. Hoover's thoughtfulness. "But any time I need the services of the FBI," Truman added, "I will ask for it through my attorney general." The agent took the message back to Hoover, and from that time on Hoover's hatred of Truman knew no bounds.

This hatred caused Hoover to break precedent and testify publicly in the congressional investigation of Harry Dexter White. White had been an important economic advisor to both Roosevelt and Truman, and in 1948 he denied charges that he had been giving aid to Communist spies. Truman said, and rightly so, that the whole damn thing was a red herring, which, of course, further outraged Hoover.

Hoover was sure that Truman had it in for him, and he was right. One day, Louis B. Nichols, then the bureau's assistant director and in charge of all press matters, public relations, and congressional liaison, called me into his office from my desk in the research section.

"Sullivan," he said, "I've thought very carefully about the matter which I'm going to discuss with you. I have decided that you are the kind of person I can rely on and the kind of man who can get some information which Mr. Hoover wants very, very badly." I was flattered by Nichols's appraisal of me and waited for the sensitive assignment which he was obviously leading up to.

"Someone in the Masonic Order," said Nichols, "is blackballing the director and preventing him from becoming a thirty-third degree Mason. Mr. Hoover believes that it is President Truman." I was stunned by the accusation but sat quietly as Nichols continued. "I have worked on this very hard. In fact, I personally have infiltrated the Masonic Order in Alexandria, Virginia, thinking that by joining them I could determine for Mr. Hoover who was blackballing him and what action could be taken to eliminate this obstacle to the director's becoming a thirty-third degree Mason." Nichols was well known at headquarters as being a man who believed himself capable of selling anyone anything. "Sullivan," he went on, "I understand that you are friendly with former Congressman Joseph E. Casey, who is, coincidentally, close to President Truman. What the director and I want you to do is to approach Mr. Casey in confidence, explain the problem, and ask him to talk President Truman into supporting the director's endeavors instead of opposing them." Nichols noticed the look of surprise on my face and said, "You're Catholic and I'm asking you to get information out of the Masonic Order. I wouldn't ask you to do this if it wasn't a matter of grave importance to the director."

I had become used to these preposterous requests but this was the most ludicrous so far. I did nothing about the request but I found out later that Nichols was grabbing everyone he could at the bureau who could assist in this "grave matter."

His effort finally paid off. Hoover finally got someone to get to persuade Truman to lift his ban and Hoover at last became a thirty-third degree Mason.

Just as Roosevelt had put us into the intelligence business, Truman almost put us out of it. With his usual vision, Hoover had the entire world staked out as fair game for the FBI, and had opened offices in a great many foreign capitals. These foreign liaison offices were considered to be plum assignments as the FBI agents' American salaries allowed them to live very well in most foreign cities. But Tru-

man was in favor of limiting the FBI to domestic intelligence investigations, and in 1947 he created the Central Intelligence Agency to
deal with foreign intelligence. Hoover sent a stream of admirals, generals, congressmen, and senators to the White House to try to change
Truman's mind, but the president wouldn't budge and we were instructed to close our overseas offices. Truman did allow us to keep a
few offices open (London, Paris, Rome, Ottawa, and Mexico City),
but the agents who worked at those offices were instructed to handle
only the international aspects of domestic cases—not to be "operational" in obtaining foreign intelligence, and not to run informants.

At that time, I was the supervisor in charge of intelligence operations in Mexico and Central America. Before we closed down,
Hoover was so furious that he gave specific instructions to my office
and all offices abroad that under no circumstances were we to give
any documents or information to the newly established Central Intelligence Agency.

Many of the men who weren't easily intimidated did turn records
over to the CIA. And although we were mandated not to, Hoover
nevertheless instructed the Mexico City office to be operational, to
run informants, to develop foreign intelligence, to operate completely in violation of our charter. We'd investigate communism in
Mexico, the CIA would investigate communism in Mexico, and the
American taxpayer would pay for the duplication.

And the duplication wasn't only with CIA. In 1946 when I was
the supervisor of intelligence operations in Mexico and Central
America, a State Department official in Mexico City in charge of his
department's intelligence operations called me into his embassy office. "Bill," he said, "I think I can talk to you safely and off the
record." I assured him that he could. He said, "You know, you should
stop having your men send in material from Nicaragua because we
have better material sent in by our own men. Further, much of your
material is inaccurate. I'm not going to dictate a report on this, but for
your own good, and the good of the bureau, something ought to be
done about this duplication of intelligence gathering, especially when
it's not in the bureau's domain." I thanked him, but I had no authority
to stop it. I was just a lowly supervisor.

In later years, on three occasions I challenged Hoover on our need for all those overseas offices, but they remained. By the time I left the bureau, they were costing us three and a half million dollars a year and we were getting nothing out of them. Ottawa and Mexico City are the only overseas offices we've ever needed—criminals and espionage agents do go back and forth across our national boundary lines. We're not operational in Ottawa and ought not to be in Mexico City. Let the CIA handle the operational side of things.

When requests came from the CIA, legitimate authorized requests, Hoover would drag his heels, meet half the request, and ignore the other half. Early on it came to a head, and I saw a scorching letter from the then director of the CIA, General Bedell Smith. It said, "Whether you, Mr. Hoover, like me or not has nothing to do with the cooperation between two government agencies and it is mandatory for you to give the CIA full cooperation within your limits." Smith went on to write, "if it is not done, if you want to fight this, I'll fight you all over Washington." Hoover put his tail between his legs and backed off at that time, even requesting our CIA liaison man to set up a luncheon with him and Smith. Hoover was cordial because whenever his bluff was called he became a coward. The trouble was that few men had the courage to call Hoover's bluff.

When Thomas Dewey, with whom Hoover had a good working relationship, entered the Republican primaries in 1948, Hoover and two of his closest aides, Clyde Tolson and Louis Nichols, secretly agreed to put the resources of the bureau at Dewey's disposal. With the help of the FBI, Hoover believed Dewey couldn't lose. He would win the nomination and defeat Truman. In exchange for his help, the director believed that when Dewey became president he would name Hoover as his attorney general and make Nichols director of the FBI. To complete the masterplan, Tolson would become Hoover's assistant. It would have been a nice set-up, because with Nichols at the helm Hoover would have had the FBI as tightly under his control as if he had never left. In addition, he would have had the entire Justice Department at his disposal.

Hoover's ambitions didn't stop at the Justice Department. If he couldn't be president, Hoover thought it would be fitting if he were named to the Supreme Court, and he planned to make his term as at-

On the facing page, above: On 18 May 1934, Hoover watches FDR sign into law the crime bills that for the first time put bank robbery and other crimes under the jurisdiction of the FBI. Roosevelt was the first president to use the bureau for political purposes when he ordered the FBI to investigate those opposed to his Lend-Lease plan to aid Great Britain in World War II. *United Press International*

Below: President Harry Truman had little use for Hoover and prevented the FBI from taking over worldwide intelligence for the United States when the CIA was created. *Wide World Photos*

On this page, above: Hoover used the FBI to help his man, Thomas Dewey, defeat Harold Stassen, the other contender for the 1948 Republican presidential candidacy. This photograph was taken shortly before their nationally broadcast radio debate in Portland, Oregon, on 17 May 1948. *Wide World Photos*

Below: On 8 November 1957, Hoover presented President Eisenhower with an FBI badge mounted on a plaque. "Ike" liked hearing the political and personal gossip that Hoover delivered to him. *Wide World Photos*

torney general a stepping stone to that end. With visions of long, black robes in his head, Hoover made sure the bureau was there to help Dewey in his primary battle with Harold Stassen. Dewey was most grateful for the bureau's support, and made use of its resources while preparing for a national radio broadcast debate with Stassen on communism that was to take place in Portland, Oregon, on 17 May 1948. Many agents—I was one—worked for days culling FBI files for any fact that could be of use to Dewey. I remember that there was such a rush to get the material to him once it was collected that it was sent in a private plane to Albany, N.Y. Hoover's idea was not to wait till the end of the Republican primaries but to help Dewey from the beginning.

Governor Dewey was an intelligent man and a skilled debater, and armed with everything the bureau gave him he demolished Stassen when they met. That was the beginning of the end for Stassen, and after the debate Stassen's political star went down and out for good. Dewey got the nomination and Hoover started planning his move to the attorney general's office. The FBI helped Dewey during the campaign itself by giving him everything we had that could hurt Truman, though there wasn't much. We resurrected the president's former association with Jim Prendergast, political czar of Kansas City, and tried to create the impression that Truman was too ignorant to deal with the emerging Communist threat. We even prepared studies for Dewey which were released under his name, as if he and his staff had done the work. I worked on some of these projects myself.

No one in the bureau gave Truman any chance of winning. The spirits of Hoover and Tolson were running high. Of course, we weren't alone in that. *Liberty* magazine was so sure of Dewey that they published an article speculating on his possible Cabinet choices, and the day after Election Day the headline in the *Chicago Tribune* read " DEWEY DEFEATS TRUMAN."

The morning after the election, a heavy gloom settled over the bureau, heavier than at any other time I can remember. Nichols sent out a one-page memo saying he couldn't understand how Truman won, but there was really nothing he could say. Hoover immediately sent out a memo of his own blaming Nichols. He wrote, "Nichols pushed me out on a limb which got sawed off. I wouldn't be in this mess if it weren't for Nichols." Hoover could never admit that he had made a mistake. You could see Hoover's anger in his handwriting—the blue penstrokes were thick, as if he had been bearing down especially hard.

Hoover never involved either himself or the bureau that deeply in a presidential election again. He started beating the drums to help General MacArthur win the Republican nomination in 1952, but MacArthur's campaign fell as flat as Hoover's had, and when the director saw there was no chance for his man, he dropped him and supported Dwight Eisenhower.

Hoover's warm and cordial relationship with Eisenhower, who called him "Edgar," was furthered by a great favor Hoover had performed. Soon after Eisenhower was elected, Hoover found out that a White House aide, the son of a senator who was one of Ike's close friends, was homosexual. The director rushed over to the White House with the news, which he only repeated to Ike to save him "possible embarrassment." Eisenhower was grateful for the tip and fired his friend's son quickly and quietly. From then on, Hoover inundated the president with gossip and with more serious information about the dangers of communism. Unlike Truman, who was skeptical of anything Hoover offered and who never made any requests for political investigations, Eisenhower blindly believed everything the director told him, never questioned a word, and made requests. Eisenhower asked us to look into the personal life of Adlai Steveson, who was in the process of divorcing his wife and was involved with another woman. Eisenhower wanted to know about that sort of thing. He may have been a great general but he was a very gullible man, and Hoover soon had him wrapped right around his finger.

The dangerous threat of communism was, of course, one of Hoover's obsessions. During the Eisenhower years the FBI kept Joe McCarthy in business. Senator McCarthy stated publicly that there were Communists working for the State Department. We gave McCarthy all we had, but all we had were fragments, nothing could prove his accusations. For a while, though, the accusations were enough to keep McCarthy in the headlines. One of his major targets was a State Department employee named Owen Lattimore who McCarthy thought was an important Soviet agent, and a lot of government money was spent on digging through FBI files for evidence to prove it. We investigated the hell out of Lattimore, read every letter and memo, everything he ever wrote, but we never found anything substantial to use against him. McCarthy's accusatons were ridiculous.

I remember sitting by a window facing Pennsylvania Avenue one day working on the Lattimore case when I heard police sirens. I looked out and saw what seemed like twenty or thirty motorcycle policemen and even more police cruisers going by, sirens going full blast. When I found out that the police had been rushing to Blair House where Puerto Rican assassins had tried to kill President Truman, I couldn't help wondering why the FBI was putting all that time and effort into helping Joe McCarthy instead of working on more important matters.

THREE

"Goddamn the Kennedys"

I WAS IN BOLTON, MASSACHUSETTS, on 22 November 1963. I had been working days, nights, and weekends for months at FBI headquarters in Washington, and when the workload finally eased a bit I took a few days off to go back home and relax. I was walking in the woods that morning, and my plan had been to walk in the woods all day. Around midday though, I got one of those hunches no one can explain, a funny intuitive feeling that someone wanted me, so I turned around and started for home. Sure enough, my sister was waiting for me in a clearing between the house and the woods, and she looked as if she'd been crying. "You have to go back to Washington right away," she told me. "President Kennedy has been shot and the FBI has been calling."

She didn't know whether the president was dead or alive. I ran for the nearest house to call the office. When they told me President Kennedy was dead, I left for Washington at once. I had been working as assistant director of the FBI's Domestic Intelligence Division since June 1961, and I knew I would be heading the intelligence end of the assassination investigation.

The trip to Washington was a nightmare. I was stunned, shocked. When I arrived at FBI headquarters, I went in to see Hoover right away. He was all business. "We want to go all out on this investigation," he said briskly, "and we want to move fast." There wasn't a trace of sadness or sorrow. All he was thinking about was protecting the bureau, avoiding criticism.

This was true too of Hoover's expression of condolence to President Kennedy's brother, Attorney General Robert Kennedy. Hoover's note to him was just one brusque line of regret over the death of the president—just enough to cover himself.

I shouldn't have been surprised by Hoover's lack of personal remorse when Jack Kennedy was killed. He mistrusted and disliked all three Kennedy brothers. "Goddamn the Kennedys," I heard Clyde Tolson say to Hoover. "First there was Jack, now there's Bobby, and then Teddy. We'll have them on our necks until the year 2000." And the director nodded in agreement.

Hoover got along with Joe Kennedy, though. Joe Kennedy thought that Hoover was quite a guy, and never caught on that he was quite a con man too. Hoover was amazing. A socialist could talk to him and come out swearing Hoover was a socialist at heart, and an hour later a John Bircher could talk to him and come out convinced Hoover was about to join the John Birch Society. As smart as he was, Joe Kennedy got taken in, but Hoover couldn't fool his sons.

In 1942 the FBI was watching a beautiful young Scandinavian woman we suspected of spying for the Nazis in Washington. We had a microphone planted in her apartment and a tap on her telephone. Hoover could hardly contain his delight when he saw Lieutenant John F. Kennedy's voice reported on our tapes. Hoover immediately reported Lieutenant Kennedy's liaison to the White House, along with a suggestion that Kennedy be transferred "for security reasons." Kennedy never knew what hit him. One day he was dating glamorous women in Washington, the next day he was on his way to command a P.T. boat in the middle of the Pacific. But the transfer Hoover suggested backfired when Kennedy became a war hero. The P.T. boat helped make Kennedy president.

During the 1960 campaign, Hoover did his best to keep the press supplied with anti-Kennedy stories. At that time, the FBI had its offices in the same building as the Democratic National Committee. Hoover, a staunch Republican, was outraged. It was as if he and his agents were forced to share an elevator with the Communist party. He made it clear that we were not to fraternize with the Democrats. When Hoover discovered that one of the committee's campaign aides had once, years before, been mixed up with the Communist party, naturally he went right to the press with the story, never mentioning that the aide's Communist affiliation was far in the past. The poor guy, who had been blameless for years, found himself in the headlines and out of a job.

While Hoover was trying to sabotage Jack Kennedy's campaign, he was quietly helping Richard Nixon. Hoover couldn't be as blatant as he had been when he openly put the bureau to work for Thomas Dewey because the complexion of the bureau had changed. Until the 1940s, Catholics were kept out of the bureau along with blacks, Jews, and Hispanics. But when Hoover needed more agents in a hurry to

Hoover didn't like the Kennedys, and the feeling was mutual, as this photograph, taken a few months after JFK's election, suggests. *Wide World Photos*

work in the newly opened field of national security, the bar on Catholics was lowered and hundreds joined. As most of these Catholic agents supported Kennedy, Hoover had to curtail his overt support of Nixon. Even so, Kennedy's election was a disaster for Hoover.

Jack Kennedy disliked Hoover in return and wanted to replace him as director, but he had won the election by such a narrow margin that he felt he couldn't afford to alienate Hoover's considerable conservative following by getting rid of him. Once Kennedy realized he was stuck with Hoover, he decided to make the best of it and made it a point to contact Hoover immediately to ask him to stay on.

Hoover wanted to make a friendly gesture to the Kennedys in return, and I have always believed that I owed my job as assistant director to this and to the fact that I was an Irish Democrat from Massachusetts. Of course, the Kennedys didn't know me from Adam, but I was the best Hoover could come up with. Nonetheless, the director never disguised his true feelings for Jack Kennedy or for his brothers when he was among his close FBI aides.

Hoover was always gathering damaging material on Jack Kennedy, which the president, with his active social life, seemed more than willing to provide. We never put any technical surveillance on JFK, but whatever came up was automatically funnelled directly to Hoover. I was sure he was saving everything he had on Kennedy, and on Martin Luther King, Jr., too, until he could unload it all and destroy them both. He kept this kind of explosive material in his personal files, which filled four rooms on the fifth floor of headquarters.

Kennedy was aware that Hoover was an enemy, of course, and he kept his distance. He never asked Hoover for any gossip or any favors. If he heard that Hoover was leaking anti-Kennedy stories, JFK would call the director right away and ask him to put the statement on the record. Hoover always did, but somehow, between Kennedy's phone call and Hoover's official statement, the director's remarks softened considerably. Kennedy couldn't stop Hoover from talking behind his back, but he could do something about Hoover's public statements, and he did. Kennedy would also call Hoover over to the White House two or three times just to remind him who was boss. Kennedy didn't say it that bluntly, but Hoover got the message.

I shouldn't have been surprised then at Hoover's cold-blooded attitude when Kennedy was murdered, but it was unsettling nonetheless.

We got going on the case right away. Officially, the Criminal Division was in charge of the investigation, but there wasn't too much to investigate after Lee Harvey Oswald, the only suspect, was killed. On the other hand, over at my shop we had to untangle Oswald's myriad subversive connections. Were the Soviets behind it? Were the Cubans behind it? Was anyone behind it? It grew into a gigantic intelligence operation with over twenty-eight hundred agents working on the case.

Oswald had spent a lot of time in Mexico, so our Mexican office played an important part in the investigation. We also had agents in Canada, Central America, England, and Italy tracking down leads. We even got a note from a man in France who said he had six letters written by Oswald which would solve the case. He offered to sell us the letters for ten thousand dollars, but he turned out to be a well-known European con man who didn't have any such letters. He was later arrested and prosecuted by the French police.

We didn't have much on Oswald in our files prior to the assassination. We knew that he had lived in Russia and that he'd come back with a Russian wife, which was unusual for a couple of reasons. First of all, we never found out just why the Russians allowed Marina to leave the Soviet Union at a time when they were not permitting any Russians to come out. Second, she was a woman of extraordinary intelligence, much smarter than Oswald. Oswald had tried to commit suicide while he was in Russia by slashing his wrists, and we developed evidence that the Soviets looked on him as a nut, a nuisance, and were anxious to get him out of the country. This information was not firm, but was reported to us from a number of sources. There were so many other more subversive characters in our files with worse records than Oswald's and we had so little on Oswald that his case was considered a "Pending Inactive" case. Lee Harvey Oswald was really a cipher, a nobody to the FBI. After the assassination, of course, he became our most important subject.

But even after we zeroed in on Oswald, there were huge gaps in the case, gaps we never did close. For example, we never found out what went on between Oswald and the Cubans in Mexico.

Although his Russian connection had alerted us to Oswald in the first place, the bureau really couldn't keep him under surveillance merely because he had been to Russia and married a Russian wife. I can imagine the reaction of the Civil Liberties Union if we had— "Can't American citizens go to Russia without being hounded by the FBI?" Oswald wasn't a criminal, just a nut, and the FBI doesn't have the facilities to keep tabs on nuts.

I always tended to doubt that Oswald was a Russian or a Cuban agent because of his unsuccessful attempt on the life of General

Edwin A. Walker. Walker was a right-winger, a John Bircher, but basically a nobody to the Russians or the Cubans. It would have been unnecessary for a valuable agent to take the chance of shooting Walker if Oswald had the assignment of killing the president. If I had to guess I'd say that Oswald acted alone, but I was puzzled by the accuracy of his shooting. Oswald didn't have a record of being an outstanding marksman and yet he hit the president with two shots while his car was moving slowly down the road. His third shot hit Governor Connally. I went to the book depository from which Oswald fired at the president and I looked out the window where he was positioned. I've been around guns all my life and I'm a reasonably good shot, but I must say that that would be quite a task for me. It was, tragically, damn good shooting.

On the other hand, it seemed extremely likely to me that Jack Ruby, a local nightclub owner who knew a lot of low characters, who was a police buff, and who had a working relationship with the local police, could easily have been a police informer. That certainly could explain Ruby's presence at the jail where he shot Oswald.

Hoover became disturbed by some of the things that started to develop. Both the Dallas police and the Secret Service began accusing us of not cooperating with them. Then it was revealed that before the assassination one of our agents in Dallas had received a note from Oswald telling the agent to stop hassling his wife Marina. The note was unfortunately destroyed by the agent.

Hoover's main thought was always how to cover, how to protect himself, so he began issuing letters of censure to men in the bureau. His theory was that if he was scored with having mishandled the investigation, he could say: "The moment the assassination occurred I looked into the matter and fixed the responsibility for what happened on individuals to whom I gave letters of censure, transferred, or both." Hoover always had someone else do his dirty work, so he appointed a friend of mine, Jim Gale, as assistant director to handle the inspection. Gale, of course, was told beforehand by Hoover what kind of a result to come up with even before he spoke with anyone or looked into a single detail. Gale didn't want the job at all, but had to go through with it. The result was that two supervisors were given letters of censure and transferred out of headquarters, which meant a demotion in salary too. Fifteen others, including me, were given letters of censure. I had never even seen the file on Oswald and had never heard of him before the assassination, but I was head of the division and was theoretically responsible for what everyone did. Hoover was once again able to cover himself.

Hoover was delighted when Gerald Ford was named to the Warren Commission. The director wrote in one of his internal memos that the bureau could expect Ford to "look after FBI interests," and he did, keeping us fully advised of what was going on behind closed doors. He was our man, our informant, on the Warren Commission.

Ford's relationship with Hoover went back to Ford's first congressional campaign in Michigan. Our agents out in the field kept a watchful eye on local congressional races and advised Hoover whether the winners were friends or enemies. Hoover had a complete file developed on each incoming congressman. He knew their family backgrounds, where they had gone to school, whether or not they played football, and any other tidbits he could weave into a subsequent conversation.

Gerald Ford was a friend of Hoover's, and he first proved it when he made a speech not long after he came to Congress recommending a pay raise for J. Edgar Hoover, the great director of the FBI. He proved it again when he tried to impeach Supreme Court Justice William O. Douglas, a Hoover enemy.

President Kennedy's death did nothing to soften Hoover's attitude toward Attorney General Robert Kennedy. "The press calls him Bobby," he once told me in a deprecating tone of voice. (Hoover also felt that Bobby demeaned the dignity of the Department of Justice by bringing his dog to the office.) But Hoover played up to him as long as Jack was president. Like his brother, Attorney General Robert Kennedy realized he would have to live and work with Hoover, and he went out of his way to make a good impression on the director just after the election. Bobby came looking for Hoover's support when Jack asked his brother to serve as attorney general, and he told the director he wouldn't take the job without his support. Hoover gushed his approval, although he told Kennedy he was not allowed to give

him a public endorsement, and he went on to compare the Kennedy brothers to John Foster Dulles and Allen Dulles.

The honeymoon was over quite soon, for the two men couldn't help but let their real feelings show. Neither Jack nor Bobby ever doubted that Hoover was actually a powerful and relentless enemy, and they kept their distance.

Hoover selected a section chief from the Criminal Division named Courtney Evans to act as liaison between the FBI and the attorney general. Evans was a fine man, and he became a pal of Bobby's and of his brother Jack. This put him in a very difficult position, as he was forced to play up to Hoover's prejudices by demeaning both Kennedys regularly in countless memos. He did what he had to do to keep his job, never dreaming that the damn memos would be made public. Evans remained loyal to the Kennedys in deed if not in word, and it was rumored that when JFK was reelected, Hoover would be out and Courtney Evans would become the new director. How I wish that that had happened!

Hoover heard that rumor too, and the day after the assassination Evans was as good as dead himself as far as Hoover was concerned. The director began to find fault with everything Evans did, making reckless charges, shooting him down as relentlessly as he later shot me down. Evans talked to me and to Al Belmont, then the number three man, about his future with the bureau. "Court," Belmont told him gently, "you don't have a future." I agreed, and Courtney decided to give up and retire.

I was present at his final meeting with Hoover, which took place in the director's office. "This is a great loss to the bureau," Hoover said with a perfectly straight face, and he presented Evans with his FBI badge to keep as a gesture of thanks for Courtney's years of service. What a hypocrite! If Courtney hadn't retired, Hoover would have fired him.

Hoover set a trap for Bobby Kennedy when the attorney general, accompanied by Courtney Evans, was visiting our Chicago office. The special agent in charge asked Kennedy if he would like to listen to some "sensitive" tapes which his agents had collected during the

Gerald Ford with other Warren Commission members (from left): Ford, Rep. Hale Boggs, Sen. Richard Russell, and Supreme Court Justice Earl Warren. *United Press International*

course of a criminal investigation. Kennedy should have refused, should have asked to have transcripts sent through the usual channels. Instead, he sat down and listened to the tapes, and by doing so compromised himself. After listening to the tapes for just a moment or two, Kennedy had to realize that they were the result of unauthorized taps. But he kept listening, which to Hoover implied tacit approval. Never a man to let an opportunity go by, Hoover insisted on and got sworn affidavits from every agent present stating that Kennedy had listened to the tapes and had not questioned their legality. Those affidavits are probably still in the files.

Although Hoover was desperately trying to catch Bobby Kennedy red-handed at anything, he never did. Kennedy was almost a Puritan. We used to watch him at parties, where he would order one glass of scotch and still be sipping from the same glass two hours later. The stories about Bobby Kennedy and Marilyn Monroe were just stories. The original story was invented by a so-called journalist, a right-wing zealot who had a history of spinning wild yarns. It spread like wildfire, of course, and J. Edgar Hoover was right there, gleefully fanning the flames.

When Bobby Kennedy was campaigning for the presidential nomination in 1968, his name came up at a top-level FBI meeting. Hoover was not present, and Clyde Tolson was presiding in his absence. I was one of eight men who heard Tolson respond to the mention of Kennedy's name by saying, "I hope someone shoots and kills the son of a bitch." This was five or six weeks before the California primary. I used to stare at Tolson after Bobby Kennedy was murdered, wondering if he had qualms of conscience about what he said. I don't think he did.

On 6 June 1968, the Los Angeles office called me at about two o'clock in the morning to tell me that Robert Kennedy had been killed. I had the damn phone in my hand, half asleep, and I asked the agent to repeat what he'd said. And then I woke up, really woke up.

There was another tremendous investigation of course, and we did finally decide that Sirhan acted alone, but we never found out why. Although he was fanatic about the Arab cause, we could never link Sirhan to any organization or to any other country. He never received a dime from anyone for what he did. We sometimes wondered whether someone representing the Soviets had suggested to Sirhan that Kennedy would take action against the Arab countries if he became president. But that was only a guess.

There were so many holes in the case. We never could account for Sirhan's presence in the kitchen of the Ambassador Hotel. Did he know Kennedy would be walking through? Intelligence work is exasperating. You can work on a case for years and still not know the real answers. There are so many unknowns. Investigating Sirhan was a frustrating job, for in the end we were never sure.

Hoover's dislike of Robert Kennedy continued even after Kennedy's death. We had a positive identification on James Earl Ray, the killer of Martin Luther King, Jr., a full day before Hoover released the news to the world that he had been caught in London. He purposely held up the report of Ray's capture so that he could interrupt TV coverage of Bobby's burial, on June 8.

Hoover was as fond of Ted Kennedy as he had been of his brothers. It was the FBI which circulated the story that Teddy Kennedy was a poor student and had cheated on an exam. By rights the FBI should have had nothing to do with the Chappaquiddick affair, but the Boston office was put on the case right away. Although Hoover was delighted to cooperate, the order did not originate with him. It came from President Lyndon Johnson.

Everything that came in on Kennedy and on Mary Jo Kopechne, the unfortunate young woman who drowned in his car, was funnelled to the White House. Hoover even assigned our local agent to dig into the affair. President Johnson asked Hoover to make the assignment and Hoover jumped through the hoop to do it.

FOUR

LBJ's Tool

AFTER JOHN F. KENNEDY was killed in Dallas, Lyndon Johnson lived in fear that he too would be assassinated. I was told by his Secret Service guards (many of whom hated Johnson's imperious attitude toward them) that after LBJ became president he usually rode slumped down in his limousine with his head below the window. When he flew anywhere in Air Force One there were always two or three fighter planes flying a couple of thousand feet above the president's plane, ready to dive down if another plane flew too close.

If Jack Kennedy's death shocked and worried Johnson, it also made him warier than ever of Bobby and Teddy Kennedy. Johnson believed that both surviving Kennedy brothers had presidential ambitions, and as president he saw himself as their natural enemy and acted accordingly. Threatened by Bobby in particular, he was afraid that there would be a groundswell of support for Kennedy's nomination as vice-president at the Democratic convention in Atlantic City where LBJ, an "accidental president," sought the unanimous support of his party. Johnson wanted to choose his own running mate, and Bobby Kennedy was definitely not on his list of possible choices.

Since Johnson felt he had to protect himself against any last-minute surprises from the Kennedy camp, he turned to the FBI for help. He asked Hoover for a special security team of a dozen or so agents to be headed by Cartha D. ("Deke") DeLoach, Courtney Evans's successor to the job of White House liaison. Ostensibly the agents would be there to guard against threats to the president, but this security force was actually a surveillance team, a continuation of the FBI's surveillance on Martin Luther King in Atlantic City. By keeping track of King, LBJ could also keep track of RFK.

With the help of the FBI, Johnson spied on Teddy Kennedy during a trip Kennedy made to Italy. One of our agents heard that Lucky Luciano, the American mob boss who had been deported to his native Italy by the federal government, had carried on a conversation with Kennedy in a restaurant in Rome. Actually, we learned that the conversation was completely innocent on Kennedy's part. Luciano had approached Kennedy in an effort to get help in his plea to be allowed to return to the United States to die, and Kennedy had refused. The agent, who knew that Hoover would be interested in anything on the subject, reported the incident to Washington. Hoover used that report as an excuse to investigate Kennedy to see if he had any ties to organized crime. We conducted a discreet but massive investigation and found out what everyone had known all along: that Kennedy was opposed to organized crime in every way, and always had been.

In 1965 Johnson used the FBI to set up Teddy Kennedy. Teddy had come to Johnson seeking a federal judgeship for Frank Morrissey, a Kennedy family friend and former aid to JFK. Johnson agreed to nominate Morrissey, but as soon as Kennedy was out the door of the Oval office, LBJ was on the phone to DeLoach ordering an all-out FBI investigation of the Boston lawyer. It was one of the most exhaustive investigations of its kind we ever conducted, far more so than our puny investigation of G. Harrold Carswell when he was nominated to the Supreme Court. We went all out on Morrissey, but we didn't find much. The worst that anyone could say about Morrissey was that he had an average reputation as a lawyer. As the courts were filled with mediocre judges who had attended undistinguished law schools, many of them put there by Johnson, Morrissey seemed to be in the clear. But a few days after Johnson received the FBI report on Morrissey, stories began appearing in newspapers and magazines calling him unqualified for the job, stories that were leaked to the press by the White House, citing his unimpressive legal and academic background as proof. It was a deliberate smear and it worked. An embarrassed Teddy Kennedy was forced to ask LBJ to withdraw the nomi-

nation. Johnson had no conrete reason to dislike Morrissey; he only
wanted to make Kennedy look bad and Morrissey's nomination presented him with the opportunity to do so.

Johnson and Hoover had their mutual fear and hatred of the
Kennedys in common—and more. As neighbors in Washington since
the days when Johnson was a senator from Texas, they had been
frequent dinner guests in each other's homes. They remained close
when Johnson served as vice-president, but there was a change in
their relationship when LBJ became president. The director was over
sixty-five by that time, past retirement age for federal employees, and
he stayed in office only because of a special waiver which required the
president's signature each year. That waiver put Hoover right in
Johnson's pocket. With that leverage Johnson began to take advantage of Hoover, using the bureau as his personal investigative arm.
His never-ending requests were usually political, and sometimes illegal. There was absolutely nothing Johnson wouldn't ask of the FBI,
whether or not it fell within the bureau's jurisdiction. And Hoover
hot-footed it to Johnson's demands. The few times he let LBJ down, it
was simply because the bureau lacked the capacity.

Whenever the occasion arose, President Johnson would use the
FBI against the press. As an example, on 15 March 1965, LBJ called
the bureau and said he was damned disturbed about a story published
by the *Washington Evening Star* saying that the president was going
to appoint Kermit Gordon (then the director of the Bureau of Budget)
to be secretary of the treasury. Johnson made it clear he was very
displeased that this had been leaked to the press and said he was
going to put a stop to it.

The president told us to "discreetly" find out who leaked the
story. We said we'd do what he asked. He reminded the bureau that
we had done this before for him and obviously we had good press contacts. What we did not tell President Johnson was that it was the FBI
who had leaked the information to the *Star* in the first place. This was
a calculated policy designed to get the press obligated to the FBI so
that we could subsequently use them. What we did tell LBJ was that
the FBI would not and could not leak any such information because

we did not know Mr. Gordon was under any consideration, a patent lie. We had had the tip early from one of our countless highly placed sources of information.

Hoover had chosen "Deke" DeLoach, a man who at times seemed to be Hoover's protégé and at other times seemed to be almost a son to the director, to act as FBI liaison to Johnson when he served in the Senate. DeLoach's relationship with Johnson continued into the White House where, much to Hoover's chagrin, DeLoach became a member of Johnson's inner circle. DeLoach and his family visited with the Johnsons at Camp David and at the LBJ Ranch, and eventually DeLoach obtained a direct line to LBJ's White House from his bedroom.

Because his advanced age put him in such a precarious position, Hoover literally turned the bureau and all its resources over to DeLoach and Johnson to use as they saw fit, and he found himself very much in the back seat, almost a captive of the president and his FBI liaison. He couldn't do a damned thing about it either, even if he had wanted to, which I doubt. All Hoover wanted was to stay on as director, to avoid retirement. Appearances were maintained, however, and Johnson, through DeLoach, treated Hoover with kid gloves and was always careful to see that the attorney general, Hoover's nominal boss, did the same.

For instance, early in 1965 DeLoach told Hoover that the president wanted Hoover to know in confidence that he had called both the attorney general and deputy attorney general into his office and had specifically instructed them that they were to get along with the director and the FBI. The president, DeLoach said, told the attorney general that the director's advice should be sought, particularly on future appointments in the department, and especially the assistant attorney generalship of the Criminal Division. The president had also instructed the attorney general to initiate luncheons or regular meetings to which he should invite Hoover. DeLoach told Hoover that Johnson was sure that Attorney General Katzenbach would not be around very long and that he hoped the FBI could put up with him for the time being.

I first became aware of Deke DeLoach when he was working as FBI liaison to the CIA. Although we had never met—we worked in different divisions—I had heard about him from some former FBI agents who were working for the CIA. The word was around that DeLoach was consciously driving a wedge between the two agencies. Hoover was jealous of the CIA's power and he had been bitterly disappointed when the new agency was formed to dominate the field of worldwide intelligence. DeLoach played on that jealousy by hint-

Cartha "Deke" DeLoach, Hoover's liaison man to the LBJ White House. *Wide World Photos*

ing to Hoover that the CIA was planning to extend its field of operations to the United States. To Hoover, that was like waving a red flag in front of a bull, and he was furious when he heard it. My CIA contacts saw through DeLoach's game and came to me in alarm to discuss the ever-widening gap between the two agencies. They asked if I could do anything to remove DeLoach from his liaison job, but I didn't have the authority.

DeLoach once acted as liaison between the CIA and me when I was asked to give a speech to fifteen hundred or so CIA employees. Accompanied by three men from the CIA, DeLoach himself drove me to the building opposite the Lincoln Memorial where the CIA held many of its meetings. When we arrived at 6:30, no one was there. The speech was scheduled for 7:00. By 6:45, when not one other person had shown up, I began to get very nervous. DeLoach told me to calm down, that the CIA was so disorganized that everyone else was probably late. At five minutes to seven, when we were still alone at the hall, DeLoach went to use the phone. He came back cursing the CIA, insisting that they had given him the wrong information—I actually had been scheduled to speak in the auditorium of the HEW building, where a full house was waiting impatiently for the speaker to arrive. The CIA men and I were full of apologies when we finally arrived at the right place at 7:15, but not DeLoach. "Couldn't help being late," he told the anxious CIA delegation who met us at the door. "It couldn't be avoided. We were working on an important espionage case."

DeLoach and I did not work together, but we knew each other rather well, enough for him to make a personal request. Somehow he had heard that I enjoyed browsing in bookstores, and he asked me if I would buy some books for him. I asked what kind of books he wanted—novels? biography? history? "All of them," he answered, "just as long as they look good and are written on serious topics." He went on to explain that he wanted the books not to read but to display in his home to impress his guests. I did send him some books, mostly used but in good condition, and he sent me grateful memos.

Although DeLoach was the number three man in the FBI before me, there was never really any competition between us. If we disagreed, it was because I felt he was giving my friends a raw deal, not me. For instance, I didn't like the way he treated an associate of mine named Arbor Gray. As the bureau's resident expert in the "dangers of communism," I was swamped with offers of speaking engagements. DeLoach hoped to lighten my load by taking over some of those engagements, but Hoover turned him down so I picked Arbor for the job. I was still breaking Arbor in when I brought him with me to speak to a group in New Jersey. I planned to handle one phase of a subject and let Arbor handle another. Our points of view dovetailed beautifully, and thanks to Arbor we gave a marvelous talk. But De-Loach wrote a memo to Hoover saying that one of his cronies from the American Legion (DeLoach held many high posts in the Legion, including national vice-commander and chairman for public relations) hated Gray's speech and that DeLoach therefore had to recommend that Arbor Gray retire from the lecture circuit.

When the director showed me DeLoach's memo I defended Arbor's performance, and as soon as I got back to my office I ran a check on the legionnaire who complained about the speech. I found out that he owed money everywhere and that he had been found psychologically unfit to serve in the army and was discharged. I reported my findings to Hoover and all hell broke loose, but when the smoke cleared Arbor Gray was back on the lecture circuit and DeLoach never mentioned it again. No other complaint was lodged against Gray.

DeLoach was happy in his job as liaison man to Lyndon Johnson's White House, and he did his best to keep Johnson happy by doing whatever the president asked. He asked a lot. When Johnson was running for president against Senator Barry Goldwater, he asked DeLoach to have our agents go through the files to see if the FBI had anything he could use against any members of Goldwater's staff. DeLoach passed the word to Hoover, who, as always, was glad to oblige, and he sent whatever information we came up with (it wasn't much) straight to the White House.

Johnson's objections to Goldwater were political, but his attitude toward Senator William Fulbright, chairman of the Senate Foreign Relations Committee, was more personal. Johnson didn't like Fulbright, and he sincerely believed that the senator was playing into the hands of the enemy when he voiced his objections to LBJ's Vietnam policy. Through DeLoach, Johnson ordered Hoover to assign a few FBI agents to monitor Fulbright's televized Senate committee hearings and analyze what was said for any signs of Communist influence. It was absurd, but we did it.

Johnson was almost as paranoid about the Communist threat as Hoover was, and, through DeLoach, LBJ ordered Hoover to post an FBI lookout near the Soviet Embassy in Washington to observe visitors. The president insisted that a record be kept of any senator or congressman who entered the embassy, no matter what his mission.

DeLoach explained the president's feelings to Hoover in March of 1966. The president, said DeLoach, spoke of the harassment being given his policies by Senator Fulbright. Johnson said that there were only about six senators who formed the nucleus of the opposition, including Fulbright, Morse, Bobby Kennedy, Gruening, Clark (Pa.), and Aiken (Vt.). All of these men, Johnson had learned from the FBI, had either had dinner at the Soviet Embassy or lunches or private meetings with the Soviet ambassador prior to the beginning of their heavy opposition to the president's policies. As for Fulbright, De-Loach told Hoover, LBJ said that he "doesn't know what the smell of a cartridge is—he's a narrow-minded egotist who is attempting to run the country." The president said that what Bobby Kennedy was trying to do was to bring embarrassment to the administration and fame and publicity to himself.

Later that same month DeLoach told Hoover that LBJ wanted the director to discuss the embassy visits during a network television appearance the president planned to set up for him. LBJ said that Hoover might want to subtly work in the "fact" that there was considerable espionage going on and that certain Iron Curtain embassies were attracting many prominent legislators and leaders of the United States into doing their bidding. The president added that this would refer to Fulbright and Morse who, he felt, on the Vietnam issue, were definitely under control of the Soviet Embassy.

Johnson didn't limit his paranoia to senators and congressmen with possible Soviet connections, though. He wanted the FBI to keep an eye on every senator and congressman who opposed his policies, whether they were Republicans or Democrats, whether they leaned to the left or to the right. He wanted anything our agents could dig up on them that might prove embarrassing or politically damaging. He leaked the information we sent to him on Republicans to the press himself, but he was reluctant to attack members of his own party and supplied whatever damaging information he had on the Democrats to Everett Dirksen, the leading Republican in the Senate.

Johnson also wanted the FBI to keep a close watch on his critics in the press. For instance, in April of 1965 DeLoach told Hoover of Johnson's instructions regarding Robert Pierpoint, the White House correspondent for CBS. According to DeLoach, Jack Valenti had called him from the LBJ ranch at night, with the president in the background giving Valenti instructions. Valenti had explained that a Mr. Pierpoint had checked in at the Driscoll Hotel in Austin, Texas, and the president wanted to know as expeditiously as possible what phone calls Pierpoint had received from Washington and what phone calls Pierpoint had made from Austin to Washington, the time, and to whom the phone calls were placed. Valenti had said that Pierpoint was believed to be with the Columbia Broadcasting System (CBS).

DeLoach told Hoover that he then ordered our San Antonio office to make a discreet check at the Driscoll. They found that Pierpoint had checked in at the hotel and had neither made nor received any phone calls through the hotel switchboard, and that a William J. Moore of CBS who had checked into the hotel with Pierpoint had also neither made nor received any.

At 12:00 midnight, DeLoach reported, Valenti had called back again from the LBJ ranch and said that LBJ wanted to know if Pierpoint had received any calls at Johnson City, Texas. DeLoach told Valenti that it was probably too late to be bothering our established contacts with the telephone company at midnight; however, a discreet check would be made the first thing in the morning. Of course, nothing ever came of this waste of FBI manpower.

And, DeLoach explained to Hoover toward the end of 1967, Johnson also wanted the FBI to spy on his critics in the population at large. Bromley Smith, executive secretary of the National Security Council, had called him and said that Marvin Watson, special assistant to the president, wanted him to send to the bureau the "negative" telegrams and communications received by the president in reaction to his recent speech regarding U.S. policy in Vietnam. The communications in question were those which were clearly critical. Smith said that Watson wanted the names of the senders checked through FBI files so that the White House could get a picture of just who was sending these communications and whether a pattern existed. DeLoach ended that report to Hoover by telling him that all those telegrams and letters were being sent over from the White House.

Though Johnson's requests knew no bounds, they were never refused by Hoover. For example, whenever there was a public objec-

President Lyndon Johnson, more than any other president, used the FBI as a personal political tool. *Wide World Photos*

tion to any of Johnson's candidates for high government positions (Frank Morrissey notwithstanding), it would be up to the FBI to come up with so many ringing endorsements for the nominee that the naysayers would be lost in the crowd. To do so, our agents would sometimes have to interview fifty or one hundred people, which was a waste of their time and of the taxpayer's money. But once we came up with something from our file on one of Johnson's nominees so serious that there was no way we could bury it under a shower of praise. Through DeLoach, LBJ requested Hoover to send the applicant's FBI file containing the disastrous information over to the White House. Assistant Director of Security Paul McNichols vigorously protested this violation of FBI policy, a brave thing to do, but to no avail. Hoover saw to it that the offending file was sent to Johnson, and McNichols never saw it again.

DeLoach was riding high as Johnson's confidant. He had the

nerve to write a memo to Hoover saying that LBJ had heard rumors
that Hoover was planning to reassign DeLoach. Of course, DeLoach
wrote, the president knew that was a lie, but he wanted the director
to know the kind of vicious rumors that reached his presidential ears.
Hoover couldn't even wait until he finished reading the memo to
agree with Johnson. "No truth to this," he wrote right between the
paragraphs, and DeLoach had a firmer grip on his job than ever.

When the size of LBJ's staff grew too unwieldy, DeLoach and
Johnson came up with the idea of putting some of LBJ's White House
people on the FBI payroll. By doing so, LBJ could conceal the huge
number of people he actually employed. Hoover went along with it,
as he went along with everything Johnson and DeLoach dreamt up—
because his job depended on it. For example, Mildred Stegall, who
acted as a personal secretary to LBJ and Walter Jenkins for many
years, was at one point on the payroll of the FBI although she never
actually worked for us.

Working so closely with Johnson, DeLoach naturally found himself spending more and more time with LBJ's closest aide, Walter
Jenkins. The two men became close friends and Jenkins a frequent
visitor to the DeLoach home. When Jenkins was arrested for making
homosexual advances to a man in the basement men's room of the
Washington YMCA, it was DeLoach who carried the ball for Johnson.

The president immediately and publicly ordered an FBI investigation of the incident. Privately, he told the FBI how to run the investigation and what its results should reveal. Johnson wanted the
bureau to prove that the object of Jenkins's attention was being paid
by the Republican National Committee and that the whole incident
was a frame-up, a Republican plot. DeLoach told Hoover that LBJ
wanted agents to bear down on the complainant with respect to his
knowledge of Republican National Committee members, as well as
once again questioning him about a possible frame-up. Bear down we
did, but the man wouldn't budge an inch. Why should he? There was
no frame-up and there were no Republicans involved.

Then Johnson decided that Jenkins's problem sprang from a dis-
eased brain. DeLoach went to see Jenkins's doctor to get a public

statement to that effect, but the doctor refused.

Johnson then asked the bureau to attempt to bring further pressure on the park policeman who filed a complaint about Jenkins's attempt to solicit him in LaFayette Park in Washington (which happened before the incident in the YMCA). DeLoach also asked Bill Moyers, LBJ's press secretary, to have Stewart Udall, secretary of the interior, bring pressure on the park policeman so that this man would "tell all," but LBJ said that Udall had already tried to bring pressure on him and that it had amounted to nothing. Johnson also asked the FBI to send a letter to the Department of Justice to consider bringing the park policeman before a grand jury.

The courage shown by both Jenkins's doctor and the policeman restored some of the faith I used to have in human beings. The doctor and the policeman both stood their ground and refused to lie, and the representatives of the president of the United States and the Federal Bureau of Investigation had to back off.

Jenkins was taken to the hospital in a state of collapse, where he was treated for "extreme fatigue." DeLoach, who by this time thought of himself as Hoover's successor and longed to hasten the director's retirement, saw in Jenkins's hospitalization a chance to humiliate Hoover. He talked the director into sending flowers and a "get well" note to Jenkins, probably by saying that the gesture would please the president. Hoover, ever eager to please, did what DeLoach suggested. Of course, the story was leaked to the press and Hoover found himself in the headlines, a national laughing stock for sending flowers to a man he was investigating. DeLoach managed to convince Hoover he had done the right thing after all, telling Hoover that LBJ had dwelt at some length on the unfortunate publicity about the flowers sent to Jenkins and said that some newspapers were not taking into account the fact that the director had ordered those flowers sent before the beginning of the investigation. Johnson wanted Hoover to know that, despite any criticism he might receive over this incident, history would record the fact that the director had done a great humanitarian deed. LBJ said that he received flowers from Khrushchev every time he had a bad cold or was laid up in bed for a day or two. This did not make him love Khrushchev any more, LBJ went on, and that the American public certainly recognized this fact. Johnson said that "good-thinking, sensible people will realize that the director had done a very kind thing."

(Our investigation actually showed that Jenkins had a previous record of arrest for the same offense. Johnson may well have known all along, but he just didn't seem to care about a man's sexuality; there were at least two other homosexuals serving on Johnson's White House staff when Jenkins was arrested.)

The Jenkins scandal broke just weeks before the presidential election of 1964, and Johnson (and, of course, the FBI) moved to prevent Barry Goldwater from using Jenkins's misfortune as political ammunition against LBJ. Jenkins had once been cleared for membership in Goldwater's air force squadron and he had accompanied Goldwater on may flights. Johnson planned to play up the relationship, and a lot more dirt that our agents had dug up on LBJ's opponent as well, if Goldwater tried to take political advantage of the situation.

LBJ told his FBI liason man DeLoach that Goldwater would find it difficult to deny that he knew Jenkins quite well personally or that Jenkins had traveled with Goldwater on several occasions.

Johnson turned to the FBI again when he felt he had a serious problem in the Dominican Republic, so serious in fact that he had already sent twenty-five thousand American marines to "save" that tiny island nation from a possible Communist takeover.

The marines had no business there at all, and the FBI had even less. The CIA had been down in the Dominican Republic for years, both overtly and covertly, and they had the situation well in hand from an intelligence standpoint. But Johnson had taken a beating in the newspapers over his decision to send in the marines, and the president felt he could balance the bad publicity with good by ordering the FBI to join the fight against the Red Menace. It made a great story, and Hoover, with his dream of a worldwide FBI intelligence network, jumped through the usual hoops to carry out Johnson's scheme. The whole phony set-up made me angry, especially as I was put in charge of the operation, and I dragged my heels before assigning any agents to go down there, putting off the inevitable. In May of 1965 when I finally wrote the memo requesting permission to send the men down, Hoover wrote "It's about time" on the bottom.

Naturally, the CIA was horrified to find the FBI operating in the Dominican Republic, as horrified as the FBI would have been had Johnson ordered the CIA to investigate a case in New York City. Richard Helms, director of the CIA, found out about it in the newspapers, so I called him to arrange a meeting. He offered to come over to see me, but I knew that thirty seconds after Helms entered the building Hoover would have been told, so I went over his way. We sat and looked at each other, almost numb with disbelief. We agreed to work together and to try to keep our agents out of each other's operations. And that was just the way it worked out, like hand in glove. Of course, this agreement had to be kept secret from Hoover or I would have been fired.

Hoover's lack of enthusiasm for the cause of racial equality in America extended to the civil rights workers who were so active during the Johnson years. Hoover managed to keep his agents out of many early racial confrontations in the South, but the disappearance of three young civil rights workers in Mississippi in June 1964 became a major national scandal, and President Johnson forced Hoover to get the bureau involved.

Andrew Goodman and Michael Schwerner, both white, had gone to Mississippi from New York City to take part in the effort to register black voters. While driving near Philadelphia, Mississippi, with James Chaney, a black civil rights worker from nearby Meridian, they were arrested for speeding by a local deputy sheriff. Lawrence Rainey, the Neshoba County sheriff, claimed that the three had been released after spending five hours in jail waiting for bail to be set, but that they hadn't been seen or heard from since then. When the local police failed to locate either the young men or their bodies, the bureau was called in. At first we thought there was a possibility of kidnapping, but we came to realize almost immediately that Goodman, Schwerner, and Chaney had been murdered.

The FBI had no office in Mississippi so we flew in agents from nearby offices to investigate. When the car in which the boys had been riding was found stripped down and burnt out in a swamp, the navy volunteered to send in two hundred sailors to help with the search. But even with the navy's help we weren't getting anywhere. We couldn't find the bodies.

As the weeks dragged by, President Johnson felt more and more pressure to resolve the case, and in turn began to pressure Hoover. The case had become a political albatross to Johnson, a southerner who felt that the public doubted the depth of his commitment to solving it, and an embarrassment to Hoover, who was tired of newspaper stories which intimated that the FBI wasn't really trying to find the bodies, or worse, that FBI agents had killed the three themselves and were covering up their crime. That story really stirred up our men in the South.

The accusations that the FBI had been avoiding involvement were true. "We're investigators," Hoover would say about his refusal to protect civil rights workers, "not policemen." When James Meredith marched through Mississippi, Hoover sent just enough men to avoid criticism, and the few he sent were under orders to steer clear of confrontations.

Our agents had infiltrated the civil rights movement to see if the civil rights workers were part of a subversive plot to overthrow the United States, but they had kept out of the way of the local white citizens who were making life so dangerous for those civil rights workers. This was in part because Hoover didn't want to offend the southern sheriffs and police chiefs who had helped the bureau solve so many cases in the past. He also felt more comfortable with and more sympathetic toward those old rednecks than he did toward blacks and students, whose motivations and lifestyles he didn't understand at all.

I couldn't agree, though, with Martin Luther King Jr.'s statement that most of our agents in the South were local men hostile to the civil rights workers. We employed many northern agents in the South, but we employed southerners too, because in certain cases a local man could be more effective than a northerner in getting information out of a southern sheriff.

After the disappearance of Goodman, Schwerner, and Chaney, Hoover's halfway measures were not good enough for President Johnson. Mindful of the news value of a good story, Lyndon Johnson ordered Hoover to go down to Mississippi personally to open an FBI office. Hoover didn't want to do it, especially since all the glory would

About two hundred men from the U.S. Navy helped the FBI search for the bodies of the three young men, and two hundred U.S. Marines were also almost landed. But it took a thirty-thousand-dollar bribe to finally locate the bodies, buried under tons of earth. *United Press International*

The three young civil rights workers, all in their twenties, killed by the Ku Klux Klan in 1964: Michael Schwerner, James Chaney, and Andrew Goodman. *Wide World Photos*

go to Johnson, but he had to do what the president asked.

Back in Washington, Hoover called me one morning to ask what progress we were making in our search for the three bodies.

"We're doing everything we can," I told him, "but we're not making any real progress."

"President Johnson will be very unhappy about that," he said. "How many men have we got down there?"

I told him how many agents we had brought in on the case, and about the two hundred sailors who were helping us look for the bodies. "Keep the pressure on and do everything possible," Hoover told me, and hung up.

I went on with my work and, as I did everyday, I read the noon headlines coming across the UPI ticker on my desk. That day I read that President Johnson had announced to the press that he had personally taken charge of the investigation, and that he had ordered two hundred marines to help the FBI find the missing civil rights workers. Where the hell, I asked myself, did he get the two hundred marines?

At that moment Hoover buzzed me on the direct line he had to my office. "Have you seen the UPI ticker?" he asked.

"I have it in my hand," I said.

"I thought you told me it was two hundred sailors." I told him I had. "Do we have any marines down there?" he asked.

"None," I told him.

"I told President Johnson it was two hundred sailors," he said in a puzzled voice. "Why did it come out marines? I've got to call the president and tell him a mistake has been made."

Hoover hung up and called back ten minutes later. He was so upset that his voice was shaking. "I told President Johnson that we had two hundred sailors in Mississippi, not two hundred marines. He told me if that was the case, to get two hundred marines down there right away."

I couldn't believe it. I thought I hadn't heard Hoover right. But it was true. The president held Hoover responsible for the mistake, and he said it was up to the director to correct it. And Hoover said he wanted me to give the bizarre order to Robert McNamara, the secretary of defense.

Al Belmont, who was then the number three man in the bureau, called me just as I was about to call McNamara. Belmont was a wonderful fellow, and had saved my neck more than once when I was out in the field and couldn't defend myself against snipers in Washington. I told him about the mix-up and about Johnson and Hoover's proposed solution. We both started to laugh, and I remember I laughed so hard the tears rolled out of my eyes.

When I finally got myself back in shape, I called Secretary McNamara, an intelligent man but a real cold fish, and told him the story.

"Just a minute, Sullivan," he said when I finished talking, "say that again."

I did, and then he made me repeat the story a third time.

"I don't understand this," he said. "I've never received such a request from the FBI. I have a direct line to the president. I talk to him every day. Why didn't he ask me? Sullivan, where did you get these instructions?"

I could understand his confusion. "I told you," I said patiently, "I got these orders from Mr. Hoover. Mr. Hoover got them from President Johnson."

McNamara was becoming irritated because I wasn't going through channels. When he asked again if I was sure I was "relaying the instructions correctly," I told him I had made careful notes of my conversation with Hoover.

"Well, it doesn't make any sense," he said, "but if they want two hundred marines down there, I'll have Joe Califano [then undersecretary of defense] handle it. I'll have him call you."

I thanked Secretary McNamara, he hung up, and I never spoke to him about the matter again. When Califano called a few minutes later, he was mad as hell, cursing and damning everything. "What the hell is going on over there?" he asked.

I knew Califano and I felt I could communicate with him. "Now look, Joe," I said, "please don't argue with me. If you want to get this thing straightened out, call the president."

"Hell, no," he barked. "This is what happens when the brass starts to do something they should leave to the working stiffs. They just don't know how things work."

I agreed with him about that.

"All right," he said finally, with resignation in his voice, "I'll get two hundred marines down there, but, goddamn it, I won't get two hundred and one."

I told him two hundred would be sufficient, and asked him to keep in close touch, as the director wanted a blow-by-blow description of the maneuver. Hoover would then relay the information to President Johnson. Califano called me back thirty minutes later to say that he had been in contact with Fort Bragg and Paris Island, and that one helicopter carrying twenty or thirty marines was already in the air, a second was ready to take off, and the rest were being lined up. I told Hoover, who in turn told Johnson.

Califano had just called again to say the second helicopter was in the air when Hoover buzzed me on the intercom and asked how many helicopters were actually on the way to Mississippi. When I described the situation, he shouted, "Stop them, stop them right away. President Johnson does not want any marines to land in Mississippi."

Hoover then explained that the president had been talking to Mississippi's Governor Johnson and Senator Eastland. Both were furious and were threatening to tell the press that marines were invading the state of Mississippi against the will of its people. The last thing Johnson wanted was this kind of publicity. The marines had to be stopped.

So I called Califano. Talk about cursing! I never heard such language in all my life. "Joe," I finally said, "stop swearing and head off those helicopters."

Califano called me back a few minutes later. The first helicopter had almost landed when Califano reached the pilot, but he did reach him in time and it, along with all the other helicopters, had turned around to fly back. I couldn't help wondering what the marines in those helicopters were thinking. They probably were never told the story behind their strange, abortive trip. Joe was still on the phone, still cursing, and I asked him how long he had been working for the federal government.

"Eight years," he replied.

"I've been at it a bit longer," I told him, "and if you don't mind,

I'd like to make a suggestion. When you get an unusual request, just try to see the humor in it—lean back in your chair and laugh like hell."

There was a long pause before Califano said very solemnly, "Well, goddamn it, I might see the humor in it tomorrow, but I'm not laughing today."

As it turned out, even if we had a thousand sailors and a thousand marines in Mississippi looking for those bodies, we never would have found them. They had been buried under thirty feet of earth. A huge hole had been dug a few days before the murders as part of a dam construction project, and the murderers took advantage of it by burying the bodies on the bottom a day or two before a bulldozer refilled the hole with hundreds of tons of earth. No one could have found them under that.

We finally cracked the case with the help of an informant, one of the people involved. We gave him about thirty thousand dollars to tell us who did the job and where the bodies were buried. He was a member of the local Klan organization, and, quite prudently, used some of the money to build a barricade around his house and buy a couple of ugly German shepherds. He had been one of a group of nineteen Klansmen who took the young men out of their car when they left jail and shot them dead in the brush. The bureau probably saved taxpayers hundreds of thousands of dollars worth of investigating hours by paying our informant thirty thousand.

Without informants, any police department—federal, state, or local—would be almost helpless. In the case of the Philadelphia, Mississippi, murders our agents were reasonably sure of what had happened and who has been involved, but they couldn't prove anything until they found the bodies. The men were charged with conspiracy to deprive Goodman, Schwerner, and Chaney of their civil rights—not murder since murder is not a federal crime—and none of those involved received more than a ten-year sentence. But they were apprehended and President Johnson was off the hook.

Johnson used the FBI as his personal political police force right to the very end of his term. In fact, just a few days before the 1968

presidential election between Nixon and Humphrey, Johnson decided he wanted us to check on the phone calls made from vice-
presidential candidate Spiro Agnew's campaign plane during the
stopover in Albuquerque, New Mexico. Johnson believed that the
Republicans were in contact with the South Vietnamese government,
and that they were trying to keep the South Vietnamese away from
the conference table in an effort to sabotage Johnson's Paris peace
talks. LBJ suspected that Mrs. Anna Chennault, an influential and
wealthy Washington widow who also headed a group called "Concerned Asians for Nixon," was carrying messages between Agnew and
the South Vietnamese Embassy. The president's orders to the FBI
(by way of DeLoach) were for the Albuquerque office to conduct a
careful check of all outgoing phone calls made by the then vice-
presidential candidate Spiro Agnew on the date of 2 November 1968,
at the time he was in Albuquerque. Johnson also wanted our agents to
put Mrs. Chennault and the South Vietnamese Embassy under physical surveillance and to put wiretaps on their telephones, which he
did.

Naturally, this was a top-secret operation, and DeLoach conveyed to Hoover the president's concern for keeping it that way late
in 1968. DeLoach reported that Bromley Smith had called him from
the White House to pass on LBJ's instructions that all copies of messages being forwarded from the FBI to the White House in connection with the South Vietnamese Embassy and Mrs. Chennault were
to be treated in the strictest confidence, and that all precautions were
to be taken to protect these communications. Smith said that this situation might very well "blow the roof off of the political race yet."

DeLoach was also concerned about the secrecy of the operation,
so he recommended to Hoover that the file concerning these taps be
maintained in the Special File Room, and that because of the highly
sensitive nature of the information contained in the file, it should be
afforded strictly limited handling.

We never came up with any damaging evidence against Agnew
or Mrs. Chennault, so after Nixon won the election Johnson called off
the physical surveillance on Mrs. Chennault and the South Vietnamese and cancelled the wiretap on Mrs. Chennault. But, as DeLoach
put it in a memo to Hoover dated 7 November 1968, Johnson "de-

sired us to keep current wiretaps on the South Vietnamese Embassy in operation."

In retrospect, perhaps the FBI should have gone full steam ahead and investigated the hell out of Spiro Agnew. Maybe we could have revealed him then for what he was.

FIVE

Flacking for the Bureau

THE FBI'S MAIN THRUST was not investigations but public relations and propaganda to glorify Hoover. Everyone who
worked in the bureau, especially those of us in high places
around him, bear our share of the blame.

Flacking for the FBI was part of every agent's job from his first
day. In fact, "making a good first impression" was a necessary
prerequisite for being hired as a special agent in the first place. Bald-
headed men, for example, were never hired as agents because
Hoover thought a bald head made a bad impression. No matter if the
man involved was a member of Phi Beta Kappa or a much-decorated
marine, or both. Appearances were terribly important to Hoover, and
special agents had to have the right look and wear the right clothes.

One day Hoover was going up to his office in the elevator when a
young man, a clerk, wearing a red vest under his suit jacket got on
with him. And as if the red vest wasn't bad enough, the poor fellow's
face was broken out. As soon as Hoover got to his office, the order
went out to find the young man with pimples wearing a red vest, fire
him, and discipline the man who recommended him for employment.

Though a bald-headed man wouldn't be hired as an agent, an
employee who later lost his hair wasn't fired but was kept out of the
public eye. Nathan Ferris, who came from the family that invented
the Ferris Wheel, began his long career with the FBI with a full head
of hair but was bald by the time he worked for me at headquarters as
the man in charge of all our foreign offices. One day in the early
1960s, Nate came to me to say that his fondest wish was to close out
his FBI career in our Mexico City office where he had once worked.
Nate and his wife, who was Latin, both loved Mexico so much that he

was willing to accept a subordinate position just to go back.

It was fine with me and I told him so, but there was one problem. The men in our foreign offices were always on display, meeting people, speaking in public—in short, spreading Hoover's public relations message abroad. "Nate," I said to him, "you know what the policy is on bald heads. How am I going to get you a job in Mexico?" Ferris admitted that he had a problem, but he wanted to try anyway, so I okayed Ferris's request and sent it on to Al Belmont, who was the number three man at the time. Belmont called me as soon as he got my memo.

"Why the hell," he wanted to know, "did you send me this memorandum on Ferris? He's bald; Hoover will never approve him." When I explained to Al how much the job meant to Ferris, he agreed to try to push the transfer through, but we both knew the odds were against Nate.

Al called me a day or two later, laughing like hell. "I finally put something over on that no-good bastard Tolson," he said. Tolson, who was Hoover's closest aide as well as his closest, indeed only, friend, saw everything that went to Hoover and he met with Belmont when he received Nate's request for a transfer to Mexico.

"Belmont," Tolson said to Al, "I seem to remember that Nate Ferris is bald."

"Oh, no, Mr. Tolson," Al told me he said, "you're thinking of another fellow," and named another agent who was totally bald, even balder, than Nate was.

Tolson looked hard at Belmont, and then his face lit up. "You're right," he said, "that is who I'm thinking of," and he approved the transfer and passed the request on to Hoover, who was the last hurdle. Hoover had a rule that no man was to be sent out to a foreign office without a personal interview with the director. But Ferris was requesting his transfer at the director's busiest time of the year, just before his annual testimony before the House Appropriations Committee. As this appearance determined the FBI's budget, Hoover prepared for it very carefully. So Nate and I decided to try to get around the personal interview by writing Hoover a letter. We flattered him for about a page and a half, saying Nate knew how busy he was and felt he couldn't possibly take up any of his valuable time and was willing to forgo his interview because of that, crossed our fingers, and sent it off.

To our amazement, Hoover agreed and approved Nate's transfer to Mexico without seeing him. It was the first time he ever did that. But Nate still had one more thing to worry about. He had to come back to see Hoover and Tolson after two years in Mexico for a review. But he had two years to think of a way to get around that situation.

Two years after his transfer, Nate showed up in Washington. His head was still bald but he was loaded down with silver gifts from Mexico. When he went in to see Tolson, he spread about seventy-five dollars worth of silver on his desk. When he went in to see Hoover, he spread about a hundred dollars worth of silver trinkets on his desk. Both Hoover and Tolson were so busy looking at all their presents that they never noticed his bald head, and Nate returned to Mexico a happy man.

Hoover's insistence on good appearances was a ridiculous policy. One of my former students from the days when I taught school in Bolton, a man called Randall, decided that he wanted to join the FBI and asked if I could help. He was a smart young man with a fine character and I was delighted to recommend him. But he was turned down. The man who interviewed him thought that he was too much of a farm boy for the FBI, that he wasn't "polished" enough, that he lacked the maniacal gleam in the eye that FBI recruiters seem to value so highly. I was furious when I heard and I went right to Hoover with it. He agreed to give the young man another chance with a new interviewer.

I made it damn clear to the interviewer that he'd better not turn Randall down. He was accepted and graduated high in his class. I followed Randall's career and noted that he was getting high performance ratings from his superiors. After a few years in the bureau Randall called to say that he wanted to speak with me in person. The next morning he came to my office and said he wanted to quit. He had been assigned to the bureau in Cincinnati and told me that they had so many men there that they were falling over each other. Randall said that when the office there put a man under surveillance that needed just one or even two agents, as many as five men were stuffed into one car and their subjects very quickly caught on that they were being followed. Randall said, "I want to work. I want to do something. What I don't want is to be superfluous and waste a lot of time and the rest of it doing P.R. for the bureau." I told Randall, "I can do two things. I can clean that office out and reassign you, or I can accept your resignation." I added, "Don't worry, it won't hurt my position if you resign." And he did. It was just one more case of losing good men to inefficiency.

Most SACs overstock their offices because Hoover kept the FBI expanding. A teletype would come into an SAC asking "How many new agents will your office take?" The SAC would look over his office and think, "I could probably get rid of three men and not miss them and now they want to know how many more I need." And he'd take what he was sent.

At the heart of Hoover's massive public relations operation were the fifty-nine FBI field offices whose territory took in every village, town, city, and county in America. Each day, out of these field offices streamed eight thousand agents going into every state, city, and town, talking to and becoming friendly with ordinary citizens from all walks of life. People working in the judiciary system on local, state, and federal levels were especially singled out by agents for the establishment of close, influential relationships. Judges, district attorneys, special prosecutors, and even supporting office personnel were developed as allies of the bureau. Important organizations—patriotic, civic, fraternal, and others—were also treated for development by our men. Some people became our informants, others our apologists and supporters of influence.

The real job of the special agent in charge of each of these field offices was public relations. The SAC was out of the office a lot, visiting the "right" people, those who molded public opinion in his territory: newspaper publishers and editors, owners and managers of radio and televison stations, corporate executives, and church officials, to name a few. The SAC also plugged the bureau line day in and day out at police headquarters, City Hall, Masonic Lodge meetings, Jaycee luncheons, even at the local college or university.

In the 1940s and 1950s everyone at the FBI knew that Hoover had a desire to get honorary degrees from colleges and universities. It turned into quite a racket because whoever would get Hoover, say, an honorary doctor of law degree would get a favored post or at least a letter of commendation with a $250 cash bonus. For example, the agent would go to his own college, speak with the dean or president, arrange it if he could, and then make sure Hoover knew, by means of a letter, something like:

Dear Mr. Hoover:
Yesterday afternoon I stopped by at my college to discuss an FBI applicant with the President. While I was discussing this applicant the President said to me, "I have long thought that your director, J. Edgar Hoover, is undoubtedly one of the greatest men that this country ever turned out, and I've been thinking that the very least we could do is to confer on him an honorary degree, and would you please convey to him my view."

Hoover always accepted, and the agent always got the post he wanted, a letter of commendation, and a cash award. But after about fifteen years of this, Hoover began to lose interest in degrees and the racket stopped.

Because of this network of field offices, and thanks to the scores of contacts made and maintained by the special agents in charge, Hoover was able to place "news" stories—invented and written in the bureau, really nothing more than press releases, puff pieces for the FBI—in newspapers all over the country. Our strength was in the small dailies and weeklies; and with hundreds of these papers behind him, Hoover didn't give a damn about papers like the *New York Times* or the *Washington Post*. Most of the men who run small local papers are used to printing stories about grange suppers on the front page; imagine how grateful they are for a story from the FBI. Of course, scores of Washington-based reporters printed stories we gave them too, and they usually printed them under their own bylines. Some of them lived off us. It was an easy way to make a living. They were our press prostitutes.

We also planted stories critical of some of Hoover's favorite targets, the CIA for instance. And of course we placed stories about Hoover's congressional critics. A negative story which appears in a newspaper published in a congressman's home district hurts him more than any article in the *Washington Post.* I remember that the FBI helped to defeat Governor Sawyer of Nevada by giving some damaging information on Sawyer to his opponent, who saw to it that the stories made the local papers. What sin had Sawyer committed? He hadn't cooperated with one of Hoover's investigations. But whether the articles were negative or positive, Hoover always remembered the local editor who printed them, and thanked him for his "support" in a personal letter.

Personal letters were one of Hoover's favorite weapons in his public relations arsenal. Over Hoover's signature, we wrote "personal" letters to everybody from children in the sixth grade to members of senior citizens' clubs. We were the greatest letter-writing bureau in the history of the United States. Letters went by the thousands to the Jaycees, the newspaper editors, the movers and shakers so carefully cultivated as FBI contacts by our agents out in the field. These field agents were also responsible for reading all the newspapers published in their territory and clipping any article or letter to the editor that mentioned the FBI or Hoover. Any favorable mention of either in any newspaper in America meant a personal letter of thanks from Hoover.

Letters were also sent to people who wrote to the bureau asking questions about the FBI, and especially about J. Edgar Hoover. Did the director take cream in his coffee or did he drink it black? How does he like his steak cooked? What kind of ties does he prefer? Shoes? Suits? The American public wanted to know.

We had two full-time desks operating this correspondence mill. They were made up of supervisors, regular agents, assistants, clerks, and secretaries. For every letter received, the sender, the organization, and its members were checked out in the FBI's central files before the letter was answered. Thousands and thousands of man-hours spent. Untold millions of the taxpayers' money squandered.

The agents who actually answered these questions and wrote the personal letters for Hoover worked for a small division of the FBI misleadingly called Crime Records. This division handled public relations for the bureau, and in doing so dealt with the press and with congressmen and senators. As Hoover didn't believe in form letters, any agent assigned to Crime Records had a full-time job. Generally, the letters were fairly innocuous: "It has come to my attention that you wrote a letter praising the FBI . . ." followed closely by "I hope I continue to deserve your confidence" and Hoover's signature. But some of them could be tricky.

The director must have once mentioned that he liked popovers, because he got quite a few letters asking for his popover recipe. An agent named Russell Asch, with whom I used to go fishing in Virginia, was in charge of the correspondence desk when one of the popover letters came in. He had already answered so many routine popover letters that he knew the recipe by heart, or so he thought, and he dictated it from memory. Before it was sent out, the letter with the popover recipe was checked by Asch's section chief, by Assistant Director Nichols's assistant, by Nichols himself, and finally by Helen Gandy, one of Hoover's secretaries. Miss Gandy called Asch after reading his letter to ask if he had gone to the file for the recipe. Asch, who felt a sudden sinking feeling in his stomach when he heard her question, had to admit that he had dictated the recipe from memory. Miss Gandy told Asch to get the file with the recipe and bring it to her. When Asch located the file (which took an hour or two), Miss Gandy pointed out that the recipe called for five *tea*spoons of baking powder, not five *table*spoons as Asch had written.

Asch knew he was in for it then. Miss Gandy reported his mistake to Hoover, who sent him a letter of censure which became part of his permanent record. A letter of censure from Hoover meant that Asch's pending promotion, and the additional income that went with it, was held up. Asch told me that when he got home that night, his wife said that she had been reading stories about the FBI in the *Washington Post* in connection with some espionage cases and some big bank robberies. Was he working on these cases, she asked. "Good God," he said to me later, "what could I tell Polly? Could I tell her I was sending out popover recipes?"

The name of everyone who wrote a letter to the FBI, whether it was a request for a popover recipe or a serious statement on law enforcement, was thoroughly checked out. Hoover relied on his files absolutely, and he also checked the file of everyone who came to visit him in his office. Because of this, Hoover was able to flatter his guests by making personal remarks to them, or bringing up subjects about which they had some expertise. He would mention golf if his visitor was a golfer or football if the visitor had played in college. The public relations never stopped.

Hoover once got a letter from a minister who said that he had been praising Hoover in his sermons for fourteen years until he heard that Hoover spent a lot of time at the racetrack and actually bet on the horses. The agent in Crime Records who answered the letter started by thanking the minister for his support over the years, and then he wrote that it was true that "I" (Hoover) do go to the racetrack. I've loved horses since I was a boy, the agent wrote, and I love to watch them run. A few paragraphs later, the agent slipped in a sentence or two explaining that Hoover did place an occasional two-dollar bet so as not to embarrass his companions, but that his primary interest was the improvement of the breed. The letter must have worked because we didn't hear from the minister again, but it was pure invention. Hoover did make a few bets at the two-dollar window, but that was just for show. He had agents assigned to accompany him to the track place his real bets at the hundred-dollar window, and when he won he was a pleasure to work with for days. He and Tolson used to be driven from the courtyard of the Department of Justice to the track in a black bullet-proof car. Although Hoover always told people that he and Tolson were going off to work on a case, it was common knowledge that they were actually rushing to make the first race.

With all these letters coming in and going out, Hoover had a huge mailing list and he sent out thousands of Christmas cards every year. To Hoover, taking a man's name off the mailing list was dire punishment indeed. When Hoover got a letter from a doctor in Baltimore who had been an active supporter of the FBI for years complaining that the John Dillinger exhibit at bureau headquarters hadn't been changed in twelve years and needed modernizing, Hover retaliated by taking the doctor off his mailing list. I'm sure he believed that he was ruining the doctor's life by doing so.

Aside from writing letters and handling the press, the other main function of the Crime Records Division was dealing with Congress. There were two ways we could help senators and congressmen: we could give them useful information and we could cater to their needs, big or small. We gave them information on their opponents, of course, and thanks to the FBI network of field offices which blanketed the country we were sometimes able to tell an incumbent who was planning to run against him before his own people knew. We dealt in more personal information, too. If a senator heard about a son's drug problem from us before the story got into the papers, he'd be mighty grateful. It was unlikely that that senator would ever stand up in the Senate to criticize the FBI. In fact, if the FBI was being criticized, he'd probably get up and defend it. It gave Hoover his leverage.

Crime Records also dealt in services to congressmen and senators, especially when they were traveling abroad. Some of these services were minimal, providing limousines, for instance, complete with an agent behind the wheel to do the driving, or arranging discounts in the local shops. But some were of considerable importance and delicacy. We set up introductions and interviews with key members of foreign governments for many a senator. After a few trips to Europe, a senator could develop a nice warm feeling for the bureau, which is just what Hoover had in mind.

What did Hoover get in exchange from some of these grateful men? In his maiden speech in Congress, Gerald Ford, who had run for his seat with the blessing of the local FBI, recommended that Hoover get a raise. When Congressman John J. Rooney of Brooklyn, New York, was asked to vote for a raise for the director, he tried to increase the amount. Once a year there was an event called the Congressional Dinner at which former FBI men who were serving in the House of Representatives gave speeches honoring their former boss.

On occasion, Hoover would extend the services of the FBI to business executives. We helped some of the top men from Warner Brothers by setting up meetings for them with foreign political leaders and businessmen; they got the same treatment that some elected officials did. All courtesy of the FBI, all paid for by the taxpayer. Hoover bragged that he had the motion picture studio under his thumb.

When Hoover's book *Masters of Deceit* came out, the agents in our field offices were put to work drumming up sales. Of course, just as Hoover didn't write the thousands of letters that went out under

Hoover, a regular racetrack habitué, would be seen making two-dollar bets while FBI agents placed other bets for him at the hundred-dollar window. *Acme Photo*

his name, he didn't write the book either. As a matter of fact, I was the one who suggested the book to Hoover in the first place, and the research and the writing were done by five or six of us at the bureau.

Once the book was published, the real work began. Every office in each state was expected to sell it. Agents all over the country made public appearances promoting it at bookstores and on local television and radio programs. Agents who were responsible for big book sales received bonuses, and agents who sold an exceptionally large number of books got raises. Our men in the field also placed reviews of the book which had been written by agents at FBI headquarters with their contacts at local newspapers and magazines. Needless to say, the reviews were excellent. We used to joke in the bureau, "*Masters of Deceit*, written by the Master of Deceit who never even read it."

I was assigned by Hoover to make a speech to boost the book to a group called the Citizens' Committee of Cincinnati. We used to talk a lot about Communist front groups in the 1950s—the Citizens' Committee of Cincinnati was an FBI front group. Its sole purpose was to sell Hoover's book. When I arrived to give my speech, I noticed some panel trucks parked outside the building. An agent with the Cincinnati office told me that the trucks were filled with copies of *Masters of Deceit* and that every member of the audience would get a free copy of the book just for showing up. The purchase of the books had been financed by a millionaire named Evan Rhodes, a well-meaning man who was being used by Hoover as the committee's figurehead.

On the stage were two American flags blowing wildly in the wind created by offstage fans. The mayor of Cincinnati, members of the council and a former Miss America were on stage too. The mayor got up and thanked everyone for coming and then went into a long, praising speech about how wonderful it was that one of the greatest citizens of Ohio had financed at great personal expense the purchase of the book *Masters of Deceit*, written by one of the greatest men in the country, J. Edgar Hoover. The audience jumped to their feet and applauded. When the noise died down I gave my required speech on national security and was about to leave the platform when one of the owners of the Scripps-Howard newspapers came up to me, all taken up by the moment, and said, "I'd like to do something for Mr. Hoover, too. What should I do?" Mason, the Cincinnati SAC who was standing next to me, didn't miss a beat. Mason said, "If I were you I'd write a personal letter to Mr. Hoover telling him that you were here today and what a wonderful day it was and that you and your newspaper want to be of assistance to him in every possible way." The fellow from Scripps-Howard stopped and said, "Fine, but what do I do—just send it to Washington?" Mason grabbed the ball again. He said, "I'll tell you what to do. Tomorrow morning I'll come over to your office and dictate a letter for you and all you'll have to do is sign it." By God, when I got back to Washington I found the letter that Mason dictated and it was signed by the Scripps-Howard executive. It was an incredible operation and it took place all over the country.

Naturally, with the awesome power of the FBI behind it, *Masters of Deceit* became a bestseller. The FBI could make a bestseller out of a calculus textbook. Being somewhat naive at the time, as one of the six men who worked like hell to put the book together I wrote a memo recommending that the considerable proceeds go to the Damon Runyon Fund or to the American Heart Association or to some charity of that nature. In response, I got a call from an agent assigned to Tolson's office saying that my memo had not been "favorably received," and I was told that the director alone would decide how best to use the royalties. I was even more astonished a few years later when I found out that Hoover had kept most of the book's profits himself. I also learned that he was annoyed when he found himself in a higher tax bracket because of those royalties.

In its first draft, *Masters of Deceit* was a serious study of communism. It had been watered down and jazzed up prior to publication, however, and I suggested to Hoover that his next book be more substantial. I suggested it be called "A Study of Communism" and that the proceeds of that book go to a J. Edgar Hoover scholarship fund at George Washington University. But Hoover, who knew a lot more about royalties and the tax law by then, set it up so that all future royalties would go into the FBI Recreation Fund instead. Although agents were supposed to share the money in the Recreation Fund, it was actually nothing more than a tax dodge. The money in the fund was available to Hoover, at all times, and he used it.

All of these special projects of Hoover's put a severe drain on the manpower in the bureau. For example, toward the end of 1962, another of Hoover's books written by the agents was at the publishers awaiting the preparation of a glossary. Assistant Director DeLoach wanted to send two of our espionage specialists to New York City to aid in the task. I got into an argument with DeLoach over this and wrote to Clyde Tolson:

October 4, 1962

Dear Mr. Tolson: PERSONAL

It has been called to my attention that a vigorous disagreement I had with Mr. DeLoach early this week over the need to send two men to the publishers in New York to prepare a glossary, etc., for the Director's book, "A Study of Communism," seems to have caused some comment. I was somewhat more than mildly surprised to learn of this. In order that I may be certain you have all the facts, I wish to very respectfully advise you as follows:

1. When I was told that both F. C. Stukenbroeker and A. W. Gray were to spend one or two days in New York for discussions of a glossary, I stated what I believed thoroughly to be true; that there is no need for both going. As you know, we are badly in need of manpower. I told Mr. DeLoach that in my view, either one or the other should go.

2. No doubt there are some who believe I should not get involved in controversy; that such harms our operations. In all sincerity, I must say, rightly or wrongly, that I have always believed most strongly in controversy as a legitimate means for obtaining legitimate ends. On some occasions there seems to be no other recourse but controversy, and I do think that it should be sharp, vigorous and penetrating without any consideration as to whether one will be liked or disliked for it. I cannot help but think that on occasions this Bureau has suffered from a lack of open, direct controversy. Whenever men "scratch each other's backs" and blink at each other's shortcomings for self-protective reasons, it impairs our efficiency. Life is essentially composed of unrelenting competition—often rough, bruising, and fierce competition. Isn't it so that men will clash and, if they have any convictions at all, must clash over ideas, principles, values, means, interests and ends. I cannot help but think that such competition is good for the Bureau and it makes for progress. Whereas the superficial bowing, scraping, smiling and namby-pamby self-protective agreements that so often 'exist may result in harm to anything to which they are related.

Sincerely,
[signed]   W. C. Sullivan

The book was finally completed. Another bestseller. Those of us who wrote it received letters of commendation that said, "I have followed your record very closely and am favorably impressed by the superior work done by you over a long period of time. I have included an incentive reward to you in the amount of $250.00. Sincerely, J. Edgar Hoover."

At times Hoover tended to overestimate the power of public relations. In 1965, Joseph L. Rauh, Jr., vice-president of Americans for Democratic Action, a liberal group, made some critical remarks about Hoover in a speech he gave to a meeting of the National Students Association. Rauh accused the FBI of not enforcing the law when it came to the area of civil rights. He wanted the federal government to take steps to protect civil rights workers in the South and charged that Hoover was "the wrong man" to head civil rights investigations because of his disparaging remarks about Martin Luther King.

Faced with a real crisis, Hoover turned to his public relations machine to cover it up instead of trying to solve it. A Crime Records memo to Hoover dated 25 August 1965 stated:

Pursuant to Mr. Tolson's instructions, we are making immediate contact with Miriam Ottenberg at the Washington Star so that Rauh's charges can be answered in the press at the earliest possible time. We will prevail on her to get an article out if at all possible this weekend. Previously approved material is being furnished her for use in the article to combat Rauh's charges in accordance with the Director's instructions.

We should also utilize other sources.

By the time Crime Records wrote their next memo on the following day, the public relations operation was in full swing:

We have been working with Miss Ottenberg today and have gotten up considerable material in order that we can effectively refute Rauh's criticisms. Miss Ottenberg says that her story will run either Friday, August 27, or else on Sunday the 29th, in the *Star*.

Additionally, we have sent material today to a number of columnists including Fulton Lewis, Jr., Paul Harvey, Bob Allen of the *Hall Syndicate*, Ray Cromley of Newspaper Enterprise Association, Ed Mowry of General Features and the Newhouse chain, Ed O'Brien of the St. Louis Globe-Democrat, Warren Rogers of Hearst and Ray McHugh of the Coply Press, among others.

We are continuing to work on this to insure that the widest possible coverage can be given to our positive accomplishments in the civil rights field.

Louis B. Nichols, who was then assistant director of the FBI, was in charge of all public relations, press matters, and contacts with Congress for Hoover. Nichols had his own solution to the growing criticism of the FBI's role in the civil rights controversy. Like Hoover's plan, it had nothing to do with real policy change but was pure public relations.

In a misguided effort to cut off the criticism of the FBI at its source, Nichols talked Hoover into hiring Morris Ernst, who was at that time head of the American Civil Liberties Union, as the director's personal lawyer. As the American Civil Liberties Union was even more liberal than Americans for Democratic Action, Ernst and Hoover were a very unlikely combination. However, shortly after he began to represent Hoover, Ernst wrote an article for the *Reader's Digest* praising the FBI. The article was reprinted and we mailed out copies by the thousands.

After that article appeared, the Hoover–Ernst relationship faded away, just as the relationship between Hoover and Walter Winchell once did. Winchell was probably the first nationally known radio commentator developed by the FBI. We sent Winchell information regularly. He was our mouthpiece. Of course, he became so obvious after a while that he finally lost his value, and Hoover lost interest in him. Winchell once had a tremendous audience, though, and he was very valuable to Hoover then, who used him practically every time he wanted to leak a story.

When I hear people talk about a "new" FBI, I know that the changes they talk about are only paper changes. This public relations operation of Hoover's, this massive attempt to control public opinion, continues to this day, and it is at the very heart of what is wrong with the bureau. Unless it is exposed, until every editor of every little weekly newspaper who ever printed an FBI press handout realizes how he has been used, the FBI will do business in the same old way.

A massive, pervasive public relations operation is no substitute for the job of investigating crimes. The FBI should conduct its business quietly and it should earn its respect from the citizens of the United States by the results of its work, not from the results of its propaganda.

In 1976, five years after I left the FBI, I got a telephone call at my home in New Hampshire from Alger Hiss. Still working on his case, he wanted me to tell him whether the typewriter that helped convict him of a perjury charge was a fake which had been put together at the FBI Laboratory.

Although I never worked on the Hiss case myself, I know that we were giving Richard Nixon, who was in charge of the investigation, every possible assistance. Had Nixon asked the FBI to manufacture evidence to prove his case against Hiss, Hoover would have been only too glad to oblige. I told Hiss that the typewriter was not made in the FBI Lab. What I didn't tell him was that even if we had wanted to, we simply would not have been capable of it.

The laboratory, described in an FBI publicity booklet as "the greatest law enforcement laboratory in the world," is the highlight of the public tour of FBI headquarters in Washington, D.C. Over the years, millions of tourists have listened, awestruck, to glowing descriptions of the lab's capabilities and activities. Unfortunately, these descriptions are nothing but a show-business spiel. The FBI Laboratory is in fact a real-life counterpart of the busy workroom of the Wizard of Oz—all illusion. Even the famous laboratory files were maintained for show. They looked impressive, but they were really incomplete and outdated.

I first heard the truth about the lab at the beginning of my career with the FBI when I worked with Charlie Winstead in the Southwest. Charlie took me with him one day when he had to get some handwriting samples from a prisoner, a deserter from the army, being held at an air force base in Albuquerque because he had been charged with assault and battery and attempted murder.

Charlie made the man write for over half an hour, a sentence or two each on twenty or thirty separate pieces of paper, before he had enough. We marked each sample with the case number, the prisoner's name, and the date, and then, before sending the samples out to headquarters in Washington, he removed ten or twelve of the slips of paper and put them in his files. I asked Charlie what he was doing, and though at first he was reluctant to tell me, he finally explained.

"If you stay with the bureau," Charlie started by saying, "this is a trick that will save you all kinds of time and trouble in the future. No one at that lab they run in Washington," Charlie continued, "knows what he's doing. After years of sending handwriting samples to them, I finally learned that no matter how many I send, they always call me a month later to ask for more. When they do, I just pull out the samples I put aside years ago, put a fresh date on them, and send them in."

In the years that followed I learned that Charlie's low opinion of the FBI Laboratory was completely justified. When we asked the boys in the lab to come up with a good wall microphone so that agents

The FBI Laboratory was the highlight of the public's tour of the bureau's headquarters in Washington, D.C. *Wide World Photos*

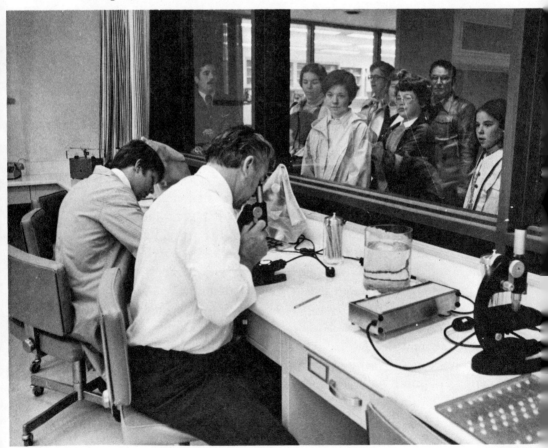

could hear what was being said in an adjoining room on an espionage case we had, they couldn't do it, and we finally had to turn to the CIA for help. When we were working on the Pentagon Papers case, we wanted to know whether photocopies we were holding as evidence were copied from an original document, from an original photocopy, or from a photocopy of a photocopy. The lab couldn't give us a satisfactory answer so we had to turn to the Xerox Company for help. The FBI Lab couldn't even come up with a simple "peephole"—a device which, when attached to a car under surveillance, would allow us to follow that car electronically when we couldn't follow it visually—that would stick to the bottom of a car. Once again I had to turn to the CIA for help.

Deciphering codes was one of the lab's major functions, but most of my men learned the hard way to take any codes that were giving them problems to the National Security Agency if they wanted results.

An old college friend of mine, a brilliant scientist who became a world-famous microbiologist, once told me that he could develop an unbreakable code by using bacteria. When he explained his theory to me I couldn't understand a word of it, and when he asked me to put him in touch with the head of the FBI Lab I did so, but I doubted whether the FBI scientists could understand my friend either. The men who were working in the FBI Lab as agent-examiners were for the most part former special agents who were chosen for their lab assignments after years in the field because they had once majored in biology or physics in college. Few of them have continued their education or updated their degrees, and therefore very few are aware of recent scientific developments. They are laboratory technicians, not research scientists.

I put my friend, the microbiologist, in touch with Donald Parsons, who headed the lab at the time. After their meeting, my friend told me that he could tell by Parsons's blank expression and by the questions he didn't ask that Parsons had gotten as little out of the theory as I had. "Don't you have a scientist up there?" he asked me. My friend finally gave his code concept to the CIA.

Why was the lab such a disaster? Starting from the top, neither of the two men who held the post of assistant director in charge of the lab, Donald Parsons or his successor Ivan Conrad, had any field experience, which seriously affected their judgment on cases which came in from the field (lab work also came in from other government agencies and from local police departments), and both men tried to make up for their lack of scientific knowledge and ability by overemphasizing clerical and administrative procedures. Because of this, agent-examiners who worked in the lab spent too much time filling out forms and not enough time doing scientific research.

This is a basic list of the FBI Lab's shortcomings during my time there:

• The document section of the lab conducted no research into optical scanners, photoelectric reading devices, or automatic imagery. Such research could have had significant application in the identification of handwriting.

• No actual research was conducted into holography, although three-dimensional holographic photographs of the scene of a crime would be an invaluable aid to investigation.

• Today, more than seventy-five years after the discovery of different blood groups, very little that has been discovered since about blood has found its way into the FBI Laboratory.

• The bank robbery note file, which, though it is one of the busiest and most productive files in the Lab, is merely a card file which is tedious to work with. The file can only be used by one or at most two people at once. Existing technology should have been utilized to improve the system decades ago.

• Of the 136 agent-examiners employed by the lab when I was with the FBI, 136 were Protestants or Catholics and 136 were white. There wasn't one Jewish, black, or Hispanic American.

• Historically, the lab has maintained a blacklist of police departments euphemistically called the "Restricted List." A law enforcement agency placed on the Restricted List may find itself completely cut off from the services of the FBI Lab. The quickest and surest way for a local department to be placed on the Restricted list was to criticize the efficiency of the FBI or to encourage the establishment of independent regional laboratories. This list still existed in 1976.

With conditions as bad as they were at the FBI Lab, it was no wonder that when I became a supervisor in the research section of the Domestic Intelligence Division in the early 1950s I was visited by the few agent-examiners who were doing good work and who believed they could do better work if there was a shakeup at the lab. These men were the thinking, honest, industrious, and concerned minority who were responsible for whatever good work the lab did turn out. They asked me to take whatever steps I found necessary to persuade Director Hoover that fundamental changes were called for. I agreed to do so, but I told them that I wanted to wait for the right moment, an occasion which would justify my stirring things up. I didn't have to wait long.

Donald Parsons was in charge of the lab at that time. Politically, Parsons was an ultraconservative. Scientifically, he was limited; professionally, he was a highly developed bureaucrat who couldn't do enough to please Hoover and Tolson. Parsons was also a close friend of J. P. Mohr, one of Hoover's closest aides, and they had a well-deserved reputation for promoting and protecting each other, irrespective of the facts involved.

Parsons believed in keeping his agent-examiners close to home. He saw no need for them to take outside courses or attend scientific meetings. After all, Parsons ran "the greatest law enforcement laboratory in the world." What did the rest of the scientific community have to teach his men? To justify keeping a representative of the FBI from attending a convention of the National Association for the Advancement of Science, Parsons wrote a memo criticizing the Association in which he implied that its members were Communists. That was my department, and I felt perfectly justified in sending Mr. Parsons a memo in which I took issue with his position. The controversy that ensued was to last for weeks.

First, Parsons wrote a memo back to me. It was characteristically pompous, authoritarian, and incorrect. He simply had not done his homework, and I proved it when I refuted his claims by using material out of his own files. Then Parsons went to see Al Belmont, my assistant director and at that time my direct boss, and asked Belmont to "keep Sullivan's mouth shut about the Lab." Al Belmont was one of the few who had risen to the top ranks of the FBI without losing his integrity along the way, and he absolutely refused. "Sullivan has a right to his opinion," he told Parsons.

A few days after Parsons's meeting with Belmont, I got a visit from Parsons's friend J. P. Mohr, then assistant director of the Administrative Division. He came by, he said, to give me some "friendly advice," and went on to tell me that I would hurt my career if I continued to speak out and to write rude memos. "No supervisor should ever criticize or attack an assistant director," he said solemnly as he left. I wrote his advice down in my diary as soon as he was out the door.

The conflict continued to rage until Director Hoover himself established a committee to resolve the issue. The committee was comprised of Parsons's men, however, and the final outcome was not satisfactory either to Parsons or me. It was a typical fence-straddling compromise, the kind Hoover was so good at, made to calm stormy waters but not to solve the problem.

SIX

Life in the Circus

A S DIRECTOR the Federal Bureau of Investigation, Hoover lived like a king, and the bureau was his kingdom. In keeping with this regal self-image, his suite of offices was lavish. Visiting Hoover was an awe-inspiring experience. An outer office housed a large glass-topped table, the kind museums often use for exhibits. Hoover's display included a hollowed-out nickel used by Rudolf Abel, the Russian spy, to pass coded messages, and pistols taken from famous criminals like Dillinger and Karpis. These pistols were the closest Hoover ever came to a real gun since he didn't know how to use one. He was with the FBI for forty-eight years, but he never made an arrest or conducted an investigation. In fact, Hoover, whose fondest wish was to be in charge of worldwide intelligence, never once left the United States.

From the outer office a visitor walked into a smaller inner room where one of Hoover's secretaries was positioned. Down a corridor, past the desks of two more secretaries, was Hoover's own office. It was an enormous room, lined with books, furnished comfortably, and its focal point was the oval table, large enough to seat ten, in the center of the room. Naturally, Hoover always sat at the head of the table.

Thanks to his loyal subjects at the bureau, Hoover lived well during his hours away from the office, too. He hated to fly; trains were his favorite form of transportation and each trip was a major operation. Someone from the Administrative Division was expected to contact the president of the railroad to insure that the temperature in Hoover's and Tolson's compartments (they always traveled together) was kept at a constant sixty-eight degrees. God forbid it might be sixty-seven or sixty-nine. When Hoover arrived at his destination, the local boys made damned sure his hotel room was stocked with Jack Daniels for Hoover and scotch for Tolson—his one deviation from the master—and lots of flowers.

Hoover was equally fastidious about his automobile comfort. He had two automobiles in Washington and one each in Miami, Los

Hoover lived the "good life" while he helped build his image by being seen and photographed with celebrities.

Below: With Shirley Temple in 1938. *United Press International*

On facing page, above: New Year's Eve at New York's Stork Club in 1938 with "society girl" Cobina Wright. *Wide World Photos*

Below: At a ball in Washington, D.C., with movie stars Wallace Beery and Lana Turner. *Wide World Photos*

Angeles, and Chicago. They all had to be prepared exactly alike. The air conditioning was set at just the right temperature in the summer, and the boys always kept a blanket in the trunk of the car in the winter in case the heater broke down. The heater did, in fact, break down one winter day, the very day that the blanket was at the cleaner's. Hoover hit the roof and demanded a full investigation from his driver, and an extra blanket was bought. Needless to say, many members of the Administrative Division received letters of censure.

None of us envied Hoover's driver but we all liked and trusted him because he had to put up with Hoover as much as we did. He told me once that it was the most nerve-wracking job he'd ever had, and like many of us he wanted to leave but was fearful that Hoover would make it difficult for him to get other work.

About two o'clock one morning the Baltimore office called me at home and said, "Bill, all hell has broken loose. Hoover's driver has been in Baltimore, drunk and in a fight. When one of the local police tried to arrest him, he clipped him and now he's in jail and in a hell of a mess." I told one of the agents to go down to the jail and see what we could do for him. A couple of hours later the agent called me back and told me, "He's still drunk and cursing Hoover like I've never heard anyone speak about the Old Man."

We knew about the kinds of pressure Hoover could bring to bear on a man and we sympathized with this fellow's going over the deep end and getting drunk to forget, even for an evening, the man he had to work for each day, so we developed a plan.

The next morning the driver was still in jail in Baltimore, but a memo from the Baltimore office arrived on Hoover's desk. The memo stated that the agents received a call from the Baltimore police and had gone to the jail intending to take very firm action against him. But, the memo went on, when they arrived at the jail, they found the offender on his knees praying. The agents' memo said that he didn't see them approach his cell so they stopped and listened. The prayer, the memo went on, went like this: "Good Lord, I'll always condemn myself as long as I live for embarrassing Mr. Hoover. I don't care what happens to me, it's Mr. Hoover I'm concerned about."

We waited with our fingers crossed. Finally, Hoover came out of his office and said, "The man's conduct is atrocious, but I'll overlook it this one time." He was saved. That's how we protected ourselves, playing on his ego.

Hoover took his royal treatment for granted, came to expect it, and was nasty when he didn't get it. Some years ago, he and Tolson were being driven to New York City to the funeral of one of our agents who had been killed in the line of duty. The agent who was acting as chauffeur was planning to drive Hoover and Tolson directly up to the church door, but he found that the street the church was on was closed for repairs. The director's arrival had been planned for the very last minute, and the driver knew there wouldn't be enough time to approach the church by going around to another street, so he suggested that the two men get out and walk. Without a word Hoover and Tolson did so. The next morning, however, that agent found himself relieved of his duties, the subject of a letter of censure from Hoover.

Another agent I knew was transferred out of headquarters after he made the mistake of asking Hoover if the director had had a nice vacation. Hoover, tanned from a recent trip to La Jolla, California (made at government expense, like all of his trips), really hit the ceiling. Hoover reddened and picked up the files the agent had just handed to him and threw them at him. Hoover screamed, "You know I never take a vacation . . . never take a vacation." That day the agent was transferred out of the front office. What Hoover should have said was that he never took a vacation that he paid for. Though his hotel rooms were always free, he actually asked for reimbursement for the price of the room when he returned to Washington.

FBI agents were used regularly to do work around Hoover's house. Once, a team of agents built him a porch. They worked so fast and did such a good job that some of the neighbors, not realizing the men were FBI agents, tried to hire them to work on their own houses. The money for the wood and for the men's overtime salaries came out of the FBI Recreation Fund. That porch didn't cost Hoover a dime.

Hoover never had to spend any of his salary. The American taxpayers paid for everything, even for Clyde Tolson's hobby. Tolson was an inventor of sorts; he would come up with an idea and try to figure out how to make it work. When he was stymied, he turned the whole thing over to the boys at the FBI Lab to work out. The patents for these inventions were always taken out in Tolson's name.

Hoover's personal accountant was an FBI employee with a thirty-six-thousand-dollar salary and whose chief duties were to look after Hoover's and Tolson's stock investments and work on their income taxes.

Though Hoover expected the royal treatment from everyone at the bureau (and got it!), he treated his agents shabbily. His policy of "enforced voluntary overtime" was particularly hard on the men. I never knew a man in the FBI worth his salt who wouldn't get up at two in the morning to make an arrest or work all night if necessary. But no man wanted to waste his time sitting at his desk if there was no work to be done. Thanks to Hoover's overtime policy, though, that happened frequently. The men were forced to come in to work at 7:00 A.M., two hours before the official workday began, whether there was work to be done or not, just so Hoover could point with pride at the long hours FBI employees worked when he went before the House Appropriations Committee. No one was paid for enforced voluntary overtime, which the men bitterly resented, and it was one of the major reasons for the low morale that existed in the bureau.

One way to make this early-morning duty more bearable was to go out for coffee with some of the boys. It helped to pass the time when there was no work. A few ambitious agents tried to turn this unofficial coffee break into a career break by reporting to Hoover that a good number of agents who were signed in for duty at the FBI headquarters could be found drinking coffee at Whelan's drugstore.

When Hoover heard the report, his only worry was that the word would get out that he forced men to work extra hours when there was no work. His solution was Operation Black Friday: he sent a team of inspectors down to Whelan's one morning in 1958 to take down the name of every agent present. I was having breakfast there myself that morning, but I had come to work too late to sign in and come back downstairs as I usually did. I never noticed Hoover's men taking names that morning, and neither did anyone else. When I finished eating, one of the inspectors followed me into my office. When I asked him what he wanted, he didn't answer but walked over to my register, opened it, and looked to see whether or not I had already signed in. I was lucky that morning, but fifty other men weren't so lucky and they were finished in the FBI.

We called those agents who spied on their fellow FBI agents "submarines" because they worked in secret, below the surface, always trying to ingratiate themselves with the director to get a raise or a promotion, even if another agent's career was destroyed in the process. Given the FBI's dependence on informants, it came as no surprise to learn that there were people working within the bureau who habitually informed on their fellow employees. I knew that two or three men in my division reported on our activities to others, and I myself had people in other divisions who kept me informed. You couldn't survive in the FBI without them.

One of the secretaries who worked in my office during my last year at the FBI was a spy for Hoover and Tolson. She had worked in Al Belmont's office for years, and I inherited her when Belmont retired and I moved into his job. She begged me to keep her on, as her husband had just died and she had only two years left before she could retire. It was a real sob story and I fell for it. She repaid me by keeping tabs on my phone calls and my appointments (Hoover and Tolson would have loved to have actually bugged my office, but I knew too many people in that line of work and one of them would have tipped me off), and she even tried to eavesdrop on my meetings. She would come in and very slowly shuffle the papers on my desk pretending to be looking for something. I loved to put her on the spot and ask her exactly what she was looking for.

"It probably isn't here now," she'd reply, and sulk out, red in the face. Of course, I used to feed her the same sort of disinformation the bureau fed to double agents, which she faithfully carried back to Hoover and Tolson. Before I left the bureau, I couldn't resist telling her that I'd known about her activities all along. Flustered and embarrassed, she finally said, "I wish you men wouldn't get us girls involved."

Hoover and Tolson were always together, and it was always just the two of them. When Lee Boardman got the number three position

The "unipersonalities," J. Edgar Hoover and his assistant Clyde Tolson in Miami Beach, 1937. They were inseparable. *Wide World Photos*

in the FBI, he thought that with the job would come acceptance by Hoover and Tolson socially as well as officially. After a few weeks, Boardman called Tolson seeking to join him and the director for lunch and Tolson agreed. A few weeks later, Boardman got a memo from Hoover saying, "I've been analyzing the different positions in the Bureau and I have concluded that the position of the Number Three man is not necessary. I am herewith transferring you to the Washington Field Office." Boardman knew the game was up and that he no longer had a future in the FBI, so he requested retirement, which Hoover quickly okayed. It was a long time before the FBI had another number three man.

As the absolute rulers of the FBI, Hoover and Tolson were not benevolent despots. When Hoover dismissed an agent for some real or imagined offense to himself or the FBI, if he were angry enough he put the phrase "dismissed with prejudice" on the man's record, a phrase Hoover coined himself. A dismissal with prejudice was a serious matter, and could make it very difficult for a former agent to find other work.

A story that may or may not be true went the rounds of the bureau that Tolson came into work one day complaining to Hoover that he was depressed. To cheer him up, Hoover gave Tolson a list of FBI supervisors. "Pick out one you don't like and fire him," the director said, "then you'll feel better." As the story was told to me, Tolson then smiled at Hoover and asked, "With prejudice?"

Following World War II we made some efforts to locate Nazi war criminals who had escaped from prosecution. The number one target was Martin Bormann. We were receiving rumors that he had escaped to Latin America and was living there under an assumed name. One of the bureau's supervisors was convinced, based on his contacts in Latin America, that he could locate Bormann, so he sent a strong memorandum to Hoover stating his case. He recommended that Hoover send him to South America to do the job. Hoover was so delighted at this prospect that he dispatched the agent at once and began to spread word of the impending capture around Washington.

The first week went by and the agent communicated to us through the embassy in the Argentine that he hadn't yet located his man. Then another week and another communication, this time from Paraguay, that he hadn't yet come up with Bormann. Another week and another message, this time from Uruguay, saying still no luck. After a month the agent asked to come back. He had exhausted all of his leads and he had no where else to look.

Hoover was furious. He had told everyone that we'd get Bormann and now it had all come to nothing, so he said, "He wanted to go down there, let him stay there."

Three full months went by and we pointed out to Hoover that the poor fellow was still in Latin America with absolutely nothing to do and wanted to come home. Hoover finally relented and let him come back.

It was not always possible to protect the men who worked for me from the worst of Hoover's wrath. When we needed another man to work in our London office, I recommended Lawrence McWilliams, a supervisor at FBI headquarters. McWilliams was the perfect man for the job, a walking encyclopedia on espionage. He accepted the job on one condition: that he be allowed to return to the United States (at his own expense) for three or four days for his parents' golden wedding anniversary. The party, which McWilliams planned himself, was to be a major family reunion.

I advised Larry to tell Hoover about the party well in advance, just in case. He did, and Hoover was agreeable. As the time drew near for the party, McWilliams sent a memo from London requesting time off and I approved it and sent it on through. A few hours later, back it came with Tolson's disapproval written on the bottom, and the director's written under his. McWilliams had only been in London for a few months, Tolson had written; there was no need for him to come back for a visit so soon.

Obviously, Tolson and Hoover had forgotten. I called McWilliams in London with the news. He was furious, and he told me that he planned to come back no matter what Hoover said. I told him that I felt the fault was mine for sending his memo to the director without making it clear that Hoover had already approved the trip months ago. To make amends, I wrote another memo putting all the blame on myself, apologizing profusely to Hoover for not making the whole matter clearer to him, pleading with him not to take it out on poor McWilliams when the fault had unmistakably been mine. Hoover eventually relented, but the episode reflected Hoover's feelings, or lack of them, when it came to a man's family. "Family problems are secondary to the welfare of the bureau," Hoover used to say, and he actually believed it. He even expected the men to inform the bureau if they were having marital problems or problems with their children. He didn't give a damn about the people involved; he just didn't want the bureau embarrassed.

I had one experience very much like Larry McWilliams's when I was selected to speak to a statewide law enforcement convention in Texas. A letter had gone out to Hoover about the speech two months before it was scheduled to take place, and he approved the engagement. When the final arrangements for the speech were being made two weeks before the convention, no one reminded Hoover that he had already known about the speech so he refused to let me go on only two weeks' notice! We straightened that out by putting the blame on everyone but Hoover, but not until an expansive and time-consuming official investigation of the whole affair had been completed. I came through unscathed that time, but some of the other men involved received letters of censure, which became, of course, part of their permanent record.

In the early 1950s we had a very popular agent in the San Francisco office who was retiring and there was a huge turnout for his going-away party. Members of the local San Francisco police force, U.S. Customs, and the Immigration and Naturalization Service, as well as about two hundred FBI agents turned up at the bash which was held at a large restaurant out there.

There was also a nude belly dancer who provided the entertainment. As always, Hoover found out and demanded an explanation of exactly what went on and a full accounting from every single agent present as to where he was during the "entertainment." Apparently the agents in San Francisco didn't coordinate with each other on their responses to Hoover's request for an explanation because virtually every man said that he hadn't seen any girl at the dinner—that he had been in the men's room. It seemed that we had two hundred FBI agents in that San Francisco restaurant's men's room at the same time.

Hoover could come down really hard when he felt he had been personally insulted. A man named Bill Wells who worked for me as a liaison man to the CIA and to Internal Revenue, got into trouble with Hoover after he attended a party in Delaware. Somebody at the party asked Wells what Hoover "was like." Wells didn't say anything, but he tapped the side of his head with his index finger a few times. The man who had asked turned out to be a member of the John Birch Society, and he reported the entire incident, including his interpretation of the gesture ("Mr. Hoover, he believes you are out of your mind") in a long letter to Hoover.

Hoover blew up. He suspended Wells from the bureau and confiscated his bureau property: his gun, badge, manuals, credentials, everything. Then he had him transferred out of headquarters to an office whose SAC was right under Hoover's thumb. I knew it would be only a matter of time before the SAC would find fault with Wells and fire him. I decided to try to save Wells's job by using one of Hoover's favorite techniques against the director himself, the letter-writing campaign.

I contacted some of the other guests at the party who kindly consented to write letters telling Hoover that Wells hadn't made a deprecating gesture, that he was merely scratching his head, and that, furthermore, Wells's behavior at the party had been a credit to the FBI and to Hoover himself. But the letters didn't change Hoover's mind or Wells's status. Wells wrote a letter himself to Hoover in which he denied that the incident had ever taken place and announced that he planned to sue the John Bircher who had written it for defamation of character.

To Hoover, a lawsuit involving the bureau meant only one thing—a publicly embarrassing situation which was to be avoided at all costs. Within days of his threatened lawsuit Wells was back at work at headquarters, but not as my liaison.

The bureau system made liars of us all. If you didn't lie you couldn't survive.

I remember the day Wells came into work on his fiftieth birthday. He had put in more than twenty years with the FBI and was eligible for retirement, his government pension assured. "I'm a free man," he said that day. Wells didn't quit when he turned fifty. When I asked him why he had decided to stay on, Wells said, "Would I leave the circus?"

It was hard to leave the circus. My whole family had been pleading with me for years to get out. After I'd put in twenty years of service, was fifty years old, and eligible for retirement benefits, they got on me even more. I kept telling them no, that I'd like to stay a little longer. I liked the work, in spite of Hoover, and my three children were either in or going to college and I needed the income. I could have retired with a modest pension and combined that with another job, but nothing else appealed to me. But there were times when I was ready to quit. At the end of my first month of training in the bureau, I had written to my intended wife Marion that I had no intention of remaining in what I considered to be "a shallow, artificial atmosphere," but an FBI friend persuaded me to remain.

Again in 1942 another friend was recruiting men for combat intelligence with the U.S. Marines. I went to the personnel office at bureau headquarters and told them that I intended to join the marines. I was told that the FBI would not give me a military leave but would allow me to be "separated" from the FBI which, I was told, was tantamount to a dismissal from the bureau. I later learned that this was not true, but it was the line that Hoover had the personnel people pass on to all who wanted to leave.

By 1945 when I was promoted into FBI headquarters as a supervisor, I noted that it was packed with draft-dodgers who worked as little as possible. All most of them wanted was the security of their paychecks.

The main thrust at headquarters was not investigation but public relations. Luckily, I was able to surround myself with good men, the most talented I could find. We worked hard and stayed together. Many of my friends were sure that I would never be promoted to higher positions in the bureau because of my dissent to a lot of Hoover's policies and the enemies I made as a result. They were sure that I would be "busted out" of headquarters and sent back to the field because I was in constant controversy over issues that I felt were important: the emphasis on public relations over investigations, the need for improving the training system, the need to employ blacks and Jews, the need to stop leaking serious information from bureau files to the press for the purpose of aggrandizing Hoover or to hurt his supposed enemies; and finally the need to put bureau manpower where it was needed and not waste it on dead issues that only resulted in public relations campaigns designed to shine the bureau's "image."

I too fully expected to be booted out of headquarters by Hoover, but for some strange and unknown reason Hoover kept moving me up the ladder. Maybe it was because I worked hard and tried to get the jobs done in spite of him. Maybe because the old vanity-ridden tyrant was a bit puzzled by me and curious as to what I would do next or what uproar I would cause.

What really kept me at the bureau, and some other colleagues as well, was that we wanted to be around for the time when we could help reform and reorganize it. We kept hoping that Hoover would retire or die. We weren't seeking the directorship. What we wanted was, quietly, without publicity, to have a hand in developing the kind of an FBI that the nation deserved and didn't have. So I too stayed in the circus.

SEVEN

Odd Man In

HOOVER ALWAYS took the public position that the United
States didn't have and didn't need a national police force.
But for all practical purposes we had one, a secret one at
that, and it was controlled by the FBI.

This national police force was made up of graduates of the FBI
National Academy's special three-week training course for police officers. It was a great honor for a member of a city or state police force
to be selected for this training—in fact, the men selected for this
training often rose to positions of prominence within their own organizations shortly after returning home. And they were suitably grateful. With good reason, Hoover felt that the alumni of the FBI training
course were his men. Thanks to this network of FBI-trained police officers, we had a private and frequently helpful line to most city and
state police organizations throughout the country. The police officer
who helped me out of a jam when one of my undercover agents was
arrested by the Chicago police at a pot party during the Democratic
National Convention in 1968 was trained at the FBI National Academy.

Having a man accepted for FBI training was quite a plum for any
chief of police. Hoover was aware of this, and he took full advantage of
the leverage. When the Capitol Building in Washington was bombed,
the only informant who knew anything at all about the case was working for the Washington Metropolitan Police, not the FBI. Although
the bombing was within our jurisdiction and was clearly our responsibility, Hoover was so angry that the police were one up on the FBI
that he refused to touch the case or let the FBI help the police in any
way. When the incident blossomed into a full-scale feud between
Hoover and Jerry Wilson, the chief of the Washington Metropolitan

Police, Hoover went after Wilson with everything he had. He crossed Wilson off the FBI mailing list and ordered the National Academy not to accept any more trainees from the Washington Metropolitan Police.

Any other police chief would have dropped the matter and waited, hoping for a change of heart. But Wilson worked in Washington, where power and influence are the name of the game, and he had a friend or two of his own in high places. Hoover was eventually forced to rescind his decision.

During the 1950s I was present at a meeting when John P. Mohr, who as associate director had jurisdiction over the Training Division, suggested to Clyde Tolson that future graduates of the FBI police training course be given a looseleaf notebook with the seal of the FBI embossed on its front cover. "They'd be proud of those books," Mohr told Tolson, "and they'd keep them out on their desks where everyone could see them. It would be a good public relations gimmick."

"The director would be opposed to that," Tolson said immediately, shaking his head. (He really believed that he could talk for Hoover, answer for Hoover, make the same decisions Hoover would make. At the bureau, we used to call the two of them the "unipersonality"—they were two people who acted as one.)

Mohr asked Tolson why the director would be opposed. "One of those police officers could go bad, could be caught taking bribes," Tolson replied. Tolson was afraid that if a rogue cop had an FBI bookcover, he and the bureau would be open for criticism.

Mohr couldn't believe it. "Damn it, Tolson," he shouted, "we give these guys diplomas signed by Hoover. Why can't we give them a bookcover too?" We could, and from then on we did.

Hoover treated local city and state police forces the same way he treated the Royal Canadian Mounted Police, the CIA, and every other law enforcement agency that wasn't the FBI. He didn't like his agents to help the police, and if any local police officer had been of assistance to the FBI, he'd get no thanks from Hoover, either publicly or privately.

It was unusual then for an FBI man to develop close ties with many police officers, but Quinn Tamm, who was at one time assistant director of the Training Division, was elected executive director of the International Association of Chiefs of Police when he left the FBI. Tamm had been a good FBI man, but he had a mind of his own. Since independent thought was heresy to Hoover, when Tamm became too outspoken the director froze him out. No cases were assigned to Tamm, his mail was rerouted to his assistants, and his phone never rang. He just sat at his desk day after day with no work to do. After a few months of that, he decided to resign.

Tamm had many high-ranking friends on police forces all around the country, friends he had made through his work at the FBI Academy, and when he left the FBI, his friends wanted to know why. Hoover had his boys spread the rumor that Tamm had lost his touch, that he was no longer able to do his job at the bureau. It was slanderous, and it didn't work. Those police chiefs knew Tamm; they had trained and worked with him for years; they liked, respected, and trusted him a lot more than they trusted Hoover. And though Hoover did everything he could do to see that Tamm was defeated when he ran for the job of executive director of the International Association of Chiefs of Police, Tamm was elected easily. He knew, of course, that Hoover had been working against him, but he took it philosophically. "I'm younger than Hoover," Tamm would say, "and I expect to be here long after he's gone."

"How does he know he'll outlive me? Does Tamm have a direct line to God?" Hoover asked Tolson when Tamm's remark got back to him—as all remarks eventually did.

There was always something of a rivalry between the FBI and local police organizations, and in at least one area—investigating organized crime—the police were way ahead of us. In fact, before 14 November 1957, when news that the New York State Police had discovered a meeting of mob leaders in a house in Apalachin hit the headlines, the FBI never officially acknowledged the existence of the Mafia. "They're just a bunch of hoodlums," Hoover would say. He didn't want to tackle organized crime. He preferred his agents to spend their time on quick, easy cases—he wanted results, predictable results which produced the statistics Hoover thrived on. These statistics—how many teenage car thieves we'd apprehended and how much the cars were worth (if a stolen car was worth eight hundred dollars, the agent making out the report automatically jacked up the price to fourteen or fifteen hundred)—were the heart and soul of Hoover's annual speech before the Senate Appropriations Committee. "This year, gentlemen," he would boast, "the FBI recovered two million dollars worth of stolen automobiles."

The senators on the committee would nod their heads, murmuring "wonderful, wonderful," and approve ever larger budgets for the FBI. What the senators never knew was that most (if not all) of the real work involved in investigating the kinds of crimes that made for Hoover's blockbuster statistics, juvenile car theft and the like, was done by local police, not the FBI, and credited to the FBI only because the perpetrator inadvertently crossed a state line.

Investigating the Mafia promised to be more difficult than rounding up juvenile auto thieves. Organized crime is far more complicated; the Mafia runs legitimate businesses as front for their illegal operations. Mafioso are rich and can afford the best lawyers, while we have to use government lawyers, some of whom are excellent, some of whom aren't worth a damn. And the Mafia is powerful, so powerful that entire police forces or even a mayor's office can be under Mafia control. That's why Hoover was afraid to let us tackle it. He was afraid that we'd show up poorly. Why take the risk, he reasoned, until we were forced to by public exposure of our shortcomings.

The Mafia has an ironclad rule—"Death to the informer!"—which makes investigating their activities even more difficult. Placing an informant in the Mafia is expensive and risky. We once found an informant in Detroit strangled and stuffed into the trunk of an automobile. Informing on the Mafia is more dangerous than informing on the Soviets—the Mafia is deadlier.

The news about the meeting of sixty-one top Mafia figures at Apalachin hit the FBI like a bomb. The meeting proved beyond any doubt that organized crime existed on a massive scale in this country. Hoover knew he could no longer duck and dodge and weave his way out of a confrontation with the Mafia, and he realized that his policy of nonrecognition left him and the FBI open for criticism. To prevent this, Hoover moved on two fronts. First, he put on a public relations show, telling the press that the FBI had long been contributing valu-

It took the accidental discovery by local police of a meeting of sixty-five Mafia members at this house in Apalachin, N.Y., for Hoover to finally admit that the Mafia existed.

Below: Four of the twenty delegates to the organized crime convention who were convicted for their refusal to reveal what really happened at their get-together in Apalachin on 14 November 1957. Clockwise, from top left: John Montana of Buffalo, N.Y.; Frank Majuri of Elizabeth, N.J.; Nat Evola of Brooklyn, N.Y.; Anthony Riela of West Orange, N.J.

United Press International photos

able information about organized crime to local police organizations, information that had helped these organizations prosecute Mafia members. That statement was somewhere between an exaggeration and a lie.

Once he took care of the public FBI image, Hoover tackled the more important issue: who would get the blame. After all, as Hoover himself was infallible, surely any mistake made by the FBI had to be someone else's fault. In this case, since investigating organized crime came under the jurisdiction of the Investigative Division, he blamed it on Al Belmont, assistant director in charge of the Intelligence Division. The only mistake Al had made was to follow Hoover's line that the Mafia was nothing but a bunch of hoodlums, so he got shellacked.

I had nothing to do with criminal investigation at that time—I was chief of the Research and Analysis Section investigating communism, espionage, and the Klan—so I was surprised when Hoover called me into his office to talk about the Mafia and even more surprised when he accepted my offer to do some research on organized crime for him. But he was like a drowning man, reaching for any help he could get to prevent future embarrassment, and he gave me the assignment.

It was my good fortune to have talented, dedicated men working for me then, men I had trained myself over the years, and I took the best of them off their other cases and put them to work full time on this project. One of them in particular, a man named Charles Peck, got so involved that he started working until eleven or twelve every night. He read over two hundred books on the Mafia and checked through the *New York Times* coverage of organized crime for the last hundred years. When I ordered him to leave the office by eight at night, he started coming in at five in the morning. He and the other men who worked on the project did a tremendous job, and we ended up with a two-volume study of organized crime that proved that the Mafia existed and had been operating in this country for many decades.

As this conclusion was contrary to the established FBI line, I was a little wary of presenting the study to Hoover. It was impossible to predict how he'd react, and if he got angry I wanted the blame to fall on me, not on my men or on Al Belmont who was forced to take

Hoover's position that the Mafia didn't exist. I bypassed Belmont and sent the five-page synopsis directly from "Sullivan to J. Edgar Hoover." I had never before bypassed bureau channels and it was also the first time that anyone who had the kind of minor job I then held had ever gone direct to the top in that way.

I also signed the five-page synopsis so that if someone was to be clobbered it would be me and not one of the men in my section.

The number three man at the time, Borden, intercepted it, read it, and sent a memorandum to Hoover saying "I have Sullivan's memorandum and in time I will review it." Almost at once Borden's memorandum with the synopsis on the Mafia came shooting out of Hoover's office. Hoover had written, "The point has been missed. It is not now necessary to read the two volume monograph to know that the Mafia does exist in the United States." The battle had been won. Hoover finally gave in.

I was proud of that study and I wanted to get it out to other people. I notified Hoover that we were sending copies of the large two-volume study to Harry Anslinger who headed the Bureau of Narcotics and another copy to Attorney General William Rogers. Like a shot Hoover called me into his office and said, "I see no need of giving Anslinger or the attorney general copies of our study." I told Hoover that the copies had already been sent out that morning. "Retrieve them at once," he shouted at me. I sent some men over and they sneaked the copies out and brought them back to me. After all, the study did prove that the FBI had been wrong. Copies were sent out to our field offices on a very confidential basis, and no one outside the FBI ever saw it.

When President Kennedy was elected and made his brother the attorney general, Hoover really began to get pressure about the bureau's efforts against the Mafia. Hoover divided the Investigative Division in two, making the second part a Special Division for Organized Crime so that he could create the impression for Attorney General Robert Kennedy that we were really getting the ball rolling. Hoover even selected Courtney Evans, an agent who had been working with Kennedy's office on the James Hoffa case and who became a close friend of Kennedy's, to head the new division. So here was a new division devoted to organized crime headed by a close friend of the attorney general. Hoover thought this move would take the pressure off him, but Robert Kennedy still kept after Hoover for results until President Kennedy was killed and the whole Mafia effort slacked off again.

EIGHT

Civil Rights and Wrongs

SOME YEARS AGO, *Ebony* magazine published an article called "The Lily White FBI," which focused on Hoover's hiring practices. The article was correct; there were no black FBI agents and there were very few black employees of the FBI at any level. Hoover, ever sensitive to bad publicity, was concerned about the article, and he decided to convince *Ebony* that it was wrong.

The sensible thing would have been to change the personnel policy and do some quick hiring, but Hoover didn't want to change the policy, he wanted to change the image. He invited the editor of *Ebony* to visit the FBI and pressed Sam Noisette, his office boy, into service. Noisette had worked for Hoover for years, and he knew how to please his boss. "I'm a black man who knows his place," Noisette used to say.

Sam's job was to show people into and out of Hoover's office, but the job was far from secure. Hoover took his frustrations out on Sam, and when he really got angry, Sam was demoted to working in the supply room in the basement. Though he dressed beautifully when he worked upstairs in Hoover's office, Sam was forced to wear work clothes when he was in exile. It was always a shock to see Sam in a little gray coat pushing a cart of stationery supplies around down in the basement. Hoover would always bring him back upstairs after a month or so, but Sam had a precarious existence during the thirty-odd years he worked for Hoover.

There were moments in Sam's job that made it all worthwhile, though, and he described one to me. Hoover was fanatic about germs, almost as bad as Howard Hughes, and flies, which he believed to be germ carriers, were a major preoccupation. One of Sam's most important duties as Hoover's office boy was to man the ever-present fly swatter. Hoover called Sam and his swatter into the office one day and pointed to a fly sitting in the middle of the conference table. Sam took aim, swatted, and missed. The fly buzzed around and around and finally landed on the back of Hoover's chair.

Again Sam swung and missed. "I started to worry then," Sam told me, "I had visions of the gray jacket and the basement." The fly buzzed around again, and this time it came down right on Hoover's arm, on the sleeve of his coat. "I was on it in a second," Sam said, "with my swatter up and ready to go. But I paused before I brought it down when I realized that I'd have to hit Hoover in order to kill the fly. Hoover didn't care about that, though. 'Hit him, hit him,' he screamed, and I brought down the swatter a hell of a lot harder than necessary."

On his own time, at night and on weekends, Sam was an artist, and every year he would hold an exhibition of his paintings at a gallery in Washington. Attendance at the affairs was mandatory for all senior FBI officials, and Hoover had spies there taking down the names of absentees. One year there was a hijacking on the day of Sam's show, and a few of us had to work right through the night. A few days later, along with everyone else who missed the show, I got a memo from Hoover saying that anyone who missed Sam's exhibit next year would be "dealt with severely." In other words, it was a command performance. I made certain to go the next year, and the day after the exhibit I sent a memo to Tolson about one of Sam's paintings. It was a lovely painting, I wrote, a pastoral scene of cows and a red barn on a green hillside. It reminded me of the farm where I grew up, but with one exception. The cows were grazing downhill. Cows graze uphill or they graze across the hill, but they never graze downhill. I was worried, I told Tolson facetiously, that an obvious error like that could reflect badly on the FBI and on Hoover himself.

My memo threw Tolson's office into a spin. He had no idea how to react to it. Should he tell Hoover? He asked advice from all his secretaries. I think he finally tore up the memo and threw it away.

When the editor of *Ebony* magazine came to see Hoover about the "Lily White FBI" article, he was ushered in to see Sam. Sitting behind a desk, dressed in his finest upstairs suit, Sam was introduced to the editor as an FBI agent, one of many black agents employed by the bureau. (During World War II, Sam had in fact been named a special agent so that Hoover wouldn't lose him to the draft.) Sam assured the editor that he'd gotten his facts wrong, and the editor left the FBI determined to write another article in atonement for the first one.

During the late 1960s when the FBI was under fire for our role (or lack of it) in the civil rights movement, the American Civil Liberties Union also showed some concern over our hiring practices. When a representative of the ACLU insisted on coming over for a look around the bureau, DeLoach was put in charge of the operation.

Out of about four thousand employees the FBI had in three levels of the Justice Department Building, only eight were black—and they were young women.

On the first floor we had an enormous room, a kind of typing pool. DeLoach pointed out that we had "a number" of black personnel working there. As the ACLU representative acknowledged that fact, DeLoach suggested that they go to the floor above. The moment the men left for the second location, DeLoach had the girls move up the stairs to the next level. When the men arrived at the second floor, the girls were seated in prearranged places among the mostly white employees. Not noticing that these were the same young ladies seen on the floor below, the ACLU representative had it pointed out to him that black FBI employees were also working there. Again, the moment the men turned to take the elevator to the third floor, the black girls were hustled upstairs before the visitor arrived. The ACLU investigator counted twenty-four black FBI employees.

Hoover saw no reason to hire blacks to work for the FBI, just as he saw no reason to involve the FBI in the struggle for civil rights in the South. We had been rightfully accused of dragging our heels and avoiding confrontations. "We're investigators," Hoover said, "not police officers. We're not going to get involved in these civil rights cases in Mississippi. We have just enough men there at this march of Meredith's so that when we are criticized and attacked we can say, 'You're wrong, we had men down there but not enough for them to engage in any activities.' If we see any of these Negroes being beaten up," Hoover went on, "we don't have to interfere, but be sure our men are right there."

By the middle 1960s, membership in the Ku Klux Klan had grown to fourteen thousand militant and often lawless racists. Responsibility for the Klan was in the hands of the FBI's Organized Crime Section of the General Investigative Division, headed by a good friend of mine, Jim Gale. Gale came to me complaining that his department was standing by watching helplessly, its hands often tied by FBI procedure. I agreed that something had to be done and I wrote a strong memo to Hoover recommending that the responsibility for investigating the Klan be shifted to my division, Domestic

The "lily white" typists in bureau headquarters, in Washington, D.C., where eight young black secretaries were shifted around so that the American Civil Liberties Union would think that there were twenty-four of them. *Acme Photo*

Intelligence, of which Hoover had appointed me assistant director in 1961.

I first encountered the Klan when I was a boy in Bolton, Massachusetts, and I can still vividly recall the fiery coffins the local anti-Catholic Klansmen burned as a show of strength in our town. They seemed like hoodlums to me then and I never learned anything about them that caused me to change my opinion. The Klan's poison even spread to my little country school, and I once wound up tangling with three boys my age in a fight that had started over religion and ended up being about a lot of other things too. I came home cut and bleeding that day, and when my dad found out he went out and beat the hell out of each of the three boys' fathers. My father-in-law also fought the Klan all his life, and they retaliated by burning down some of his buildings and taking a shot at him from a passing car.

When I took over the investigation of the Klan I was accused of trying to build my own empire within the bureau, but empire building was the last thing on my mind. I was already burdened with more work than I could handle. I wanted the Intelligence division to investigate the Klan because they were getting away with murder and had been for years.

One of my agents once told me, "Thirty years ago, FBI headquarters divorced the field offices and the two have been living in adultery ever since." The "Seat of Government," as Hoover called FBI headquarters, suffered from an enormous lack of knowledge, information, and techniques because it dealt only with official reports, so decisions by headquarters were often unsound. The ideas, problems, and techniques of the seasoned agents out in the field were never taken into account.

I arranged for a two-day conference in Atlanta with veteran agents from all over the South and from a couple of Midwestern states. It became clear that the plan of operation against the Klan drawn up in Washington was unrealistic. I abolished it and drew up a practical program based on the experience of the agents who attended the meeting.

Klan members were shooting into the homes of black people, blowing up synagogues, and burning churches. Things got so bad in some parts of the South that citizens started to raise money to protect themselves. When the situation was at its worst in Mississippi, a local Klan group decided to demolish the home of a Meridian businessman who had been acting as one of the main fundraisers. Most of the money he raised had gone to pay informants, and through one of these informants I found out about the plot and alerted the local law enforcement officers.

On 30 June 1968, the Meridian police were there waiting when a twenty-one-year-old Klansman named Thomas A. Tarrents III drove up. He got out of his car with enough dynamite to demolish not only the businessman's house but also the houses on both sides of it. He carried a machine gun too, and when the police called out to Tarrants to stop and put up his hands, he dropped the dynamite and started firing the machine gun in the direction of the voices. The police returned the fire, and in the exchange of gunfire, Tarrants was hit and a woman friend he'd brought with him in his car was killed. Tarrants survived the gunfight although he had fourteen bullets in his body when the police finally picked him up.

The counterintelligence techniques we brought to our fight against the Klan have been thoroughly damned by the press and the public, but our successful use of these techniques is what finally broke them up. As far as I'm concerned, we might as well not engage in intelligence unless we also engage in counterintelligence. One is the right arm, the other the left. They work together.

Actually, these counterintelligence programs were nothing new; I remember sending out anonymous letters and phone calls back in 1941, and we'd been using most of the same disruptive techniques sporadically from field office to field office as long as I'd been an FBI man. In 1956, under Assistant Director Belmont, five years before I came in to take over the Domestic Intelligence Division, the decision was made to incorporate all counterintelligence operations into one program directed against the Communist party. I merely redirected the use of those techniques toward investigating the Klan.

Although we certainly wouldn't have broken the Klan without them, informants could cause tremendous problems for the bureau. After they've been working for us for a while, informants get to know the kind of information we want and many of them tailor their stories to suit the occasion. It's very easy to embellish a little at first—a small exaggeration here and there will convince the bureau that it's getting its money's worth. If our informant starts to run out of facts altogether, however, little exaggerations can turn into great big lies.

That's why we always try to have more than one informant in the same group. Three in a group of thirty would be ideal. Each would be unknown to the others, of course, so that we could compare three separate reports of the group's activities. That way it's easy to spot major discrepancies in the reports, run it out ourselves, and see who is mistaken or lying.

When I left the bureau we employed over three hundred full-time informants who reported from all over the country. Most of them were involved in crimes like hijacking, bank robbery, murder, and kidnapping. But some were members of the Black Muslims, the Black Panthers, the Ku Klux Klan, and the Minutemen—we heard about everybody, right across the board. During the late 1960s and the early 1970s the bureau must have spent a million dollars maintaining informants in the antiwar movement.

Sometimes an informant can become an agent provocateur who ends up participating in and perhaps instigating and even leading the activity he was being paid to report on. Of course, life isn't easy for informants, and they must walk a fine line between observation and participation. If our man is one of a group of three or four and the leader says "Let's go shoot up a house and burn down a church," it would be hard for our man to say "I told my wife I'd be home early." The others would assume he was working for the FBI. Informants must make decisions which are always difficult, never clear-cut.

But because of our informants, we created suspicion throughout the whole damn Klan, which was their undoing.

After the Philadelphia murders we had set up a Mississippi office. Toward the end of the summer of 1964, Roy Wall, the special agent in charge of that office, called me. I told Roy, "Let's destroy these fellows, just utterly destroy them." I trusted Roy; he was an outstanding agent. He said that in Mississippi there were three different Klan organizations and that we were in a position either to keep them separated and have them compete and fight with each other for support, or to merge them into one organization. I asked

Roy, "If you merge them into one, can you control it and if necessary destroy it?" Roy said, "Yes, we can do that." I told him to go ahead and merge them, through the use of our informants. From that time on, the Klan never again raised its head in Mississippi.

We had a man in one Klan organization whom we pushed up to the point where he controlled all the downstate Klan organizations in his area. At our suggestion he made a speech to them one night saying, "What we've been doing in the past is stupid, and none of us wants to be stupid. We've been engaging in violence and you all know the result; the damn federal agents have been investigating us. If we continue being stupid they're going to destroy us. Let's outsmart them by not violating any laws. What we'll do is throw all our resources in propagandizing the Klan and try to use legal means to get what we want." By God, he sold them a bill of goods and the violence stopped just like that.

Once, in Alabama, the Klan had a nationally known Klansman as a speaker before about eleven hundred members. Unknown to the Klan audience, the speaker had two of his own trusted henchmen there, one in the rear of the hall, the other up in front. He gave a rousing, emotional, inflamatory speech about "Whites' Rights" and the rest of it, and when he finished the entire audience was on its feet applauding him. Suddenly one of the speaker's men got up and shouted, "That's just the kind of talk we need. I'm going to pledge fifteen dollars for that man." The audience, of course, didn't know that it was a con job, so they started passing a large basket and everyone began putting money in it. In case the spirit of the moment was missed by anyone, the speaker's other crony shouted that he was going to put in twenty-five dollars. The three men picked up over a thousand dollars and drove away to a motel. FBI agents trailed them the fifteen miles to their room and watched as they divided the money. We made it known to the Klan that their own prejudices and ignorance had made them patsies for their own people. Immediately afterward we had one of our informants suggest to his fellow Klan members that they take a lie detector test to weed out the FBI informants among them. We suggested that because we knew that the test is an expensive process that would drain them of funds and a lot of time. Our informant said that if anybody opposed the test he would be a suspect. Because of the expense and the effort involved, a lot of them back down on submitting to a lie detector test, and the more they backpedalled, the more our informant would raise hell. They all ended up suspecting each other.

In 1965, Gary Thomas Rowe was on the FBI's payroll as an informant the night he was riding in an automobile with the Klansman who shot and killed Viola Liuzzo in an Alabama marsh. Mrs. Liuzzo was a Michigan housewife who had gone South to work for civil rights, and her murder horrified most of the country.

When I got hold of Rowe, I really gave him hell. Why hadn't he grabbed the gun, or hit the killer's arm and deflected his aim?

"I couldn't," he told me. "There were five of us in the car. I was in the back seat behind the driver. We were driving along very slowly when suddenly the guy sitting in the front passenger's seat, way out of my reach, drew his gun and fired. I knew he had a gun, and I knew that the others had guns too, but there was no reason to think anyone would use one."

We had to take his word for it. Rowe had said he couldn't prevent the murder, but his eyewitness evidence did break the case for us. His testimony, however, failed to convince an all-white jury in Haneyville, Alabama, and it took a second trial to obtain a conviction.

After he gave his testimony, the Klan would have killed Gary Rowe, so we moved him to another part of the country where we gave him a new identity and a new job. But he continued to be the damnedest guy, always getting in trouble, very hard for us to control. We would beg him to stay out of fights, but whenever our agents inspected photographs they had taken of riots and brawls that took place in Rowe's new territory, we would always spot our informant right in the middle of the worst of it. We once had a picture of him holding two men up against a car, pounding the hell out of both of them. The picture only showed his back, but Rowe was powerful, a six-foot-two redhead weighing two hundred twenty pounds. There was no doubt that the man in the picture was Rowe. "Where's my face?" he asked when we showed him the picture. "That's not me, you can't see my face," he told us. But it was Rowe all right—he was a real hell raiser.

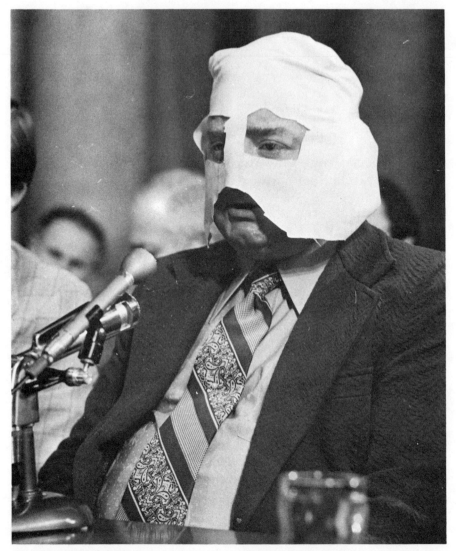

Gary Thomas Rowe, Jr., was an FBI informant who was "hard to handle." In 1975, testifying before the Senate Intelligence Committee, he wore a white hood to protect his identity. *Wide World Photos*

Once, in Alabama, after staying out all night Rowe went to get a cup of coffee at a roadside stand. He had just given his order when four members of a local Hell's Angels–type motorcycle gang roared up. One of the young toughs told Rowe he'd have to wait to get his coffee until the four of them were served. Rowe hauled off and belted him, knocking him silly. With that, the rest of them jumped on Rowe, and when it was over three of the men went to the hospital. The fourth ran off and left his motorcycle.

The night after we shipped Rowe out of Alabama he got into a fight in an alley behind a saloon. The fellow he hit wound up in the hospital with a concussion and three broken ribs. Rowe was a real headache, but he was a good man for our purposes and he served us well. We must have paid him eight or nine thousand dollars a year.

It was my habit, when I had the chance, to go incognito into the field to get a feel for the people and the situation that was developing.

During the Poor Peoples' March on Washington, a number of the civil rights workers had taken up residence in "Resurrection City" and Stokely Carmichael was one of them. Dressed in old clothes, I went up to him and asked how he thought things would work out. Carmichael, well composed and neatly dressed, answered by saying, "This is one of the most important public protests that we have held. I'm sure that it will be successful." He said that with a lot of other people listening in. Privately, he was sure that the march was doomed to failure. We knew his personal feelings because his body-guard, a man who called himself Peter Cardoza, was our informant.

Cardoza was another tough customer and was a real discipline problem for the bureau. But there's absolutely no point in hiring Boy Scouts as informants—they just don't have access to the information we need. The FBI can't be too choosy when it comes to the moral fiber of its informants, and Cardoza earned his FBI salary by telling us everything Carmichael was thinking and doing.

Our agents never could keep Cardoza in line either. He had a maddening habit of going off on trips around the country without informing the bureau. One Sunday, about a month after his "final" warning to keep the bureau informed of any sudden moves, I got a call at home from one of my assistants. "We're in terrible, terrible trouble," he said, "so bad that I can't talk about it on the phone."

I went right down to the office to find out what had happened. The boys couldn't wait to tell me. Cardoza had gone to Louisville, Kentucky, without telling anyone at the bureau, and had been part of a group that started a riot in which two men were killed. When the

Louisville police arrested him, Cardoza told them that he had been acting under the instructions of the FBI. It was a very sticky situation. We had to cut our ties with him, and he ended up in jail.

My program of using established FBI techniques, techniques that we had used successfully in the past against groups like the Communist party, paid off. By 1971 the Klan was reduced to a disorganized and impotent forty-three hundred members.

We knew what we were getting into and what kind of risks we were taking when we put informants like Rowe and Cardoza on the payroll. We sought them out and asked them to help. For a fee, of course. Hardly anyone does this kind of work out of conviction or as a public service, and we tend to look on people who do volunteer with a very wary eye, as they often turn out to be double agents.

NINE

Martin Luther King, Jr.

WHEN I TOOK OVER the Intelligence Division in 1961, the FBI's counterintelligence operation was already in existence and the King investigation was one that I inherited along with thousands of others. Martin Luther King, Jr., had been the subject of FBI scrutiny as far back as 1957. In my initial talk with Hoover, after he appointed me to the job of assistant director, he explained his policy regarding sensitive and major investigations. Hoover singled out the King case, emphasizing the need to extend great care and discretion in the wiretaps and other techniques that were being used against King. Hoover told me that he felt that King was, or could become, a serious threat to the security of the country. He pointed out that King was an instrument of the Communist party, and he wanted it proved that King had a relationship with the Soviet bloc. Hoover also made it clear that he wanted evidence developed that would prove that King was embezzling or misusing large sums of money contributed to him and his organization.

The original basis for the taps that Hoover had placed on King relate to men whom Hoover considered to be Communists or pro-Communist and who were confidants of King. In addition, Hoover was concerned by indications that King had been interested in establishing contact with the Soviets to see if he could get money from them to finance his movement. But at bottom Hoover was concerned about King's repeated criticism of the FBI and its alleged lack of interest in the civil rights movement. I personally believed that Martin Luther King, Jr., could be the leader his people needed. I was one hundred percent for King at that time because I saw him rising as an effective and badly needed leader for the black people in their desire for civil rights.

I knew that Hoover didn't like King on general principles, but though we had been tapping King's telephone in Atlanta since the late 1950s, no damning information on him had been unearthed. I thought that King should visit me at the bureau the next time he was in Washington. King was "on his way up," I wrote, and he "could be of great assistance to the Bureau in the future." You always had to say this to Hoover because his interest in King or anyone else was purely pragmatic. He didn't care whether or not King had the makings of a great leader, or if he could actually improve the racial situation in our country. He just knew that if we didn't get King on our side, someone else would, so he approved my request for the interview—but only on the condition that Deke DeLoach sit in with me. He expected that DeLoach would faithfully report every word we said.

The Crime Records Division sent out the invitation that I had proposed, but Dr. King, in a brief note, replied that he was too busy to join in a discussion at the FBI. Hoover told me that he knew that the FBI would be snubbed by Dr. King and that I too should have known that and should not have extended the invitation to him. I think King made a serious mistake when he turned down the invitation.

It was shortly after this that Hoover started piecing together the fragments of information agents had gathered about King, tiny fact by tiny fact, and came to the conclusion that King was a dangerous, subversive Communist who needed to be watched closely by federal agents at all times. Avid for more evidence of any kind to prove his case, Hoover would chastise me for not finding more, saying, "If I'd appointed someone else assistant director instead of you, I'd have the information I want by now." Hoover went so far as to tell me, "If you didn't have the job that I gave you, Dr. King would no longer hold the position that he has and would no longer be a prominent national figure."

There was only one man who could make the decisions in the FBI and although we were able to keep some matters from him, if he was on to something, if he was up on a case, there was nothing we could do. All the well-meaning people in the bureau did exactly what he told them, for if they didn't, they'd be pounding the pavements. They had to carry out his orders if they didn't want to sell their homes and take their children out of school. So I had to play to his dusty conclusion that King was a Marxist, no matter how mistaken he was.

Hoover berated me, "I kept saying that Castro was a Communist and you people wouldn't believe me. Now you're saying that King is not a Communist and you're just as wrong this time as you were with Castro."

What was Hoover's proof? Hoover believed that King was a Communist because King once said publicly that he was basically a Marxist. And if that wasn't enough, two of King's associates (he must have had thousands) had been linked to leftist groups and Marxist causes. Hoover presented his case to Robert Kennedy, then attorney general, and asked for Kennedy's authorization to step up FBI surveillance on King. Kennedy admired King and he didn't want to do what Hoover asked, but Hoover kept twisting his arm. I was under orders from Hoover to send Kennedy anything I got indicating pro-Communist sympathies on King's part to "keep up the pressure." Kennedy finally met with King at the Justice Department and warned him to stay away from the two "Communists" ("You don't need these people," Kennedy said to King—I know, because I read a transcript of their whole conversation). But when King continued contact with one of the two (a lawyer who had been deeply committed to the civil rights movement and to King personally from the beginning), Kennedy reluctantly gave in to Hoover's demands. He was afraid that Hoover would leak his information to the press if he didn't. Whether it was fiction or fact, the story could hurt John and Robert Kennedy, as they had both publicly supported King.

I don't think King ever had any real ideology, though, and he certainly wasn't a Communist. King wasn't interested in ideology— he was an organizer, an orator. There were many black men in this country who were head and shoulders above Martin Luther King, Jr., in terms of ability, but he had charisma.

Hoover believed that King was a Communist, though, and he went out after him with his biggest guns. No one, not the Kennedys and certainly not anyone at the bureau, could stop the surveillance and harassment to which King was subjected until his death in 1968. It was a classic confrontation: Hoover vs. Communism, blacks, and social change, and Hoover gave it everything he had, which in his case was considerable.

Hundreds of memos were written to Hoover during those years from all the top men at the bureau, including me, all of us telling Hoover that King was a dangerous menace and that Hoover was doing the right thing, all of them telling Hoover what he wanted to hear. No matter how well meaning a man might be, no matter how much he disagreed with Hoover's ideas and tactics, he went on with the investigation. No one in a top job at the bureau got there because he refused to follow Hoover's orders, no matter how distasteful they might have been. There was only one man at the bureau who made important decisions and the rest of us carried them out.

I had under my jurisdiction a lot of important criminal and espionage cases that I determined were more vital than the investigation of Dr. King. But Hoover was monomaniacal about that case and kept after us all, even though valuable FBI manpower was being diverted from essential investigations. Many of us, myself included, sent Hoover memos that would echo his attitude toward King just to get him off our backs so we could get on with our more important work.

There were, at the top, no fewer than fourteen men with high-ranking positions who not only never objected to the investigation of King, but because of Hoover's pressure were vigorously behind it. At the top, of course, there was Hoover, with Tolson at his side and Tolson's assistant beside him. Then came the number three man in the bureau, at that time Alan Belmont. Below him was Cartha DeLoach and then me, director of the Intelligence Division. My division, in turn, had two branches with an inspector heading each one, Security and Counterespionage, and the Intelligence branch. A section chief from Intelligence was assigned to the case; under him was an assistant section chief who handled the King case when his superior was away; under him was a unit chief; and below him were supervisors, the bedrock of the administrative structure. On the everyday working level it is the supervisor who follows the day-to-day communications between the field offices and Headquarters.

Hoover's motives for pursuing King, as far as I can see, were:

1. Hoover was opposed to change, to the civil rights movement, and to blacks.

2. Hoover really believed that King was a Communist, or at the

very least pro-Communist, all evidence to the contrary notwithstanding.

3. Hoover resented King's criticism of the FBI.

4. Hoover was jealous of King's national prominence and the international awards that were offered to him.

Hoover felt that King was a deceiver because on the one hand he talked of God, the Gospel, and morality, and on the other Hoover saw bureau reports that indicated that King led a high life on which he spent large amounts of money gathered from his supporters.

Hoover believed it all and we backed him up. "The director is correct . . ." is the way many of our memos to Hoover would begin. We gave him what he wanted—under the threat of being out on the street if we didn't agree. Hoover told me that his view of King was reinforced by many citizens from "bellhops to nationally known figures." He cited Norman Vincent Peale and Roy Wilkins. Roy Wilkins of the NAACP did visit the FBI headquarters and, according to DeLoach, who at that time was the head of Crime Records, Wilkins knew of some of Dr. King's personal activities and "expressed strong disapproval of them." Wilkins, said De Loach, was opposed to exposing Dr. King because he thought that the civil rights movement would be hurt as a result. But Hoover wanted King "exposed," and instructed us that all derogatory information about him be used to inform King's important financial backers, key field workers, influential churchmen, and community leaders. Hoover insisted that speeches be prepared for congressmen about King's activities. He also kept agents busy preparing information about King for the press, partially to block him from getting honorary degrees by spreading this information to various institutions.

Hoover's hate overcame his judgment during a press conference he agreed to hold in 1964 with a group of women reporters headed by Washington veteran Sarah McClendon. When one of the reporters asked Hoover about King's allegations that the FBI wasn't effectively enforcing the law in the South, Hoover called King the most notorious liar in America.

Hoover's "on the record" remarks about King were too much for Lyndon Johnson, who was then in the White House. Suddenly the Hoover–King feud had gone public and had become a political embarrassment to the president himself. Johnson ordered Hoover to meet with King and patch things up.

A meeting was set up and Hoover did all the talking. He always did. I think it was because he was afraid that someone would bring up a topic other than the FBI. Hoover didn't feel qualified to talk about anything except the bureau and the exploits of its agents, so he tended to dominate the conversation.

The meeting went smoothly, but nothing was really accomplished. The next day, we overheard King describe the meeting to one of his friends on the telephone. "The old man talks too much," he said. Hoover, of course, thought he had captivated King, really charmed him. When he found out what King had said about him, King was lost.

We were on him night and day. Because of this constant surveillance, we got every aspect of King's life on tape, including his love life. Hoover had always been fascinated by pornography, and if any that came to the bureau during the course of an investigation was kept from him, he'd raise hell.

There was an iron-clad rule at the bureau that any material of this sort that went into FBI files had to be taped shut, but within hours a file with compromising photographs would be opened and closed so many times that the tape would lose all its adhesiveness.

When we raided the apartment of Angela Davis during her fugitive days, the agents found a series of photographs of her and her boyfriend taken while they were making love and word of the pictures got around . . . to everyone but Hoover.

Hoover called the SAC in New York about a hijacking case, and when the conversation was almost over, the SAC, without thinking, said to Hoover, "What did you think of those photographs of Angela Davis and her boyfriend?" Hoover said, "What pictures? I haven't seen any pictures!"

The buzzer in my office rang. It was Hoover on the phone. He asked, "Have you seen the pictures of Angela Davis and her boyfriend?" The truth was that I had heard about them but hadn't seen them and I told him so. Hoover shouted, "I want to see them immediately and I want to know why I hadn't been sent those pictures before." I called the agent who had them and who had been holding them back because, like all of us, he wanted to get on with his work and not be interfered with by Hoover. He brought them into Hoover's office and received a scorching letter of censure. He was unable to get the promotion that was due him for six months.

Dr. Martin Luther King, Jr., arriving at FBI headquarters on 1 December 1964 to meet Hoover, who had recently called King "the most notorious liar in the world." LBJ asked King and Hoover to end their feud. After the meeting King said about Hoover, "The old man talks too much." *United Press International*

There were no pictures of King, but there were tapes, and Hoover listened to all of them. Just in one seventeen-month period, from 5 January 1964, for example, fifteen separate wiretaps were placed in as many hotels as King traveled throughout the country. From New York City to Milwaukee, Detroit, Washington, Sacramento, and Honolulu.

Hoover instructed us that tapes made in King's hotel rooms were to be made available to some members of the press, to some select congressmen, and to President Johnson. Thinking that wasn't enough, he had the FBI send derogatory information about King to the pope prior to King's visit to Rome for a papal audience. The pope ignored Hoover's information and the meeting took place as scheduled in August 1964.

As the feud between Hoover and King grew, Hoover's one wish was to silence King's criticism of the FBI.

Late in 1964, Alan Belmont (then the number three man) called me into his office and told me that Hoover and Tolson wanted some excerpts of tapes obtained by bugging King's hotel rooms sent to King's wife Coretta. I told Belmont that even if the tapes were sent anonymously, Coretta King would know they were from the FBI.

Belmont told me that Hoover had already made the decision, and that since the case was in my division, I was to arrange to have a package of the tapes prepared by the FBI Laboratory sent to Mrs. King from Tampa, Florida. A laboratory employee brought a box containing the composite tape to my office. I called in a veteran agent whom I trusted and gave him the assignment of flying to Tampa and mailing it from a post office there.

Enclosed in the box with the tape, I learned later, was an unsigned note to Dr. King warning him, "your end is approaching . . . you are finished." The letter suggested that the tape might be publicly released, and ended, "You are done. There is but one way out for you. . . ." The purpose of the tape, according to Belmont, was to silence King's criticism of Hoover by causing a break between King and his wife which would reduce King's stature and therefore weaken him as a leader.

I had not heard or seen the tape, and I did not know about the unsigned note until it surfaced in the press.

Experiences are really not transferrable, but it is important to have an understanding of the weird circumstances in which we worked. I had literally thousands of cases under my jurisdiction, and because of the weakness of Hoover's administrative policies, the workload on some key officials like myself was enormous. As assistant director in charge of the Intelligence Division, however, I believed in delegating responsible work to responsible men. I had nine assistants at that time, all of them making about thirty thousand dollars a year, so I used them as much as I could to lighten my load. We did what we could to keep Hoover off our backs, and when we had to, we gave him exactly what he wanted. The King investigation seemed to dominate Hoover's attention and all matters relating to King originated with Hoover and the follow-up was reviewed by him.

Three days before the tapes were sent, Hoover had branded King "the most notorious liar in the country." Now King was prepar-

J. Edgar Hoover with his assistant and close friend Clyde Tolson on 15 July 1964.
Wide World Photos

ing to go to Stockholm, Sweden, to receive the Nobel Prize and Hoover wanted to scare King off from getting that prestigious honor.

Early in 1964 when I saw that Hoover and King were on a collision course, I suggested to Hoover that we recommend to the NAACP that another man be chosen as a successor to King. My recommendation was approved by the then number three man in the bureau, DeLoach, and even by Tolson himself, who rarely agreed with me about anything. My memo fed Hoover the rhetoric about King required in all matters relating to him, and then went on to name Dr. Samuel Riley Pierce, a black educator with a fine reputation. I had never met Dr. Pierce, but we had mutual friends who thought him to have high character, ability, and the capacity for leadership. I had even recommended Pierce to lecture in my place when I could not accept an offer myself. Although there was interest in my suggestion, the entire matter ended because Hoover was still preoccupied with King.

In a way, Hoover was responsible for some of King's power and prestige. As the revelations of Hoover's actions against King leaked out, Martin Luther King, Jr., became even more important as a

James Earl Ray
in a photograph issued by the Royal
Canadian Mounted Police, which
was responsible for tracking Ray
down. Hoover, however,
never gave them the credit.
United Press International

leader of the civil rights movement. If he was important to Hoover, it followed that King should be important to his people, more important than other black leaders who were ignored by Hoover.

I was convinced that James Earl Ray killed Martin Luther King, but I doubt if he acted alone. Ray was so stupid that I don't think he could have robbed a five- and ten-cent store. He was not only stupid, he was sloppy. He left the rifle he used to shoot King in an alley, and he left beer cans covered with his fingerprints in the trunk of his abandoned car. Ray could have left the gun in his room, or if he was smart he could have opened a hole in the wall and hid it there. He could even have broken the gun down into two pieces and carried it out in a small box, but he was sloppy. And stupid.

Someone, I feel sure, taught Ray how to get a false Canadian passport, how to get out of the country, and how to travel to Europe because he could never have managed it alone. And how did Ray pay for the passport and the airline tickets? Ray's brother told the FBI, "My brother would never do anything unless he was richly paid."

Thanks to all the clues he'd left we knew we were after Ray, but we had a hell of a time finding his whereabouts. As the weeks passed, the pressure on the FBI to find him grew. Johnson was giving us hell because Ray was a political liability and would remain so until he was in custody. There were rumors about Ray and the FBI: first, people said that we didn't want to find Ray; then they started saying that the FBI itself had a hand in King's murder. We had a lead that Ray had gone to Mexico, but we couldn't find him there or anywhere else.

As a matter of course, I had asked the Royal Canadian Mounted Police to help us find Ray. One night in early June, two months after King was shot, I got a call at home at eleven at night from Bill Kelly, deputy commissioner of the RCMP and a close friend. "I think we've solved your case," he said. The RCMP had painstakingly gone through 250,000 passport applications, checking pictures and handwriting, until they came up with Ray's alias. It worked; they traced him for us from Canada to Portugal (where he had been living with prostitutes) to England. He had tried to rob a bank in England to get some money, but naturally he bungled the job. We asked the British to move in and pick him up, which they did.

At our request, the British forgot about the bank robbery attempt so that we could bring him back to the United States on a murder charge.

Ray was in custody in London for two days before Hoover released the story to the press. He waited until the day of Bobby Kennedy's funeral to break the news so that the FBI could steal the headline from Kennedy one last time. I told Hoover that we should give the credit for Ray's capture to the RCMP. Hoover said no and the FBI falsely got the credit.

TEN

The New Left

THE CIVIL RIGHTS MOVEMENT which began in the late 1950s gave organization and impetus to the antiwar movement of the late 1960s. The tactics of direct action against authority that proved successful in the earlier struggle were used as a model for the students of the New Left. The two were tied together because although there had been some campus protest about the war, the riots of 28 April 1967 following the death of Martin Luther King, Jr., really started the whole thing rolling. And we weren't prepared.

A few weeks after King was shot, we at FBI headquarters were astonished when we got to our offices and read the morning papers. A student riot had broken out at Columbia University in New York City.

The trouble at Columbia came as a surprise to the FBI, as much of a surprise as our discovery of the true strength of the Mafia when we raided their meeting in Apalachin. Before we read the headlines and saw the pictures of Mark Rudd smoking a cigar with his feet up on Grayson Kirk's desk, we didn't know the New Left existed.

I teletyped the New York office and asked them what was behind all this and demanded to know what information they had. That afternoon I received a memorandum from New York that had attached to it a number of newspaper articles. I teletyped New York again, saying, "I don't want newspaper clippings. I want to know what you have in the files about the student uprising at Columbia University." New York got back to me again with the terse response, "We don't have anything."

Suddenly we had a new cast of characters to deal with, and the FBI found itself in a new business overnight as it had during the 1930s when there was a rash of kidnappings, and after the explosion of bank robberies in the late 1930s and early 1940s.

The FBI took the uprising at Columbia very seriously. We wanted to know whether, because of the Vietnam War, a revolutionary situation was developing at Columbia or on any other campus in the country. We didn't want to interfere with what the students were saying or thinking. After all, protest is nothing new in this country. A third of the population was opposed to the American Revolution and another third neutral. During the Civil War, soldiers had to be bribed to fight. But when the students started to blow up buildings, student unrest became FBI business.

After the Columbia riot, the New Left was fair game. By 1968, the Communist party, Hoover's number one fixation, was old, tired, and harmless, but if Hoover could tie CPUSA to the young, vital, and dangerous New Left, he'd really have something he could go with. Here was Hoover's chance to renew his fight against the Communist menace in the United States. When Gus Hall, longtime head of the CPUSA, said in a speech that the Students for a Democratic Society was an arm of the Communist party, that was all the proof Hoover needed.

"Maybe this will convince Sullivan that the Communist party is a terrible threat to our society," Hoover wrote on the bottom of a memo on Hall's speech, and for a month or so after that he kept writing the same sort of comments: "Sullivan better read this" he would write, or "Sullivan better remember this." There was blue ink everywhere.

Though Hoover used this connection between the New Left and the Communist party as a wedge to drive us into investigating the New Left, the connection wasn't real, and the only people who believed in it were Gus Hall and J. Edgar Hoover (I have my doubts about Hall). The New Left never had any important connection with the Communist party; as a matter of fact, the New Left looked on Hall and the Communist party as a joke—hidebound, retrogressive, and outside the mainstream of revolutionary action. The average age of CPUSA members was forty-nine; the New Left was made up of young people almost without exception. Just in case SDS leader Tom Hayden was not aware that the average party member was forty-nine years old, the FBI sent him an anonymous letter to that effect.

Hall, trained in Russia and a graduate of the Lenin school there, had been an effective organizer and leader during the 1930s, but by 1968 he had become a member of the middle class, and very fond of his nice apartment in New York and of having a new Oldsmobile every year.

Hall was so far from the mainstream of revolutionary action that on 15 November 1969, the day over a hundred thousand people marched in Washington to protest against the war in Vietnam, there were only about two hundred Communists present and they had no leadership at all. Hall himself was fishing in Maine. Some of his people were at the march, and when they realized that it was turning out to be a significant event, they gave Gus a call and told him to put down his fishing rod and get on a plane to Washington right away. He stayed in town just long enough to get his picture taken in front of the Washington Monument before he flew back to Maine, but Gus Hall was there!

Even though the CPUSA was finished we kept after them. Early in 1969 we learned that the Soviet Union planned on sending Hall a gift of some expensive stallions and mares which Hall planned to ship to his brother's farm in Minnesota. They expected to breed thorough-breds and sell the colts to help fill the coffers of the party. On learning about the impending Soviet gift to Hall, one of the imaginative men in my division came up with an idea. He had contacted a veterinarian, and without telling him what it was about, got the doctor to agree to inject the horses with a substance that would sterilize them before they were taken off the ship in New York. But for some reason the Russians never sent Hall the horses.

There was no question (as there had been in the case of the Klan) which division of the FBI would investigate the New Left. It was the job of the Domestic Intelligence Division. We used the same general investigative techniques against the New Left that we had used successfully against the Communist party: wiretapping, informants, hidden microphones—the lot.

The first thing I did was take a number of men off the investigation of the Communist party without telling Hoover about it. The men I took off the CPUSA investigations were instructed to concentrate on the violent aspects of the New Left because there were real differences in the kinds of people we were operating against. Building were being blown up, innocent students were getting wounded or killed, and education throughout the United States was being disrupted.

The New Left was active on college campuses and in the academic world; the Communist party never had been. We'd find the CPUSA in union halls, not universities. They were interested in the working man, not his boss's Ivy League son. Every member of the Communist party was a true believer, and they all believed the same party line. But the New Left was a diverse group. A few of them were Communists, some were Socialists, and others were liberals, conservatives, radicals, Republicans, or Democrats. The only thing that those in the New Left had in common was their opposition to the war. When we finally did pull out of Vietnam, the New Left disappeared.

During its main years, however, it flourished on campus. Next to their opposition to the war, the students seemed most unified in their opposition to their own university administrations. In the course of our investigation of the campus situation, we couldn't help but notice that in many cases the students were right. Many of the colleges and universities were poorly run, and it showed in the way the administration reacted to the uprisings.

The administrators who allowed their students complete freedom were rewarded by having their building bombed, while at the University of Denver, when the president warned that any student who seized a university building would be dropped as a student and that the matter would be turned over to the Denver police, no buildings were seized. At Dartmouth, when students threatened to seize two buildings, the president warned that he would call in the state police if they did. Thinking he was bluffing, the students seized the buildings. They were arrested, prosecuted, and fined a hundred dollars each. Dartmouth never had any trouble after that. When the administration wouldn't get tough, however, the students started blocking passages to classrooms, grabbing professors and locking them in closets, and blowing up buildings.

Though universities were the major battlefield of the antiwar struggles of the late 1960s, the churches were also going through political turmoil because of the war. Naturally, Hoover decided that any clergyman who spoke out and acted against the war was a Communist, but I knew that the activist clergymen were loyal Americans who were supported by many decent people in their communities. The most prominent of the dissenting clergymen, however, were the Berrigan brothers who were playing at being revolutionaries. They had begun to embarrass the hell out of us because we couldn't locate them. While a fugitive, Dan Berrigan once gave a sermon in a Methodist church in Connecticut. It was played up in the press and Hoover was furious.

Their father had been an active labor leader. Their mother, a German woman, was very religious and she tried to sway them from their father's influence. So the boys pleased their mother by entering the priesthood, but within the church the Berrigan brothers were still rebels. Daniel Berrigan was a first-class scholar; he made a name for himself as chaplin at Columbia University, and he was also considered to be a good poet. Philip, on the other hand, didn't have Dan's academic reputation or credentials; he was a run-of-the-mill clergyman. But both brothers were committed to ending the war, and they and their followers were willing and able to break into federal government property to publicize their cause.

On the evening of 8 March 1971, a group of dissenters, followers of the Berrigans, broke into our resident agency in Media, Pennsylvania, and the documents they stole from us and released to the press caused a national uproar. They stole eight hundred documents in all, most of them relating to our criminal work, but the documents relating to our security investigation proved beyond a doubt that the FBI was investigating students as if they were criminals. It cost us hundreds of thousands of dollars to put in safety precautions in all of our offices throughout the country.

Our men in the field had no trouble getting information about the New Left because the majority of the students, although they were against the war in Vietnam, were also against the violence that was going on. There was no difficulty in recruiting informants who were asked to report to us only information that related to violence

that was hampering their schooling. Some agents, especially some of
the younger ones, infiltrated many of the groups in spite of Hoover's
insisting to me that no agent should wear long hair, dress in jeans, or
wear a beard. I said "the hell with it" and made the decision myself to
go against Hoover's dogmatic ruling.

Everyone's workload began increasing during this period. One
agent might have three or four cases relating to the New Left while
still pursuing espionage and intelligence operations. The hard-working agent out in the field who rarely ever got to headquarters began
getting upset with the new cases. I had always had good rapport with
my men throughout the country and they felt free to let me know
what was on their minds. From all over I began getting personal letters from agents telling me that they were uneasy about investigating
these youngsters because they felt that many of the cases were political and not security investigations. Politically motivated investigations were nothing new to the FBI, though, and Hoover reminded us
that Franklin D. Roosevelt had set the precedent for these kinds of
investigations when he asked the FBI to investigate people who opposed his Lend-Lease program.

Through an informant we found out that the same group of dissenters who broke into our Media office was planning an entry into
another federal office building nearby. We knew who the members of
the group were—and we knew their leader, John Grady. But we
didn't interfere with their new plan because we wanted to catch them
red-handed.

Thanks to our informant, on the night of the break-in the target
building was surrounded by eighty FBI agents hidden in cars and in
various other buildings. I was on the telephone to the agent in
charge, directing the operation from Washington.

One of the buildings we were using as a hiding place was a funeral parlor across the street from the federal building. So as not to at-
tract attention, we took the agents in and out in a hearse. As business
was going on as usual at the funeral parlor, the men were forced to
wait for the break-in among the corpses. Unfortunately, their wait
was in vain.

"Grady changed his mind at the last minute," our informant told
me the next day. There were two more nights like that, our agents

going into the funeral home in a hearse and waiting in vain surrounded by dead bodies. After three disappointments, though, our
informant and I both felt that the time for a break-in had really come.
Our men were stationed all around the federal building when Grady
and his friends arrived. They walked over to one of the walls of the
building. "Where's the ladder?" Grady asked.

Each of the men looked at the others. There was silence. "Didn't
anyone bring it?" Grady demanded. Nobody had. Grady was so angry
that he wanted to call it off, but our informant, who had been catching
hell from me over all the false alarms, pleaded with him. "Let's do it
tonight," he said. "Let's go back and get the ladder." After a brief
debate, Grady agreed and the group left. All the agents stayed in
place, waiting. The men came back with the ladder about an hour
later and went into their well-rehearsed break-in routine. They had
been practicing for weeks. They kept the ladder out at a farm which
had a barn with a second-story window the same height off the ground
as the second-story window at the federal building. They had the
whole operation mapped out and timed, and they went through it
perfectly that night to an appreciative audience of FBI men.

Part of their plan was for some of the men to stay outside the
building to remove the ladder once the "gang" was inside. As soon as
the ladder was removed, the agent who was on the phone to me
wanted my permission to let the men move in.

"No, not yet," I told him. "If we move in now, all we'd have
against them is trespassing in a federal building. Let's give them some
time and get them for destroying federal property." After the three
false alarms the men were edgy, ready to move in at once, but I made
them wait almost two hours before I gave the signal to go. When I
did, there were agents everywhere. Some of them grabbed the men
who had stayed outside with the ladder and the rest swarmed into the
building. They found Grady's friends busily smashing file cabinets
and promptly arrested them, but we couldn't find their leader. He
had slipped through our fingers. The agents asked where he was and
were told that he was asleep at a Lutheran minister's house. Sure
enough we found Grady there, and our boys had to wake him from a
sound sleep in order to arrest him.

The Berrigans and their followers dreamt up and discussed

hundreds of wild schemes to break into buildings and destroy federal
property, ninety-nine percent of which never got beyond the discussion stage. But as these discussions were usually overheard by the
FBI or reported on later by an informant, we were aware of most
plans that came up, whether or not they were eventually rejected.
The Berrigans and their followers had no desire to hurt anyone, they
just wanted to call attention to their cause. Their most grandiose
scheme was a bombing-kidnapping plot; the kidnapping of Henry
Kissinger and the destruction of a tunnel area under the Capitol
Building. My division was right on top of the case and I was waiting
for the Berrigans to move so that we could have an air-tight case
against them, but Hoover was immediately aware of the shock value
and headline potential. He decided to make the Berrigans and their
radical plots the centerpiece of his annual speech before the Senate
Appropriations Committee.

Tolson called me a day or two before Hoover's Senate appearance to ask for anything I had on the Berrigans. "We can't publicize
that," I told Tolson. "If we do, they won't take any action and we'll
never get them. Besides, if Hoover tells the world about our surveillance, I don't think we'll even have a case against them, and they
could have a case against us."

"What's the use," asked Tolson, "of having this information in
our files if the director can't use it?" One of my own informants in the
bureau told me that Tolson decided to go around me and get someone
else to prepare a document of the Berrigans which Hoover could use.
It was like telling the press in a small town where a bank robber lives
and when he's going to do it. I was so alarmed that I sent Hoover a
very sharply worded memo advising him not to testify on the Berrigans. To protect himself, Hoover did ask that the Senate go into executive session so that what he was about to divulge would be kept
confidential. But one of the senators included in the executive group
was Byrd of Virginia, a charter member of Hoover's senatorial stable.
Byrd was Hoover's man, one of the few senators to be honored with
an invitation to listen to Martin Luther King's motel room tapes. It
was understood that Hoover would speak to the Senate off the record,
that Byrd, with Hoover's connivance, would leak the information to
the press, and that Hoover could say with authority, "I spoke off the

record." After all, a story about a group of radicals—probably Communist radicals to boot—blowing up Washington and kidnapping Henry Kissinger was too good to waste on senators.

Hoover's testimony backfired, as I warned him it would. Though Hoover had been a master of public relations, he was allowing personal prejudices to cloud his judgment. He had publicly implicated the Berrigans in a plot before any charges had been filed against them. The press throughout the nation pointed that out and Congressman William Anderson led an attack against Hoover in the House, while Senator George McGovern called for a congressional investigation of the FBI. Hoover and Tolson looked around for somebody to blame and called me into the office. "You should have warned me," Hoover said. "If you had warned me," he scolded, "I wouldn't have mentioned this information." He got red in the face as all the while Tolson was sitting behind him nodding his approval of Hoover's admonishment.

I got out a copy I'd saved of the memo I'd sent to Hoover advising him not to testify and put it on his desk. Hoover read it, looked up at me, and glared. "Why didn't you tear up that memo?" he asked.

"I thought I might need it for protection," I answered. A hush fell over our little group.

"You know you don't need that kind of protection in the bureau," he replied, smiling. It was like watching Dr. Jekyll and Mr. Hyde. If I hadn't saved a copy of that memo, he would have fired me then and there.

The late 1960s could be a dangerous time. A young professor got killed in his lab when angry students blew up the building he had been working in, and a young girl in Southern California lost an eye and one arm when a mailbox blew up as she was mailing a letter to her parents. The most famous explosion took place on West Eleventh Street in New York City. A group of Weathermen had been using an expensive Greenwich Village town house (Dustin Hoffman lived next door) as a bomb factory. The house was owned by Joe Wilkerson, a broadcast executive, and while he and his wife were out of town, their daughter Kathy invited her Weathermen cohorts to take advantage of their absence to use her home as their temporary headquarters. Kathy survived the explosion, but two of her friends did not. When we went in there after the explosion, we found enough bombs that hadn't gone off to level the whole block.

The majority of the students (and others) who made up the New Left, however, were not violent. They were completely loyal to this country. They just wanted us to get out of Vietnam.

I used to go out during demonstrations and mingle with them myself. I'd wear old clothes and I wouldn't shave so as not to put them off. I'd always try to find out what they thought about the FBI, and in many cases I was amazed by their ignorance of the bureau. Some of them confused us with the Secret Service, others with the Department of Commerce! They were obviously not hardened revolutionaries; they were seventeen- or eighteen-year-old kids who knew almost nothing about the government they were attacking.

But attack it they did, there was no doubt about that. One day I walked from the office over to Constitution Avenue and Ninth Street. The Department of Justice Building was all but surrounded by demonstrators and I found myself standing next to a young black fellow who was wearing an old U.S. Army knapsack. He turned to me and said, "We're going to win this struggle, we're going to win it." A signal was given and forty or fifty demonstrators started throwing rocks at the windows of the Justice Department. As he threw his rock, the young man next to me said, "The revolution has begun!" He really believed that his rock would be the rock felt around the world. Then the district police moved in with tear gas and I got a helluva dose myself.

Hoover didn't know anything about my trips to the streets of Washington until he read about it in a newspaper. I had been working at my desk while a demonstration was going on downstairs when I got a call from one of the agents with the crowd in the street in front of the Department of Justice building. "It looks like they're going to break into the courtyard," he told me.

If they broke into the courtyard, I knew they could get into the building itself. I went right down to see if I could help. He was right; the crowd was surging right up to where the police were blocking the entrance to the courtyard. One young demonstrator ran right into me in his rush to get past the police. As he tried to push me aside, I clipped him and knocked him down. I didn't hurt him—he was just knocked off his feet. Ken Clawson, then a reporter for the *Washington Post*, saw the whole thing and wrote a story about it.

Hoover gave me hell when he read it: "A high-ranking official of the FBI should not engage in physical contact with a demonstrator—with anyone."

It didn't take an undercover investigation for the FBI to learn that there was going to be trouble in Chicago during the 1968 Democratic National Convention. Many of the young people who planned to demonstrate against the war and against the convention were open, even boastful of their plans. At a rally in Chicago's Grant Park, SDS leader Tom Hayden told the five thousand young people gathered there to confront the police of the city so that the Chicago authorities would "charge around like a dog gone mad." At another rally, Jerry Rubin told his followers to go into the streets and "kill the pigs" and Chicago's Mayor Daley. As the time of the convention approached, a great mass of material, fact and fiction intermingled, flowed into the FBI.

• Ground glass would be sprinkled into the food in Chicago restaurants.

• Certain buildings would be firebombed.

• There would be sniper fire close to Convention Hall.

• Police would be lured into isolated areas where they would be assaulted by gangs of violent youths.

• Every effort would be made to prevent the Democratic convention from taking place at all.

• Large quantities of drugs were to be transported to Chicago to be consumed by the demonstrators.

• Demonstrators would protest in front of all Selective Service Boards in Chicago.

• Welfare Boards would be picketed.

• Delegates to the convention would be stopped as they arrived at the airports and railroad stations, and those who did get through the lines would be harassed and prevented from leaving Chicago after the convention.

• Demonstrators would sit and lie down in the streets in large numbers to stop all traffic on the streets leading to Convention Hall.

• Guns were being stored in a Chicago church.

• Large numbers of demonstrators would stop military and police cars. Members of a Chicago street gang would shoot at the occupants with high-powered rifles.

• All grocery stores in the ghetto would be destroyed.

• One head of an organization that would participate in the demonstration was seen and identified buying a holster for the revolver he was carrying.

• The following men would be assassinated during the convention: Mayor Richard Daley, Vice-President Hubert Humphrey, Senator Eugene McCarthy, Lester Maddox, Roy Wilkins (head of the NAACP), and Edwin King (a member of the Freedom Democratic Party of Mississippi).

In view of the assassinations of Martin Luther King, Jr., John F. Kennedy, and Robert Kennedy, this information had to be given serious and constant attention. I wanted our men to be able to infiltrate some of the groups making these threats. But how the hell could a well-dressed man with a handkerchief in his pocket mingle with the Yippies on the streets of Chicago without becoming a laughing stock? Given the seriousness of the situation, I again asked Hoover if we could send a few agents out in disguise, but the old fool wouldn't budge an inch. "As long as I'm director of the FBI," he shouted, "I'll not have any agent wearing old clothes and long hair."

I called the head of our office in Chicago, a tough-minded Swede named Johnson who was a friend of mine, and told him about my conversation with Hoover. He wasn't surprised at Hoover's obstinance, and when I offered to give him my own authorization to allow five or six of his agents to stay away from the office long enough to grow some hair, he was willing to take the risk. He knew we'd both be in trouble with Hoover if he found out, but Johnson felt as I did—sending our agents to penetrate these various groups was necessary.

Johnson picked men who had already been working on cases involving the New Left. The men he picked were young and single so they could be free to stay out all night if necessary without arousing the suspicions of their new companions.

Those agents did a remarkable job. They told us which of the threats were just rumors and which were actual fact. One of the groups was planning to seize the television network operation at Convention Hall, and we were able to give the police enough information to prevent it.

We had a bad moment, though, when we found out that one of our men had been arrested and put in jail. He was such a success in his role as a protester and demonstrator that he had been one of a dozen young people invited to attend a top-level pot party/strategy session. He had just been selected to serve as one of the leaders in an attack on Convention Hall when the Chicago police arrested the whole bunch of them.

Johnson called me as soon as he heard what had happened. The first thing I thought about was fingerprints; as soon as our agent's fingerprints were checked, it would come out that an agent of the FBI was in jail. When Hoover found out who was behind it, which wouldn't take long, Johnson and I would be fired.

We kicked the problem around for a few minutes and decided to take a high-ranking official of the Chicago police, who both of us knew and trusted, into our confidence. He was part of our underground "national police force," a graduate of the FBI Academy school for local police officers. We felt that he had enough power to help us and enough brains to keep his mouth shut. With his help, we got our man out of jail the next morning without arousing anyone's suspicions.

At the convention, and throughout the campaign, Hoover kept his distance from Hubert Humphrey, the Democratic nominee. Hoover was friendly with Nixon and supported his candidacy, and he didn't want Nixon to think that the FBI was helping Humphrey in any way. In fact, I don't think he ever gave Humphrey adequate protection, and neither did Humphrey, because his people were always asking us for additional security.

A week or two before the election, Deke DeLoach made Hoover even more wary of Humphrey when he told Hoover that he had heard a rumor that Humphrey planned to remove both Hoover and

DeLoach from office if he was elected. That story was nothing but a rumor, one that probably originated with DeLoach himself in an effort to upset Hoover and to show him that DeLoach, so close to Johnson, had also developed a source in Humphrey's camp.

Hoover believed every word of it, however, and he was terrified. In his fear, he turned to me, one of the only Democrats he actually knew. "Do you have any friends who are active in Democratic party circles?" he asked. As it happened I did know someone, a lawyer in Chicago. "Talk to him," Hoover said, "and find out if DeLoach has his facts straight." My friend in Chicago told me that Humphrey was much too busy trying to get elected to worry about J. Edgar Hoover and hadn't given him a thought. Hoover was relieved, but he didn't really relax until Nixon won the election.

There was no doubt about George McGovern's intentions, however, for he was quoted in *Life* magazine as saying that he'd definitely fire Hoover if he were elected president. Hoover turned the heavy guns on McGovern after that. Any malicious piece of gossip we unearthed was leaked to the press immediately. Hoover, through Tolson, also insisted that every top-ranking official of the FBI send a letter to McGovern condemning his statement.

I was indiscreet enough to oppose this in a conference with DeLoach. "Surely," I told him, "McGovern will see through the barrage of letters and realize that the letter-writing campaign had been a command performance." But I couldn't change his mind. Everyone had to write a letter.

Within a few days twenty of the other senior officials of the bureau had written and sent out their letters to Senator McGovern. To a man they called McGovern an irresponsible, reprehensible opportunist. McGovern did exactly what I anticipated he would; he had every single letter published in the *Congressional Record*—every letter but mine. When Tolson saw that omission, he sent one of his men into my office. The agent told me, "I've been instructed to tell you that this is a test of loyalty. Write the letter and you pass the test. Don't and you've failed." I was the last holdout. I had to write the letter. I tried to word it so that it was a letter I could live with—a lot of meaningless, general statements such as "Hoover needs no defense from me," and "His record speaks for itself"—but I found the whole thing so distasteful that I went home that evening, the letter was still on my desk, unmailed. I finally had to ask Jim Gale, my friend from the Organized Crime Division, to mail it for me.

Gale had already sent his letter in. The next day Tolson's man called me. "Have you written that letter?" "Yes," I replied. "Did you mail it?" "No," I said, "I didn't." That confused him and there was a moment of silence until I finally said, "Jim Gale mailed it for me." A few moments later Gale came into my office and said, "That damn fool Tolson just called me. Told me it was very confidential and not to speak to anyone about the conversation." Tolson asked him, "Did Sullivan give you a letter to mail to Senator McGovern?" Gale told Tolson that I had. My letter was published three weeks after the others in the *Congressional Record*. I'll never forgive myself for it.

But, after nearly thirty years with the FBI, I had passed the loyalty test.

ELEVEN

Espionage

THERE HAVE ALWAYS BEEN two schools of thought on the effectiveness of Soviet intelligence in this country. Some people believe that the Russians are bunglers who never succeed, while to others they are ten feet tall, brilliant, and invincible. The truth, of course, is somewhere in between. Some of their operations were failures while others were so successful that the FBI found out about them only by accident—or they are still undetected.

Like the Russians, the FBI did outstanding work on some cases and inferior work on others, but even if we had been the supermen Hoover made us out to be, we would still have had a hard time catching Russian spies, thanks to Hoover's restrictive policies. Though the pressure was always on for our boys in the field to identify Soviet agents and to gather evidence against them, Hoover was reluctant to give them the proper tools for the job.

For example, when our agents in the Philadelphia office discovered that a local couple was gathering material for the Russians on U.S. radar installations along the mid-Atlantic coast, Hoover refused to grant permission to put a microphone in their apartment because they were U.S. citizens. I knew, just as the FBI agents who were working on the case knew, that we could not gather information on professional Russian agents, which these two definitely were, without using the right equipment, so we made our own microphone and put it in. I kept after Hoover, though, and when he finally did back down, we just replaced our own microphone with a better one from the FBI inventory.

It only took one or two experiences like that to teach a man in the field to take matters into his own hands and find ways to get around Hoover's impossible restrictions. One reason I had good rapport with the men was because I'd always stick my neck out for them and remove as many of Hoover's obstacles as I could, at least at my level.

Another reason for our less-than-perfect record at catching Russian spies was a basic fault in the organization of the FBI itself. Every other major country in the world has two domestic investigative agencies—one to deal with criminal cases, one to deal with security problems. In England, for instance, criminal cases are handled by Scotland Yard, intelligence by MI 5. The French, the Dutch, and the Israelis all have separate criminal and security agencies to handle criminal investigation and security operations. The Royal Canadian Mounted Police never mix criminal files with security files. Not separating the two is like mixing oil and water. In contrast, the FBI's files are a hodgepodge. When the FBI is finally reorganized, this issue deserves serious attention.

When the two fields of investigation are separated at last, they must be staffed by men with very different ways of looking at their work. The man who goes into criminal investigation thinks in terms of black and white. To him issues are clear-cut, and he expects results when he acts. If a bank is robbed, he knows he must find out who did it, locate the criminals, and take them into custody.

The man who excels at criminal investigation would be lost in intelligence. Instead of having clear-cut black-and-white issues, intelligence is full of gray areas. In intelligence, a man can investigate for years without getting any real results. A man who enjoys solving tantalizing and complex problems, who likes to experiment, would be bored stiff catching bank robbers and belongs in intelligence. In the FBI, both types of men are misused and disappointed at least some of the time because most agents have to deal with both types of cases every day.

Despite being hampered by Hoover's restrictions and FBI policy, we did meet with some success in finding Russian spies. One case I remember particularly concerned a woman agent who was operating in New York City in the early 1960s. Her "cover" was as a beautician, but the agents in the New York office were convinced she was working for the Soviets and they couldn't break the case using the conventional, traditional investigative techniques.

In this instance, we had Hoover's permission to act, and I ordered the men in New York to kidnap her out of her apartment and bring her to a "safe house"—a place that we rented anonymously and that was beyond any suspicion of belonging to the FBI—that we kept in a suburb close to the city. At first she claimed to be an American citizen, and she had the documents to prove it. She warned the men that she intended to file a complaint with the police when they let her go. But they kept her there, never letting her out of their sight or out of the sight of a nurse who worked for us, for one second. They were at her night and day, asking questions, showing her the evidence they had against her, telling her to confess. Finally she realized that they had so much on her that she broke down and admitted the truth. She turned out to be a lieutenant colonel in the G.R.U., Soviet army intelligence. She agreed to work for us as a double agent and we let her go back to her apartment in Brooklyn.

We kept in touch with her every day for months. One day when one of our agents tried to call her there was no answer at her apartment. She wasn't at work either, so he called me. "There's only one thing to do," I said, "break into her apartment." A moment later I called Hoover to get his permission to go into the apartment, which, surprisingly, he gave the first time I asked. When our men broke in they found her, but she was dead. She'd left a note for the agents, a very proper and polite note, thanking them for their courtesies and then explaining that she couldn't bring herself, one of the highest-ranking women in Soviet intelligence—and proud of it—to serve as a double agent. She knew that if she returned to Russia, which was her only other option as we wouldn't let her stay in the United States without working for us, she would break under their interrogation just as she had under ours, and admit that she had been compromised by the FBI. "There's only one way out," she wrote, her handwriting getting worse by the word, "and I'm taking it." She finally stopped writing in the middle of a word. There was a line down to the edge of the paper and the pen was lying on the floor.

The boys searched her apartment and removed all of her espionage paraphernalia: code books, forged documents, including her passport; and a large amount of cash which we turned over to the U.S. Treasury Department. Then one of my men called the police, pretending to be "someone from the building" who hadn't seen his neighbor for a few days and was getting concerned. The police found her body, which was never claimed, and she was buried in Potter's Field.

Another case that worked out well concerned Cornelius Drummond, a black yeoman in the navy who had been recruited by the Russians while he was stationed in London shortly before he was due to be transferred to Newport, Rhode Island. When Drummond was invited out to dinner by a charming and generous Russian diplomat, he wasn't surprised when his host proposed a business deal over dessert. Soviet agents were known to single out and approach black enlisted men like Drummond who had access to classified information.

The Russian offered Drummond two hundred dollars to deliver a naval base telephone book that was not classified, that was easily and

Yeoman First Class Cornelius Drummond, a sixteen-year navy veteran, was arrested on 29 September 1962 by the FBI at Larchmont, N.Y., on charges of spying for the Soviet Union. *Wide World Photos*

legally available to anyone, and that was not worth more than fifty cents. It was an easy job for Drummond and a profitable one, and by the time he reported for duty in Newport he was hooked. Drummond had no ideological basis for his disloyalty. He was only interested in the money.

About a year after Drummond's return to the United States, we heard through an agent we had in the Soviet apparatus that the Russians were getting extremely classified top-secret information about our radar defense system, and that the information was coming from someone in the navy. Because of this leak, millions of dollars had to be spent to devise a new radar defense. The public was never told, and some of the senators and congressmen who complain so loudly about high defense budgets never knew either.

The navy asked the FBI to find the leak. By analyzing the kind of information that was being passed to the Soviets, we narrowed the focus of our investigation to four naval installations, one of which was Newport, Rhode Island. We then went through the record of every person at each installation who might have had access to the information. It was an expensive, exhaustive process, and we came up with the names of a dozen or so possible spies. One of them was Cornelius Drummond.

When our agents took a close look at Drummond's life, they discovered that he only worked at his job with the navy for a few hours a day and that some days he didn't work at all. No one in the peacetime navy had ever questioned Drummond's work habits, which left him with plenty of time for other pursuits. One was a restaurant and lounge, a damned nice place, which Drummond owned outright. How, our agents wondered, could an enlisted man with a wife and children afford to buy such a fine restaurant without even taking out a mortgage?

I told the boys to take a closer look at Drummond. They started by searching his car. When they found nothing suspicious, they opened the trunk. There wasn't a damn thing inside except a spare tire and a filthy old sponge. You don't overlook anything in this business, though, so one of the boys reached in and squeezed the sponge. It was hard in the center. He opened it carefully. There was a tiny

Minox camera inside.

After discovering Drummond's camera, we put a hidden television camera in the room where the secret radar documents were kept. Sure enough, a few days later, like a scene from a spy movie, there was Yeoman Drummond on closed-circuit TV, photographing the paper with his Minox.

We wanted to catch Drummond in the act of transferring information to the Soviets, so we put a physical surveillance on him. But he made it very, very hard for us to track him to his rendezvous: he used to drive down the Merritt Parkway, in Connecticut at sixty or sixty-five miles an hour, and then, all of a sudden, speed up till he was going ninety. Now, how in the hell can you follow someone inconspicuously at ninety miles an hour? Another of Drummond's tricks was to slow down, cross over the center divider, and head back to Rhode Island for ten or fifteen miles, then cross over again and continue on toward New York. It finally took a two-hundred-mile surveillance to track Drummond, and even two hundred agents weren't enough the first time we tried it.

We posted fixed agents with walkie-talkies in the woods and brush all the way from Rhode Island to New York. As Drummond passed each relay point, no matter how fast or in which direction he was going, the agents traced his route on their own closed-circuit network radio. When Drummond finally hit New York City traffic, a forty-car team was waiting to move in. One car would stay on him for no more than three or four minutes before the next car took over. It was all very natural, very unobtrusive, and although Drummond kept a sharp eye on his rear-view mirror, he never saw anything to alarm him. Just when it looked as if we had him though, Drummond drove right through a red light. Hell, we couldn't follow him through a red light. He'd be onto us right away. So we lost him—it was heartbreaking. There are a lot of disappointments in this business.

The next time Drummond drove to New York City, we repeated the fixed roadside surveillance, and when our mobile surveillance took over in the city, they followed him all the way to Larchmont, in Westchester County, N.Y. At one point Drummond turned the wrong way down a one-way street. Of course, we didn't follow him, but, luckily, one of the agents in the car that was on him at that moment lived in the neighborhood. He knew that the street was a cul-de-sac and that if he followed Drummond he would give himself away, so he radioed the next car to be ready to take over when Drummond came back out. They did and followed him to the parking lot of a nearby diner.

Drummond sat in his car in that parking lot for half an hour before a second car pulled in and parked next to his. Drummond got out of his car and got into the other one.

Our boys at the diner recognized the second car as belonging to the Soviets and spread the word to the other agents nearby. Almost immediately, twenty FBI agents had the two cars surrounded. When they saw movement in the Russian car, they moved in fast and opened both car doors just as Drummond was handing photographs to one of his two contacts from an open attaché case on his lap. One of the Soviets put up a hell of a fight when he realized what was happening, but our boys just knocked him cold, picked him up, put him in one of their cars, and hauled him down to the New York office. Drummond didn't offer any resistance at all, but the boys gave him and the other Soviet agents a beating just for good measure.

I got a call from New York shortly after the agents arrived with their catch. "We've got them," one of the agents told me, "and we've been calling the Soviet Embassy, but we can't seem to get anyone who wants to talk."

"Keep at them," I told them, "and keep in touch with me."

The Soviets claimed that they had never heard of our "prisoners," but after a dozen or so phone calls, an embassy official finally came over to get them. They were never prosecuted and they left the country three days later.

Drummond, who cost this country millions, had been paid at least forty-eight thousand dollars for his work. The Soviets are penny pinchers when it comes to paying for information, and that was a lot of money by their standards. Obviously, they felt the information Drummond was selling was very valuable.

We had an airtight case against Drummond. He couldn't explain why he kept a Minox camera inside a sponge in the trunk of his car.

He couldn't explain his driving habits, and he certainly couldn't explain his television performance. But Drummond's trial ended in a hung jury.

One of the jurors, a black woman, believed that Drummond had been framed by the FBI because he was black. The trial was held in 1963 during a time of terrible racial disturbances in the South, and the sound of one of our agents testifying against Drummond in his Mississippi accent was enough to convince the black juror to vote to acquit Drummond. There were race riots in Birmingham, Alabama, at the time, and in her mind it was not Drummond, the Russian spy, who was on trial but the treatment of blacks in the South. That's not logical, but it is human. Of course, we couldn't let Drummond go free, so he was retried a few months later and sentenced to life in prison.

In the case of Cornelius Drummond, we had time to watch him in action, to set him up before we caught him red-handed. But intelligence cases aren't always long, drawn-out investigations. When I got a telephone call at two in the morning saying that an army enlisted man who had been working on top-secret projects called the Russian Embassy offering to pass on what he knew (which, as he had a photographic memory, was plenty), I had to take action right away. The projects he knew about were so secret that the army didn't want to admit they existed. In fact, the army was so sensitive about his disappearance that they had never declared him AWOL, though he had been missing for over a week.

The Russians professionally and correctly assumed that their telephone was tapped, and when the soldier called, they offered to talk to him but told him that they were not interested in his information. We called the military police as soon as we heard about it and found out that the soldier was not only unofficially AWOL but homosexual to boot. I sent about three hundred agents, as many as I could muster at that hour, to search for him in New York City's homosexual bars. Find him they did, about two hours later. Although we had no legal right to do so, FBI agents kidnapped the soldier, brought him to the New York office, and then called me to ask what they should do.

I telephoned a general who worked for Department of Defense intelligence to tell him the good news, and though he was delighted to hear that we had the soldier, when I told him I was wary of holding the man without his being charged with a crime (after all, he wasn't even officially AWOL), he said he couldn't help me and told me to call back in the morning. I knew right away that I was up against a stone wall there, so I went over the heads of the Pentagon military brass and called Cyrus Vance, then assistant secretary of defense under Robert McNamara, to ask if he could help.

Vance said he could. He knew all about the case, and he was happy and relieved to hear the soldier was in FBI custody. "This is tremendous," he said. "I'll have my men in New York come right over for him." Vance was a man after my own heart; he listened to the facts, evaluated the situation, made a decision, and went into action, all within five or ten minutes. Vance said, "We'll have a plane fly down to New York City at once, pick him up, and bring him back to Washington." And he did. Army security officers took charge of him in New York and brought him back. He was held in custody by the army while they tried to rehabilitate him because no charges were ever brought against him for fear that the sensitive information that he held would become public. He wasn't ideologically motivated, but like Drummond he was interested in the money that he could get from the Soviets.

We kept a surveillance on him after he was returned to the Washington area because he was discharged honorably from the army, had been given a good job, and a nice place to live. Our hope was that the information he had stored in his remarkable memory would eventually become hazy or that his information would, after some time, no longer be valuable. We kept up the watch on him for a couple of years, even when he took vacations. He developed a good rapport with our agents, but to this day we have him under surveillance.

We found out some months later that it had been the army's own fault that such an unstable individual was allowed to work on such a secret project. One of his commanding officers had put it right in his record that this man should never be allowed to get near classified material. But that was overlooked somehow, probably by an officer who needed a man with a good memory and was willing to take a chance.

Another case that demanded fast action involved the arrival of a Russian assassin in Washington. The Soviets actually have an assassination squad, and when I learned through an informant that one of its members was assigned to report to the Soviet Embassy, I knew he hadn't been sent from Moscow just for the trip. He had a cover, of course—he was posing as a businessman who was in the United States to buy aluminum for export to Russia. Periodically, we were successful in developing a Soviet official and getting him to work for us, and this is one of the times that it paid off. We had successfully penetrated the Russian intelligence network a few months before and our man had informed us of the arrival of the assassin. We set up our own phony aluminum company and got in touch with him by proposing an attractive business deal, telling him that we'd seen his advertisements for aluminum in the newspapers. He expressed interest in meeting with our company's representatives, so we set up a meeting in a Washington hotel room.

Two of our agents, posing as aluminum salesmen, offered the Russian a very attractive price for the metal, and then they told him that the price could go even lower if he would just tell them what his "real business" was in the United States. The Russian looked at the two salesmen closely, then shouted "you're FBI," and headed for the door. One of the agents, a redhead, stopped him by blocking him at the door and punching him full in the face. He was put back in his chair, but he never admitted to anything more than being an aluminum buyer. They finally let him go, and as he was on his way out one of the agents said to him, "Get the hell out of this country, and fast!" At the door he turned to the agent and said, "You redheaded son of a bitch, when we take over you're going to be the first man I kill." The Soviet assassin left that same day on a Russian plane headed back for Moscow. From then on, the threat of assassination of Soviet agents under our control was always on my mind. (There were at least two cases I was sure of where they killed defectors in the United States.

One man was run over by a car in New York City, *after* he had been killed. The other, a Soviet army officer who defected, was killed in his hotel room in Washington, D.C.).

One of our most successful operations concerned a Russian intelligence officer who came over to us, although the Russians didn't know it. For three years we fed him disinformation, false intelligence data. He reported this information to his superiors who assumed it to be correct. The Soviet government spent countless millions of dollars in fruitless experiments trying to duplicate what they thought to be an actual article of U.S. military equipment, one which in fact never existed. Finally, when the game was played out and the Russians began questioning the authenticity of our man's reports, I had him "come out"—defect.

We gave him a job and a new identity, but I still feared for his safety. When an espionage case came up in New York City he was needed as a witness to testify against an American he knew to be a Soviet spy. I learned through another Soviet agent contact of ours that there was a plan to kill our defector before he could testify.

I had two of my men, Agents Rathburn and O'Toole, rent a house in an upper-middle-class suburb of New York City and I instructed them to stay with our defector twenty-four hours a day—to eat with him, walk with him, live with him—until the trial.

After a week up there the neighbors living near the three men began to act strangely. None of the neighbors talked to them and they even turned away when they passed our men on the street. It went on for weeks—everyone shunned them.

Finally, their closest neighbor leaned over his fence and called to O'Toole to join him. The neighbor, pointing to the other house adjoining ours, said, "See that house over there . . . the man bought a rifle to protect his children."

"To protect them from what?" asked O'Toole.

"From what . . . from what?" the neighbor stammered. "From you three men . . . from you three homosexuals." O'Toole was stunned. "You live together, eat together, walk together. None of you ever is with anyone else. Not one of you this past month has had a date with a woman."

O'Toole reached into his pocket and showed the man his FBI credentials and said, "Look, we're not gay, we're here for reasons I can't explain and we're going to be here for only another week or two."

The funny thing was that the neighbor looked carefully at the credentials, handed them back to O'Toole, and never said a word to him. He just walked away shaking his head. During the next two weeks they were there the neighbors continued to avoid them. Just part of the hazard of being an FBI agent.

The FBI and the Russians were always trying to infiltrate each other's intelligence apparatus, and we, at least, were periodically successful. I say *periodically* because once we'd developed a man, anything could happen. He could be transferred back to the Soviet Union or assigned to some other country. He could even turn against us and start to work as a triple agent. The Soviets had the same problems. And we both had the same ways of solving them. One way was by using sex.

Sex has been used as a lure, persuader, and bargaining point by espionage agents for hundreds of years and things haven't changed. They try to recruit American citizens to work for them, we try to recruit their people to work for us, and we both use men, women, and compromising photographs to bolster our efforts. I don't know how the Soviets worked things, but we went out of our way to cater to individual tastes. Once we found out that a Soviet code clerk (we didn't need to deal with ambassadors when code clerks, who read all the documents, knew just as much and sometimes more) wanted to "experience" a black woman, for instance, we saw to it that he met a black woman who was on the payroll (not the regular payroll, however—we had a special fund for this type of work) of the FBI. We would set up these "chance meetings" to get information, but the game got more serious when either side resorted to sexual blackmail.

An American scientist who was invited to Russia for a Soviet–American scientific conference was given a farewell banquet by his Soviet colleague on his last night in Moscow. The meal lasted for hours and the liquor flowed on even longer. The next morning the scientist found himself in bed in his hotel room with no memory of getting there under his own power. A few months after returning to the United States, he was invited to lunch by a Russian businessman who surprised him by removing a stack of pictures from his briefcase and passing them across the table for the American to see. They were pictures of the American scientist, naked, in bed with another man. The Russian told him to provide classified information or else he would make the photographs "public."

The scientist realized immediately that his luncheon companion was no businessman but a Russian agent. Since he was not a homosexual he knew that he had been set up on his last night in Moscow. He didn't know what to do, so he very wisely took his problem to the FBI. And we took care of him. We let the Soviets know that we knew all about their plan, and we did the same thing to one of their people and the two cancelled each other out. It's all part of the game.

We could and did play as rough as the Soviets. When we found out that a commercial attaché in the Yugoslavian Embassy was having an affair with the wife of a colleague, we decided to use that knowledge to try to turn the attaché into a double agent. We watched them to see when and where they met—it was at a motel just outside of Washington on the Dixie Highway—and we set up a one-way mirror and a small photography studio in the next room.

Once we had the evidence, we decided to approach the Yugoslav in his natural habitat, at an embassy party. Armed with the compromising photographs, one of our agents struck up a conversation with him, reminding him of their last, but imaginary conversation at another embassy party some months ago. Of course, being a diplomat, the Yugoslav pretended to remember him, and he even agreed to give our agent a ride home ("it's only a few blocks") when he asked.

"Take a right here," our agent told him in the car, "then turn left, now down a block, now right again." The directions went on and on. After many rights and lefts, they found themselves at the end of a dead-end road.

"Where to now?" asked the Yugoslav, thoroughly irritated. "I can't drive you all over Washington."

"I'll get out here," replied the agent, "but I have something to show you before I do." He reached into his briefcase and handed the Yugoslav a picture of himself and his colleague's wife in their motel room. The Yugoslav looked at the picture for a long time. He didn't say anything, but the expression on his face kept changing. Finally, he handed the picture back to the agent. "Good photography," he said.

"Here's another one," the agent said, handing him a second picture, "just as good. And another." In all, he showed the Yugoslav twelve photographs, all different and all "good." When he finished looking at them, the attaché took the whole stack of pictures and slammed them against the car's dashboard.

"Goddamn you, you're an FBI agent, and now you think you've got me. Well, I'm not going to work for you," he told the agent, "get out of the car." Because he wouldn't work with us, we sent the pictures to the ambassador and the attaché was sent back to Yugoslavia, his career ruined. It's a rough business.

When a prominent American journalist traveled to the Soviet Union, he was the subject of a series of photographs taken of a homosexual encounter. In this particular case the pictures were not faked, the encounter not trumped up. The Russian KGB showed him the pictures and tried to turn him into what we call an "agent of influence": someone who is not a spy, but one who can influence policy in accord with Soviet objectives.

When he returned to the United States he did an extremely courageous thing; he came right to the FBI to tell us of the problem and the Soviet pressure. "Just because I'm a homosexual," he said, "doesn't mean that they can force me to become their rubber stamp and to write what they tell me to write. I just won't do it." We told him what to do. He went to the Soviets in Washington and told them that he had told the whole story to the FBI. The Soviets never bothered him again.

Of course, sex isn't the only lever we used to convince people to work for us. Joseph Sizmonic was a code clerk working for the Polish Mission to the United Nations in New York City. He was a key man, someone we really wanted to turn into a double agent, and we had had him under surveillance for months. He never did anything out of the ordinary, but one Sunday morning when his wife left the house alone, we decided to follow her. She took a long, involved route to another part of the city and ended up at a Catholic church in Brooklyn, just in time for Mass. We kept our eye on her after that and found that she attended church regularly. At that time religion was under attack in Poland and her Catholicism was just the opening we had been searching for, the chink in Sizmonic's armor.

One of our agents, a man who spoke Polish, approached Sizmonic while he was shopping (an agent would never approach a possible recruit at work, or anywhere near his colleagues) and struck up a conversation, in Polish, of course. The conversation quickly turned into an ideological debate, communism vs. capitalism, East vs. West, but it was kept on a philosophic plane. No attempt was made to win him over at that point. The same agent "just happened" to bump into Sizmonic again a few days later in another part of town, but when he tried to resume their conversation, Sizmonic, looking frightened refused to talk and walked away. After that the FBI man would arrange to bump into Sizmonic once or twice a week, and every time they met, he would smile and say "Hi, Joseph," and walk on. He did that 111 times over the period of a year. The 112th time he said "Hi, Joseph," Sizmonic put out his arm and stopped the agent from going by.

"I want to talk to you, and I want to bring my wife," he said. Normally we like to meet with just one person at a time, but the agent agreed to meet both of them for lunch the next day in a restaurant in Queens.

At lunch, our agent tried to resume the ideological debate, but the Pole stopped him after a sentence or two. "You don't have to convince me," he said, "I've convinced myself during the past year, and my wife has always been convinced. I will work for you, and in exchange, when I am ordered back to Poland, you will let me and my family stay here and help me to get a job. I want to bring up my children in the Catholic church and I can't do that in Poland." We agreed, and he was our man for over two years. Because of him, we knew everything that went on in the Polish Mission and everything that came in through their communications system. Information like that was of enormous importance because it meant that our diplomats could sit down at the conference table knowing as much as their opposite numbers.

After two years, though, when he still had one more year to go at the United Nations, Sizmonic was asked to return to Poland for a two-week refresher course. He was ordered to leave immediately. He was worried, but willing to go back if we thought he should. We knocked it around at FBI headquarters and some of the men thought he should go. But I was the one who had to make the final decision, and something told me that they were on to him and that if he returned to Poland, he'd be executed. It was time for Sizmonic to "come out."

He went to the United Nations early the next morning and came back out soon afterward carrying two enormous suitcases, each one crammed full of secret Polish government documents. The suitcases were so heavy that he literally staggered to First Avenue, where our boys were waiting in a car at the curb, and that was the end of Sizmonic's double life.

We had a similar experience with a code clerk named Tisler who worked in the Czechoslovakian Embassy in Washington. Tisler was an extremely valuable man, and thanks to him we were party to all the Czechs' top-secret information. In exchange for his help, we promised to help him when his time in Washington was up; we agreed to give him asylum and a new identity. As he was really working as an intelligence officer for the Czechs (almost every employee of the Soviet bloc embassy is an intelligence agent, no matter what the official job), we would also reward Tisler by giving him information, something that wouldn't hurt us but that would make him look good. Our problem was that we made him look too good. Back home in Prague, they thought Tisler was doing such outstanding work that they wanted to bring him back to Czechoslovakia and give him a promotion.

We didn't want to lose Tisler, and he certainly didn't want to go back, but we didn't think the time had come for Tisler to defect. He was simply too valuable to lose. So we exposed Tisler's announced successor, another Czech embassy employee, as an intelligence agent (which wasn't difficult—we could have done the same to almost anyone at any of the embassies of the Iron Curtain countries) and had him expelled from the United States. It was a year before the Czechs came up with another successor to Tisler, and when they finally did, it was time for Tisler to defect.

Tisler arranged to meet my men at the Czechoslovakian Embassy in the middle of the night. He planned to empty out the embassy's vaults and filing cabinets, and to throw their contents out the window to the waiting agents, who would scoop it all up and stuff it into large bags. Once full, the bags would then be whisked away to our Washington field office. Tisler himself planned to leave the embassy at 3:30 A.M. by way of the window in the file room, sliding down a rope into the waiting arms of the FBI.

Everything went as planned, and our agents were stuffing documents into bags and bags into cars for over an hour. But at 3:30 there was no sign of Tisler at the window. Our men waited and waited. Four o'clock came and went, so did 4:30. Finally, at 5:00 A.M., as dawn was breaking, down he came out of the window. The agents put him into their car just as two Czech officials were arriving at work. As Tisler and the FBI agents drove to the Washington office, he explained why he had been so late.

At 3:30, as he had been preparing to leave the embassy by way of the window, there was a knock at the door. The file room was in complete disarray, empty file drawers on the floor, the safe open and empty. Tisler didn't know what to do. He opened the door a crack, just enough to see who was there without allowing whoever it was to see in. It was a colleague, a fellow clerk, who couldn't sleep and had come to work early. Tisler joined him outside the file room and closed the door firmly behind him. "Let's go for a drink instead," he said, and while the FBI was nervously waiting outside, Tisler was drinking with his friend, waiting for him to get drunk and pass out, which he finally did at about 5:00 A.M. One of the boys asked Tisler what he would have done if the other man had insisted on going into the file room. "I would have shot him," Tisler answered.

The two Czechoslovakian diplomats who were arriving at work just as we were leaving with their code clerk discovered at once what had happened. The Czechs had no way of communicating directly with their own country; they had to go through the Soviets. They called the Soviet Embassy to tell them about it in code. "We have a very, very sick man here in the embassy," they said. Of course the Soviets and the Czechs assumed that their telephones were tapped by the FBI. Why did we tap their phones if they spoke in code? Because sometimes they would slip and give us just a tiny insight, a small fragment of information that might fill in parts of a jigsaw puzzle.

The Czechs continued speaking to the Soviet Embassy, "Not only is the man sick, but we don't know whether he's going to live or die so we'd like to have some of you come over to our embassy right away." Almost at once a team of Soviet intelligence officials drove out of their embassy and headed toward the Czech Embassy. They didn't stay there very long before they knew what we had done, so they headed back toward the Soviet Embassy. The Russians contacted headquarters in Prague to give the coded message (which we intercepted), "There has been an explosion in the Czechoslovakian Embassy in Washington." That meant that the United States government walked off with all their codes, all their records, everything.

Our men were no slouches when it came to entering embassies and breaking into vaults. Usually, we didn't need the man inside to help—we just went in and photographed the material we wanted. The men who did that kind of work were specially trained for it at headquarters and at Quantico, Virginia. We called the training program "Sound School," an innocuous name like "crime records." The agents who went to the FBI Sound School learned to use classic bank robber's techniques, techniques we knew so well from working the other side of the street. They would study the neighborhood for weeks, "casing the joint," gauging the flow of pedestrian and automobile traffic, finding the quietest time (usually two or three in the morning) to break in. A group of agents would be posted outside the embassy with walkie-talkies, two more men with walkie-talkies were posted inside, and finally, in communication with both, were the men in the vault. If someone came too close to the embassy, the men in the vault were ready to grab their lights and cameras and run. It takes a very special man to do this work. I've known agents who couldn't even take the pressure of surveillance and began to believe that they were the ones being followed. We never got any complaints from the countries whose embassies we broke into because they were up to their necks in illegal activities themselves, and they didn't want the delicate balance of illegality to tip.

Not all of our successes in counterespionage were the result of good hard work by the many excellent men we have in the field. Some of our most publicized cases were "walk-ins," cases that were successful only because we were given the information needed to find a Russian intelligence agent at work in the United States.

The capture of Colonel Rudolf Abel was hailed as one of the FBI's biggest espionage coups, but even though the Russian master spy was handed to us on a platter by one of his fellow agents, we almost messed up the case and lost him. Abel was the highest-ranking Soviet espionage agent known to have been in the United States. He lived under cover in Brooklyn, New York, for ten years or so—as his cover was successful, we could only guess how long he had been operating. We would never have found out about Abel at all if it hadn't been for one of his associates, Reino Haynahan, who told us all about him.

Reino Haynahan was a Finn who became a Soviet KGB agent in 1939. At the end of 1952 the KGB sent him to New York and two years later he was assigned to Colonel Abel. Haynahan was also an alcoholic, which proved to be his downfall and the end of Abel's career in the United States. Long before we knew about Abel we were onto Haynahan, and we had him under surveillance since he was operating as a courier for Soviet intelligence operations. Once in the 1950s we followed him up to West Point, near the military academy. He was seen to walk in the woods, retrace his steps, and then walk back again to his original position, as if he was looking for something. He was. He was looking for what we call a "bank" or a "dead drop," which is a small, protected cache like a hollow tree trunk, a loose brick, or a simple hole in the ground that is not likely to be spotted by a casual observer or disturbed by animals or children. He found his dead drop and took something out of it and put it in his pocket. Years later when he was under arrest, we asked him what he had taken from that hole. He told us, "It was five thousand dollars that the KGB had put there that was to go to the wife of a U.S. Communist party member that was in jail. She needed the money for her lawyer. I took it and kept it and used most of it to buy liquor during the next year."

Because he was an alcoholic, Haynahan kept fouling up most of his assignments for Abel, so in 1957 the Russian colonel ordered him back to Moscow via Paris to make a delivery of some of Abel's intelligence information to KGB agents in Paris. That was Abel's mistake.

When Haynahan got to Paris he went right to the American Embassy and asked to speak to a representative of the FBI. He was directed to our legal attaché, a nice enough fellow but a man whose head was in the clouds, not in the world of spies and counterspies. When Haynahan told him about Abel, our man in Paris told the Finn that the FBI had no interest in that kind of information and our agent took him outside and put him into a taxicab with instructions on how to get to the CIA's offices, telling him, "It's clearly a case for the CIA." As soon as a CIA agent heard Haynahan's story, he got on the phone to our legal attaché. "This guy doesn't belong to us," he told him, "he belongs to the FBI." With that, the legal attaché cabled Washington. Haynahan was sent to the United States and Abel was arrested on 21 June 1957. The arrest was hailed as a counterespionage success by the FBI. In 1962, when Abel was exchanged for Francis Gary Powers, the CIA pilot who was shot down in his spy plane over Russia, the Soviets got the best of the bargain, for we gave them a brilliant man and got back a run-of-the-mill pilot. Back home, Abel was put in charge of all intelligence operations concerning the United States. Powers went to work as a helicopter traffic reporter for a Los Angeles radio station and was killed on the job, flying the freeways.

We were pleased, of course, every time we caught an enemy agent operating inside the United States, even if the capture was a fluke. But at the same time, we were also a little frightened and upset. We'd have to ask ourselves how many more of them were out there operating without our knowledge.

We did solve many of our cases by doing good, hard work, but we solved many others, famous cases like the Rudolf Abel case, through sheer luck. And as in the Abel case, we came close to losing our quarry through stupidity or inefficiency more than once. One of

Reino Hayhanen, a Finn who worked for Russian intelligence, gave himself up to the
FBI and told the bureau about his boss, Colonel Rudolph Abel.

Below: Colonel Rudolph Abel, the Soviet spy who was discovered only because
his associate turned him in.

the best examples of this inefficiency occurred early in World War II. One of our agents in the New York office got a phone call from a man who claimed to be a member of a Nazi sabotage squad. He said a group of them had landed off the coast of Long Island on the previous day from a German U-boat and he wanted to turn himself and the others in to the FBI. The agent laughed. "Yesterday Napoleon called," he told the desperate German and slammed down the phone. Somehow the German gathered up what was left of his courage and called back the next day. Luckily another agent answered the phone. When the newspapers wrote it up, the headlines read "FBI CAP-TURES GERMAN SABOTEURS" and the story praised the bureau for its "brilliant investigative work."

When it came to the realities of espionage, J. Edgar Hoover was as much a head-in-the-clouds amateur as our legal attaché in Paris. He didn't believe that an agent of the FBI would ever defect or sell information to the enemy. I knew that the men in the FBI were human, though, and I always worried that their personal or financial problems could leave them vulnerable to our enemies. Hoover also put Capitol Hill off-limits for FBI surveillance. If an FBI agent had a Soviet or Czech or Rumanian agent under observation, he could follow his subject to the bottom of Capitol Hill but no further. Of course, once the Soviets and other eastern bloc agents caught on to Hoover's policy, Capitol Hill became their favorite place to meet. It was fortunate that Hoover never realized his ambition, which was to direct worldwide intelligence.

Hoover's domestic policy of noncooperation with other U.S. intelligence agencies extended to noncooperation with other countries. This was not a new policy. When World War II ended, the FBI was the beneficiary of a tremendous number—literally, a roomful—of Soviet intelligence communications between the Soviet Mission in Washington and Moscow. The messages had been gathered by a United States Military Intelligence officer who kept them all through the war without telling anyone what he was doing. When the war ended, he told the FBI what he had. As soon as Hoover saw how many communications were involved, he realized that there was so much valuable material that he had to share some of it. He kept most of the material for the FBI, of course, but he did send copies of some of the communications to the CIA and to British intelligence. But Hoover refused to give anything at all to the Royal Canadian Mounted Police.

Hoover had always been jealous of the Canadians, and he didn't like the RCMP commissioner, a stiff-backed old boy named Harvison, who had talked back to Hoover once or twice. It was to be ten years before Hoover changed his mind and decided to share the Russian communications with the Canadians. When he did, he asked me to help. "I want you to go to Canada," he told me in 1954, "to see Commissioner Harvison and cut them in on the Soviet material."

What a hell of an assignment! "When he asks why we kept it from them for ten years," I said to Hoover, "what will I tell him?"

"Blame it on the CIA," replied the director of the FBI. "If Harvison gets his back up," Hoover continued, "just pour it on. Don't take anything from him. The FBI doesn't have to answer to the Royal Canadian Mounted Police."

When I did go to see Commissioner Harvison, he was furious. I admitted that the FBI had been at fault, which helped a little (God knows what Harvison would have done if I'd tried to shift the blame to the CIA), and begged him to forget the past and make use of the material now that he had it at last.

While I was in Canada, I met the chief inspector of the RCMP, a man named McCullen. We became fast friends, each of us poking fun at our bosses, and without McCullen at my side I don't know how I could have faced Harvison. A few years later McCullen succeeded Harvison as RCMP commissioner, and when he did, he couldn't do enough to help the FBI. He'd give us permission to send our agents into Canada to surveil any subjects who tried to escape the FBI by leaving the country. We'd let them do the same thing, and when they came up with anything valuable they would share it with us. This kind of cooperation was always kept secret from Hoover.

Hoover didn't like the British, didn't care for the French, hated the Dutch, and couldn't stand the Australians. He wouldn't meet with the director of British intelligence, not even as a courtesy. "Those damn British come to Washington all the time," he said. Quite by accident, I once discovered some year-old information on the Profumo case that we had inadvertantly kept from them. They had always leveled with me despite the way Hoover treated them, and I decided to tell them truthfully what had happened and give them what I had one year late. They were very gracious about it, and a few days later the British intelligence liaison man in Washington called me to say that the British were everlastingly grateful that they didn't received the information on schedule. As it turned out the information was wrong, given to us by a double agent who was under Russian control. Had the British gotten the infromation when it was first received by the FBI, their liaison man told me, it might have caused them great harm.

A Dutch intelligence officer had once done something to irritate Hoover, and Hoover had even long forgotten what it was, but from that moment on any Dutch intelligence officer was *persona non grata* at the FBI. Fourteen years after the original incident with the Dutchman took place, the director of Dutch intelligence paid a visit to Washington. I knew better than to suggest a meeting with Hoover, but I hated to let the opportunity to exchange information go by. So, together with Sam Abbott, our CIA liaison, I spent an unauthorized afternoon with the Dutchman.

Sam decided to send a carefully worded, low-key memo to Hoover about the meeting. After all, fourteen long years had passed. A day or two later, looking sick, Sam came in to see me. Sam had once played professional football. He was a huge man, and crumpled in one of his enormous hands was a piece of paper. "I think we're in trouble," he said in a worried voice, handing the piece of paper to me. It was his memo to Hoover about our meeting with the Dutchman. Across the bottom of the the memo, Hoover had written "Have nothing to do with this man."

The incident that set Hoover against the Australians concerned a Soviet agent named Vladimir Petroff who had been operating in Australia in the late 1940s and early 1950s. The Australians had done a nice job of breaking the case and arresting the fellow. On 3 April 1954, Petroff defected and began to cooperate with the Australians in earnest.

When we learned that Petroff was telling everything he knew, we wrote to the Australians asking them to send us any information he gave them concerning the United States. It was a common request, and there was nothing out of the ordinary about the reply we got from Sir Charles Spry, director of Australian intelligence. "We will be glad to comply with your request," Sir Charles wrote, "but that will take a while longer, as we are still interrogating the subject about matters concerning Australian security."

"This is a brush-off," said Hoover, and he wrote "Have absolutely NOTHING to do with the Australians" right on the bottom of the letter from Sir Charles. And so, single-handedly, Hoover broke off intelligence relations between the FBI and Australia, rather like a sovereign who could make or break relations with any country at will. Behind Hoover's back I personally maintained good relations with Sir Charles, and whenever Sir Charles came to visit Washington, I would send a memo in to Hoover, begging him to relent and meet with the Australian. But Hoover always said no. "I don't want to see Spry," he would write on the bottom of my memos, "he gave me the brush-off in the Petroff case."

Sir Charles never knew why Hoover refused to see him, and six years after the alleged brush-off, I told him the whole story during one of his trips to the United States. At first he was stunned, then angry. He ranted and raved about Hoover for about ten minutes and then asked me about my part in the whole thing. I didn't want to argue, so I said something brief, diplomatic, and meaningless. When I finished, there was dead silence. Sir Charles looked at me. Then he spoke. "Bullshit!" he said.

Finally, twelve years after the "brush-off," Hoover gave in and agreed to see him. Sir Charles came to see me before he went in to see Hoover. By this time we had a very good relationship and I felt I could speak frankly. "Sir Charles," I said, "I want you to promise to do exactly as I tell you to do when you see the director. Flatter him," I said. "Handle him the way we do."

He agreed, and I warned him that Hoover might blame him for the rift in Australian–American relations. "If he does, I want you to get up on your feet and say, 'Mr. Hoover, you're absolutely right.' "

Sir Charles grinned. "By God, Bill," he said, "I'll do it." Fortunately he didn't have to, because Hoover behaved himself for once and we resumed "official" intelligence relations again with Australia.

I remember a physicist who worked for the National Security Agency who was aware that the FBI was not cooperating with NSA. "I'd like to talk to Hoover myself," he told me. "I think I can break down some of the barriers." When he finally met with Hoover, though, the physicist couldn't get in a word. Hoover took over the conversation, just as he always did, telling the story of the FBI. He talked about John Dillinger and "Pretty Boy" Floyd and Ma Barker and went on through organized crime and the Communist party to the "swado" intellectuals and "swado" liberals. And nothing changed between the FBI and NSA, which was just the way Hoover wanted it.

I was responsible for all espionage cases from 1961 through to 1971 and I knew that there were some fine men out in the field responsible for the true successes that we did have. One great disadvantage for us was that Hoover had never investigated any cases and had never had any practical experience in intelligence work. All his knowledge came to him while he was sitting in his swivel shair . . . in the form of memoranda and investigative reports. He had never been out on the firing line in the very field where he held the ultimate authority.

Czechoslovakian intelligence, operating in the United States, spent six years of careful planning before accepting a State Department employee to spy for them. They trusted him, but they didn't know that he really worked for the FBI. They gave him the job of planting a microphone–transmitter in a State Department office that handled Czech affairs. They hoped to know everything about United States policy toward their country, current and future. They also hoped to determine what intelligence we had about them and where it came from. The device the Czechs wanted our man to plant behind a piece of furniture was in a wooden container about two by four inches. It contained a very sophisticated system that would run for a year before the batteries gave out, and would clearly pick up everything that was said in the room. We tested it and it was incredible. It could transmit, clearly, from the Lee Mansion in Washington, D.C., all the way to the Lincoln Memorial and even to the downtown area of the district. Our laboratory tried—but failed—to come up with anything as good.

I told Hoover that the Czechs had accepted our man, and now we had a wonderful opportunity to take some of the State Department officials into our confidence and feed the Czech intelligence service misleading disinformation. We could, I told Hoover, drive them crazy with false information.

But Hoover, more interested in headlines than the work we were supposed to be doing, got as mad as hell at me and said, "No! Arrest the Czechs responsible."

I argued with him for days. Richard Helms tried to talk Hoover out of his decision, but Hoover persisted. Of course we couldn't arrest them, they were embassy officers, so the State Department declared them *personna non grata* and they had to leave the country. We lost an opportunity, but Hoover got his headlines.

He never hesitated to make a decision that would be harmful to the nation if it was helpful to him and built up his image. Hoover's passion for headlines even endangered the life of one man, a double agent, who was working for us in the Soviet Union. When Hoover read a report based on some information that this man had given us, he decided to release it to the press. I said, "Mr. Hoover, you're jeopardizing the life of this man. He's in Russia now and the Soviets will know how we got the information." "No," said Hoover, "nobody will know about it and he'll be all right." Sure enough, the KGB grabbed our man in Moscow and questioned him for hours. He managed to talk his way out of it but he never worked for us again.

The situation that disturbed me most during my thirty years in the bureau was Hoover's refusal to allow me to act on what I am convinced was Soviet intelligence operations that directly affected the FBI, and the security of the United States.

We had been, from time to time, successful in persuading Soviet officials to defect. Then all of a sudden the defections stopped. Programs that had worked in the past were no longer working, and that began to trouble me. Then I learned that the Washington field office was missing three top-secret documents that were connected with naval operations. I had a thorough search instituted but we never could find them. A Soviet defector who had come over to us before this period told us that an FBI agent had sold the files to the Soviet

Embassy. We asked the Russian for his name but he said he never knew it. But he knew that the agent had gone to the Soviet Embassy, to their naval attaché, and asked for ten thousand dollars for the three documents. For the first time my worst fears seemed to come true; the Russians had bought one of our men.

One agent in the Washington field office was suspect because of his unusually large gambling debts and because of information defected Russians gave us. We narrowed our investigation to him, and we learned that he was contacted by Soviet agents from a certain phonebooth at certain hours. To prevent the agent's realizing that we were onto him, I had men from the Baltimore office surveil him. At the exact time we were told he would be in telephone booth, he arrived. The phone in the booth rang; he spoke for a while to the caller and then left. On his way out, unfortunately, he recognized one of his colleagues from Baltimore and drove quickly away. We learned that he broke his contact with the Soviet KGB and although he would never admit to selling out to the Russians, he requested, and received, early retirement from the FBI.

Even though that agent, who I believe was a Soviet spy, retired, I was still sure that there were more leaks in our operation.

But two can play that game. The next time the Soviets had an FBI defector on their hands it was a put-up job. I instructed one of the agents in the New York office ostensibly to defect to the head of Russian intelligence, a man, who worked out of their United Nations Mission. It took our man about three years, but he finally persuaded the Russians that he was the genuine article: an FBI man who wanted money in return for secrets.

His one caveat was that although he'd try to give them what they wanted, he would never reveal his real name. He told them that he was a "watcher," a person who conducts surveillances. Men like that usually have a limited knowledge of highly sensitive information so the Russians were content to let him give them what he could. He gave them a lot over the next two years and he was very successful in persuading them that it was important. The Soviet Union spent millions of dollars on fruitless experiments trying to duplicate sophisticated military equipment that didn't work. We knew it didn't work because we had directed scientists to develop information that was wrong but would take the Soviets a lot of time and money to find that out.

Our man was paid thirty-eight thousand dollars by the Soviets for this disinformation, and we turned it over to the Treasury Department.

One evening the Russian intelligence chief asked our man to meet him in Riverside Park in New York City—at one o'clock in the morning. They met and walked in silence for about ten minutes until the Russian said, "In case anything goes wrong we have set up this escape route for you through Canada to Russia and I've got to have your right name." For the first time in two years our man slipped and gave the Russian his real name. The next day the whole operation was dead. The Russians wouldn't have any contact with him again, although he tried and tried to reach them.

This is what happened: the Russians learned that our man was not a "watcher" at all, but the number three man in our espionage squad in the New York office, and we have hundreds there doing that work. They knew that he not only lied to them about his position but that he was indeed a very important counterespionage agent who would never defect and who was, all that time, operating against them. There was no doubt in my mind that the Russians could learn our man's real job just by knowing his name only if there was a Russian spy in our New York office.

The leaks continued to vex us. I told Hoover what had been happening and recommended that we begin gradually transferring people out of the espionage section in New York. I wanted to replace them with all new men. It was the only way we could hope to get rid of the fellow on the Soviet payroll, a man we had been unable to discover.

Hoover said, "Find out who he is." I repeated to Hoover that it was impossible, that whoever it was was too deeply covered to allow himself to be revealed by any of our internal investigations. Then he said, "Some smart newspaper man is bound to find out that we are transferring people out of the New York office." I repeated to him that it could be done quietly and gradually, and that no one would know. And I told him, "Mr. Hoover, your reputation is going to be severely tarnished if the public ever learns that we have been penetrated by the Russian KGB." Hoover said, "I know that, but no transfers." The next day I sent him a sealed memorandum, one that is hand-carried and can only be read by the person to whom it is directed. In the memo I repeated the details that proved we had been penetrated by the Russian intelligence service. Hours later my memo was returned to me and on the margin Hoover had written, "As I told you, find out who it is."

Hoover never asked me a question about it after that. He never asked "How is it going?" Nothing. He never again brought it up. At the time I left the FBI in 1971, the Russians still had a man in our office and none of us knew who he was.

When I was named assistant director of the FBI's Intelligence Division in 1961, Hoover also appointed me bureau representative to the U.S. Intelligence Board. I remained a regular member until I was forced out of the bureau ten years later. The USIB is the nation's highest, most prestigious intelligence body. All foreign and domestic intelligence that is relevant to the security of the country is funnelled into the USIB.

Its members are the top-ranking officials of the American intelligence community: CIA, Defense Intelligence Agency, National Security Agency, FBI, and the intelligence divisions of the army, navy, air force, State Department, Treasury Department, and the Atomic Energy Commission. The board's chairman is always the director of the CIA, and because he acts as chairman, the CIA has an additional representative on the board itself.

We met regularly once a week at CIA headquarters in Langley, Virginia. Security regulations, I found, were always more rigorously enforced than at FBI headquarters. We always sat in the same seats around a long rectangular table, and each of us had one or two staff people sitting behind us as back-up. They did the real spade work, and they had all the facts at their disposal. When a question came up that I couldn't answer, one of my staff officers would fill me in.

When I first started attending USIB meetings, unless one of the other members asked a question which directly related to the FBI I mostly sat quietly. But as I listened, I became increasingly impressed with the knowledge and ability of the intelligence veterans sitting around that table. I was particularly impressed by the attitude of the military men on the board, who, contrary to their image, pursued worldwide peace as actively as their civilian counterparts. I was relieved to see these admirals and generals acting as apostles of peace.

I was also impressed by the free exchange of ideas. Everyone was uninhibited; every man spoke his mind. There was very little back-scratching going on; these were able, intelligent men who had done their homework and the stakes were high. A lot of hard-headed arguments took place at that table.

Because of the delicate nature of our meetings, any leaks could be damaging to the security and foreign policy of the United States. Imagine if when Henry Kissinger sat down to negotiate with the Soviets they already knew all his bargaining positions. The negotiations would be a failure before they even began. Whenever the board members discussed a particularly sensitive subject, during the Cuban Missile Crisis, for instance, or after the capture of the U.S.S. *Pueblo*, we held a special executive session and all the staff people had to leave the room. After sitting in on some of these executive sessions, I couldn't help but realize that without a very comprehensive intelligence system, we could not hope to play in the same league with other major countries.

Under Dulles the meetings of the USIB were conducted informally. No bombast, no stuffiness, and everyone had all the time needed to speak out without being cut off.

After Dulles, John McCone assumed the chairmanship of the board. McCone's background was not intelligence, but he was a cold, analytical, able man.

He didn't remain in position long before he was replaced by Admiral Raburn. Assuredly, Raburn was knowledgeable about naval affairs, but he was inexperienced in intelligence matters and was therefore at a serious disadvantage as director of the CIA and chairman of the USIB.

Richard Helms became the next director of the CIA and therefore the next chairman of the USIB. I had known Helms for years when we were both moving up through the ranks of our respective agencies. We had even cooperated together on cases behind Hoover's back when we felt the issues were important enough.

On one occasion, for example, Hoover had cut back on funds that we needed to pay an informant on a vital national security case. Richard Helms gave me nine thousand dollars from the CIA so that we could obtain the very important information that was needed.

In my years on the board, Helms was the best chairman we had. He had a great knowledge of intelligence operations but in running the board he always avoided any parochial approach. Under him, the board was handled somewhere between the looseness of Raburn and the rigidity of McCone.

When the problem of press leaks of national security information arose at one meeting, the USIB unanimously requested the FBI to investigate the case. Unanimously, that is, except for the FBI. The subject was the Pentagon Papers and the president and the National Security Council wanted to know the identities of the people leaking these highly classified materials.

I went to Hoover that day and told him of the request. He told me to take the position that the FBI was not responsible for leaks occurring anywhere outside of the FBI and that he would not assume the investigative responsibility. I told Hoover that we should go ahead, that it was indeed our responsibility. I told him that most of the other agencies on the USIB had neither the manpower nor the skill for the investigation. Further, even if they did, it would make no sense for one agency to investigate itself because of the tendency for self-protection. Hoover was adamant and wouldn't budge.

It is significant to realize that not one among this prestigious board comprised of brilliant men, including Helms, could take a stand against Hoover and say, "Look here, you're responsible for intelligence investigations within the United States. You *are* responsible. Now get off your ass and do it." If anyone had, Hoover would have backed down. We finally got forced into the thing by the White House and Hoover reluctantly gave us the go-ahead.

On another occasion, in 1971, Helms asked me if we would look into the conduct of some former CIA employees who were suspected of being agents of the Soviets. I went to Hoover, but again he refused on the grounds that it was the responsibility of the CIA. However, in this case he realized that he might be put in a compromising position by suggesting that the CIA conduct domestic investigations, so reluctantly he told me to go ahead, but he instructed me to conduct just the semblance of an investigation. I believe that this intransigence on the part of Hoover forced the CIA to begin its own activities within the country which resulted in the subsequent criticism of them by the Senate.

On at least one occasion Hoover's lack of cooperation with other intelligence agencies was laughable. The situation seems trivial but it really explains the psychology underlying Hoover's leadership with respect to his reluctant dealings with the USIB.

Every member of the board was asked to bring in the seal of his particular agency. They were all to be the same size, approximately twelve inches in diameter. They were all to be round—not oval, triangular, or square. The chairman, Richard Helms, wanted them all exactly the same size and shape so that they could be hung along each of the long walls behind the large rectangular table of our meeting chamber.

The following week, before leaving for the USIB meeting, I stopped at headquarters to pick up our seal. From the size of the carton it was packed in I knew something was wrong. When I checked to see if there had been some mistake, I was told that Mr. Hoover himself had approved the seal. The package was too large to carry under my arm, so I carried it by the cord wrapped around it and drove to CIA headquarters. When I got to the meeting and unwrapped the package, my worst fears came true. The FBI seal was almost three feet in diameter, almost three times larger than the others. I was embarrassed, but couldn't do anything about it.

The following week, at our next meeting, all of the seals were hung on the walls and ours stood out like a sore thumb. The other members of the board began to needle me. Admiral Noel Gayler, who headed the Defense Intelligence Agency, said, "Sullivan, I suggest that, with Mr. Hoover's approval, you make up an FBI seal twice the size even of this one and we'll hang it alone on one bare wall and the seals of all the other agencies on the opposite wall. In that way we'll have a perfect balance."

If I had gone back to Hoover with that suggestion there is no doubt he would have approved it.

TWELVE

The Nixon Years

RICHARD NIXON and J. Edgar Hoover had been political allies since Nixon served in the House of Representatives. In fact, it was Hoover who helped make Nixon into the great anti-Communist congressman, and Nixon always felt indebted to the director for that. I spent many days preparing material based on research taken from FBI files that I knew was going straight from Hoover to Congressman Nixon, material which Nixon used in speeches, articles, and investigations.

A few years later, when Nixon became vice-president, the bureau continued to feed him anti-Communist information. When Kennedy was elected and Nixon moved to California, Nixon lost interest in our material and sent all of it back to us. Most of it had never been looked at. Hoover was so embarrassed that he never mentioned it to Nixon, or to anyone else.

Hoover was also very sensitive about the fact that the FBI had rejected Richard Nixon when he applied for the job of FBI agent in his precongressional days. Whenever anyone (including Nixon himself) asked Hoover about it, he always said that Nixon had been turned away only because the bureau was not hiring any new agents at the time he applied. Actually, we were hiring—we just weren't hiring Nixon. The agent who interviewed him didn't think Nixon would make a good FBI agent because he was "lacking in aggression."

Over the years, Hoover and Nixon grew to be personal friends. Nixon frequently had dinner at Hoover's house, and Hoover was a regular dinner guest of the Nixons' at the White House. Of course, Hoover liked to claim to be a personal friend of whichever president was in office, but in Nixon's case it seemed to be true. "The president calls me regularly," Hoover used to tell me proudly, "even on matters that aren't related to the FBI and law enforcement." Hoover loved that.

But even their friendship didn't keep Nixon from joining the ranks of Hoover's potential blackmail victims. Before Nixon was elected president, I got a letter from our legal attaché in Hong Kong informing me that Nixon and his friend Bebe Rebozo had taken two trips to Hong Kong, once in 1966 and again in 1968, when Nixon was in private practice in New York City as a partner in John Mitchell's law firm. Our men were always on the lookout for anything they could dig up on the personal lives of public figures to send to Hoover, and even though Nixon was a private citizen at that time he was still very much a public figure. These trips, our agent in Hong Kong wrote, were brightened for Nixon by his friendship with a Chinese girl named Marianna Liu. (Nixon was also tailed by the Hong Kong police, presumably as a safety measure, and they reported that they spent time together.)

Richard Nixon was an old political friend of Hoover's, starting back in 1948 when Nixon was a congressman.
United Press International

Marianna Liu, the former
Hong Kong hostess
who was visited by Richard Nixon.
Wide World Photos

"I'll handle this one," Hoover said gleefully when I passed the
letter on to him. He took the letter to the future president immediately. "I know there's no truth to this," he told Nixon. "Someone
must be misleading our legal attaché. I'll never speak of it to anyone,"
Hoover concluded with great solemnity. It was one of his favorite
speeches, one he gave often to politicians.

About a year after Nixon became president, I got another letter,
this one from one of our agents on the West Coast. He enclosed a
newspaper clipping—a picture of President Nixon shaking hands with
a good-looking Chinese woman who was standing next to a Chinese
man. The accompanying article explained that the woman and her
husband were emigrating to the United States; in fact, they were
moving to Whittier, California, Nixon's hometown. The agent attached a short note which explained that the woman in the picture
was Marianna Liu, the Chinese man was her husband, and that their
imminent admission to the United States had been given top priority.

Once again Hoover went to Nixon to give him the "news" of Mrs. Liu's good fortune.

Hoover had done a remarkable favor for Nixon when he was first elected president. When Nixon asked the director to suspend the usual FBI investigation of nominees for cabinet posts and approve John Mitchell's nomination without any investigation at all, Hoover agreed. To my knowledge, it was the first time that an attorney general was not investigated before he assumed his post. I never found out what it was Mitchell was hiding. All I ever knew was that Hoover never had Mitchell investigated before the confirmation hearings as was done with all other attorneys general. By merely making the request of Hoover, however, Nixon put himself right in the director's pocket.

Never a man to let any advantage go to waste, Hoover took advantage of his leverage with Nixon when the president called him over to the White House (at the urging of his top aides) to complain about the quality of domestic intelligence being supplied by the FBI. Hoover already knew that the FBI's performance had been far below par in the area of domestic intelligence. In fact, the fault was his and his alone—he had personally called a halt to our most effective, if illegal, operations. Even if it meant sitting on the sidelines doing nothing, Hoover wanted to keep the FBI out of the line of fire and out of the headlines.

As he was perfectly satisfied with the domestic intelligence situation, Hoover smoothly changed the subject from domestic to foreign intelligence and sold Nixon on the idea that he should be permitted to expand our international intelligence network. Hoover proposed that Nixon allow the FBI to reopen the overseas offices that had, with some exceptions, been closed or only minimally functional for so many years. "When these offices are fully operational, Mr. President," Hoover told Nixon, "I will give you better information than the CIA." He was very persuasive—and Nixon agreed.

John Ehrlichman and Bob Haldeman, who had been instrumental in setting up the meeting between Hoover and Nixon, and who had primed Nixon to force Hoover to step up the FBI's domestic intelligence operation, couldn't believe how the meeting had turned out. "That goddamned Hoover," I was told Ehrlichman had shouted when he heard, "he swung Nixon around."

By the time I left the FBI on 6 October 1971, Hoover's foreign offices were costing the American public three and a half million dollars a year, and we were getting practically nothing for our money. We were making a lot of people angry, though. Our men overseas were under instructions from Hoover to send everything straight to him, without clearing it first with the ambassador, the CIA, or the State Department. Two of our men in Israel sent in some incorrect information, and when Hoover unwittingly sent it on to Kissinger and Nixon, the people at the State Department hit the ceiling. A real flap developed, and Nixon finally had to tell Hoover—it couldn't have been easy—that our agents had to clear their reports through the ambassador and the CIA before sending them on to the United States. That really cramped Hoover's style. He liked to go around ambas-

President Nixon with Hoover in 1970. *United Press International*

sadors, the CIA, military intelligence, and everyone else who stood between the director and the president.

Over the years my opinion of Hoover grew worse and worse. By 1968 I was so fed up with the way Hoover was running the bureau that despite the fact that I was married and had a family, I asked the director for military leave to go to Vietnam. When Hoover refused, our personal relationship began to deteriorate seriously. In spite of our differences, though, Hoover chose me to replace Deke DeLoach in the number three job in the FBI when DeLoach resigned in 1970 to go to work for Pepsico.

I really didn't want the job. In 1969, anticipating my retirement from the FBI, I bought a house for my family in New Hampshire. My wife Marion never liked the FBI, and she liked it less and less as the years went by. When I became eligible for retirement back in 1962, she begged me to leave the bureau. My children complained that they never saw me. In 1963 I was offered the job of director of the Hoover Library, located in former President Herbert Hoover's hometown near the University of Iowa. I could have broken with the bureau then. But we were running so fast in those days, running some great operations against the Soviets in spite of the director, that I couldn't bear to leave. I liked the work—the real work, not the politics, or the playing up to Hoover.

Besides, my men asked me to stay. I always made it a point to work with the most talented men I could find. I had put together a good team and my men wanted us to stay together. The longer I stayed on at the bureau, the harder it got to leave. Hoover couldn't go on forever, and I wanted to be around to help reform the bureau when he finally died or stepped down. It was to have been my reward for all those years of working under Hoover.

I wasn't seeking the directorship myself, and had I wanted to be director I would never have asked for a transfer to Vietnam, and I certainly wouldn't have acted the way I did toward Hoover in my final months at the FBI. Not that I wouldn't have loved the job. A thirty-year veteran, the son of immigrant parents—it would have been a storybook ending to my FBI career. But I never gave it any serious thought. I wasn't a lawyer or an accountant, and I didn't think the president would appoint a director who lacked the proper credentials for the job. As I told Robert Mardian, I just wanted to be there to help the new director take up the reins and reorganize the bureau.

When DeLoach resigned, my wife, fearing the worst, told me that she and the children had had enough of the FBI and of Washington. They were going up to live in the new house in New Hampshire. If I wanted to stay on at the bureau, and especially if I got DeLoach's job, I'd be staying alone.

With Marion's words in mind, hoping that Hoover would not offer the job to me, I wrote the director a letter reminding him that he had once decided that the number three position was unnecessary and had abolished it. Why not do the same thing today, I asked Hoover—why not just leave the position unfilled?

In case Hoover didn't see things my way, and in case he still wanted to appoint someone to the job, I included a list of eligible men in my letter. Each of the men I named would have been a good choice for the job. I mentioned Jim Gale, an old friend from the Investigative Division; Marlon Johnson, who had retired after heading our Chicago office; and J. Patrick Coyne, who left the FBI to work for Admiral Strauss and who was working as secretary of the President's Intelligence Advisory Board at the time I wrote the letter. I even recommended that Hoover consider J. P. Mohr, who had warned me when I was a supervisor and already beginning to speak my mind that "no supervisor should ever criticize or attack an assistant director." I knew that Hoover and Tolson personally liked every man on my list. And despite that, I got the job.

When Hoover called me into his office a few days after I sent the letter, I had an uneasy feeling that I wouldn't be seeing Marion and the children for a while. "I've read your letter," Hoover said, "and while I do think highly of each of the men you mentioned, I don't think any of them is right for this job." With a sinking feeling, I realized that the conversation was going in the wrong direction. "In fact," Hoover continued, confirming Marion's worst fears, "I'm going to appoint you."

After thanking Hoover, I gently reminded him that J. P. Mohr, who had been his top administrator under Tolson, was better suited for the job than I. "No," Hoover said, "after what Clyde Tolson told

William C. Sullivan (right), talking with Kingman Brewster, Jr., president of Yale University, at the UPI conference in Williamsburg, Va., on 10 September 1970: the day Sullivan "downgraded" the American Communist party. *United Press International*

me, I won't appoint Mohr." I was astonished. For years I thought Mohr had Tolson wrapped around his finger. "Mohr drinks too much," Hoover explained. "We can't have a man like that in the number three job in the FBI." What more could I say?

In June 1970 I took the job, but things didn't get any better between the director and me. Four months after my appointment I was asked by the United Press to speak at their International Editors and Publishers Conference which was held in Williamsburg, Virginia. My speech concerned violent movements in the United States, and I included the Black Panthers, the Weathermen, and other groups that were troubling us. During the question-and-answer session that followed I assured the group that it was nonsense to link antiwar radicals with any Communist plot, and I went further by telling them that the American Communist party no longer posed any kind of threat to the United States. When I got back to headquarters, Hoover had already seen the wire service report on my comments about the CPUSA. He called me into his office and berated me for "downgrading" the Communist party even though he knew as well as I did that everything I had said was true.

Things began to get worse but I wasn't the only one in the bureau who was having problems with Hoover. I had kept in touch with many of the men I'd worked with over the years as I had always felt that it was important to keep the lines of communication open with men at all levels: special agents, field office supervisors, special agents in charge, and others. When I moved into the job of assistant to the director, I was aware that Mr. Hoover's failing leadership had resulted in a groundswell of resentment, and that serious dissatisfaction was sweeping the bureau. But underneath the dissatisfaction, some of us were hopeful. We looked forward to a future without Hoover, and we wanted to be there to help the new director, whoever he would be, to reshape the FBI. I didn't think Hoover would outlast me, and I didn't think my end in the FBI would come so quickly.

THIRTEEN

No More Risks

BY 1970, HOOVER HAD BEEN director of the FBI for over forty years. He was an American legend, and he wanted to die with his image intact.

Hoover had started to lose his taste for taking risks during the 1960s, and by 1970 he was reluctant to allow his agents to break into embassies, tap telephones, or open other people's mail, even though these were the very investigative techniques to which he owed his publicized successes. Though for decades he had approved the use of these techniques, with or without court orders, he felt that the current climate of opinion was sufficiently hostile to law enforcement and intelligence gathering to keep his agents out of compromising situations. He was certain that his luck was running out, that our agents would be caught by the police like common thieves, or that news of their illegal activities would be leaked to the press. By refusing to give his approval of the use of these techniques, Hoover in effect put the Domestic Intelligence Division of the FBI out of business. Our hands were tied; it became virtually impossible to do our job. In the intelligence field we had come to a sterile stop.

A few months after Hoover outlawed the use of "illegal" investigative techniques, I began to receive complaints from the rest of the intelligence community. Hoover had been stingy with information before, but this was ridiculous— *nothing* was coming out of the FBI, and army intelligence, naval intelligence, and the CIA, to name just three, were hurting. The armed forces maintained small investigative units of their own, but they didn't compare with us when it came to manpower and resources. The CIA could take care of themselves overseas, but they needed the FBI to coordinate with them at home in order to really do their job right.

I passed off the first wave of complaints, but when they kept coming in I took up the matter with Hoover. "We're not in business to serve the CIA and the army," he thundered. "Let them do their own work."

Two known Soviet agents were in the United States at that time posing as businessmen, and the CIA requested FBI surveillance and telephone taps for the pair. "Tell Mr. Helms," Hoover told me, "that if he wants those people surveilled, he can do it himself." It wasn't Helms's responsibility, though, it was ours—and Hoover knew it. The CIA had no legal right, no charter to do any kind of investigative work in this country.

"Bill," Helms said when I told him about Hoover's position, "I'm not going to order my men to do a surveillance in New York City. We have no right to do it. So if you folks won't do it, it's not going to be done." If Helms had overstepped his authority and had ordered a CIA surveillance in New York, Hoover probably would have leaked it to the press. He was always setting people up.

Hoover could ignore the complaints of the CIA and the Defense Department, but he couldn't ignore complaints about the scarcity of FBI intelligence that came from the White House. President Nixon and his aides had been disappointed in the performance of the FBI for quite a while: the bureau seemed incapable of dealing with the domestic turmoil—the bombings, murders, and riots—of the 1960s. The Nixon White House wanted the FBI to be more aggressive, not less. Hoover's refusal to bug, tap, and open mail was the straw that broke the camel's back. The time had come to apply pressure.

The bad news came to me first, in the form of a phone call from a man who introduced himself (we had never met, nor had we ever had any prior contact) as Tom Charles Huston, a lawyer who worked at the White House. Huston told me that the president was dissatisfied with the quality of the intelligence he was getting from the FBI, so dissatisfied that he had instructed Huston to do something about it.

Huston and I met in his office in the Executive Office Building next door to the White House a day or two after we spoke on the phone. He was a young man, just twenty-nine, with dark framed glasses, a slight build, and an intellectual, thoughtful look to him. As we talked, I found myself admiring him more and more. I didn't know anything about his background at the time of our first meeting, but I learned later that Huston had been a member of Phi Beta Kappa, a leader of the Young Americans for Freedom, a respectable campus conservative group, and that he had given up a good law practice back in Indiana to go to work for President Nixon. As far as I was able to tell his only interest was in doing a good job for his country, and his faith in the Nixon administration was total and sincere. The fact that I, a liberal Democrat, could find so much to admire in Huston only proved to me that a man's politics have little bearing on his true worth.

"President Nixon," Huston began, "has designated me to look into the entire intelligence operation in this country to see whether we can improve it." Then he ran down a list of our recent failures. He mentioned the young professor who was killed by a bomb while he was working in his laboratory at the University of Wisconsin, the riot at Columbia that caught the FBI completely by surprise, and a lot else besides. On top of that, Huston said, our lack of cooperation with other intelligence agencies was jeopardizing national security. Hoover refused to allow his men to develop contacts at the United Nations, for instance, claiming that that should be the province of the CIA. The FBI knew that illegal foreign agents were operating in the United States, but things had gotten so bad that we couldn't identify a single one of them.

It was as if he had said two plus two equals four. Huston was right and we both knew it. Because his criticism was cogent and factual, I agreed with him.

Huston went on to say that he had been given a mandate by the President to take any necessary steps to correct this grossly inadequate situation. His approach would be open and proper in all respects, he told me, and he also said that he didn't plan to limit his analysis to the FBI. He planned to review the work of the entire American intelligence community. Actually, I never believed that the White House cared all that much about army intelligence or the National Security Agency or the others, but I guessed that President Nixon didn't want to offend Hoover any more than necessary by singling out the FBI for criticism.

I assured Huston that he would get my full cooperation—and I meant it. I was as dissatisfied with Hoover's performance as he was. In fact, I had outlined the same problem in a classified personal letter to Richard Helms, the director of the CIA, before I heard from Tom Charles Huston, but Helms felt that there was nothing either of us could do about it as long as Hoover was in control. Helms was an able, intelligent man, and he, as well as others in the intelligence business, knew that we were not solving cases. After Helms got my letter he said to me, "Bill, I'm with you, you know that. But as long as Hoover remains in the bureau there's not a damn thing that I can do and I don't think anyone else will back you either." I replied, "Well, I'll try to do something on my own." Helms responded, "You haven't a chance, but if there's anything I can do to help without coming out into the open as an opponent of Hoover, then I'll back you."

The barriers that Hoover had erected between the FBI and the other intelligence agencies had led to a condition of total isolation for each organization. None of us was operating up to the maximum level of efficiency. All of these little empires in the intelligence community—the FBI, State Department, NSA, and the others—had built fences around themselves. I had never seen anything like it. We wouldn't share our information with anyone, and no other agency liked to give us anything because Hoover would leak it to the newspapers and use it against them if he could. To me, Huston looked like manna from heaven. A serious, informed analysis of the nature, functions, and objectives of intelligence had never been undertaken in this country. Perhaps, with my help, Huston and the White House could reorganize the entire intelligence community.

As soon as I left Huston's office ("You'll be hearing from me," were his parting words), I dictated a memo to Hoover describing our meeting. I had to do it; it was dangerous to meet someone like Huston without writing a memo to Hoover about it. "Sullivan," he would say, "why didn't you keep me advised? Why didn't you dictate a memo?" Sometimes when he was dissatisfied even after I'd sent a memo, he'd say, "You should have made your memo more detailed, more vigorous."

My report on the meeting with Huston was so bland as to be antiseptic. I realized that my news wouldn't please him, and I hoped that by keeping it low key I could avoid a major blow-up. I've known men who built their careers in the bureau by writing inflammatory memos to Hoover, but I was never one of them. The more some of these bureau sycophants would feed Hoover information about someone he disliked, the warmer Hoover would feel toward the man who fed him the material. In spite of my precautions, however, Hoover hit the roof as soon as he read it. His immediate reaction was one of indignation and defensiveness. He absolutely refused to recognize and accept unpleasant reality.

He called DeLoach into his office and the two of them sent a letter to Nixon which detailed every FBI success story in the last ten years, never, of course, mentioning any of our shortcomings. It was the way Hoover had operated for years. He had first tested the one-sided propaganda blitz on President Roosevelt. Roosevelt was under great stress, particularly during the war, and he couldn't take the time to stop and figure out which part of Hoover's reports were fact and which were fiction. He just assumed that Hoover was a responsible man (after all, he was director of the Federal Bureau of Investigation) and he accepted what Hoover said as the truth. What had worked with Roosevelt would work with other presidents too, Hoover figured, and by and large he was right—until Nixon.

On 5 June 1970, Hoover was summoned to attend a meeting at the White House with the president and Huston to discuss the intelligence situation. At this meeting, Huston made it clear that the president was not interested in Hoover's one-sided version of FBI history. From that moment on, Hoover hated Huston. He never called him by his right name, and in our conversations he never referred to him by any other name except "that hippie," taking his cue from Huston's two-inch sideburns.

Hoover called me into his office as soon as he returned. He was visibly upset. "I've just returned from the White House," he said. "They don't like our performance, our intelligence operation. On top of that," he went on, "all the heads of the intelligence community were there . . . Richard Helms, Admiral Gayler, and the others." Hoover was really depressed as he continued, "They're making up a committee of the heads of the different intelligence agencies and they're going to make me the chairman."

I realized the minute he told me about the committee (they

called it the Inter-Agency Ad Hoc Committee) that he was going to unload the whole thing on my shoulders. "The only way to handle this," he said, "is to form a subcommittee working committee, and I'm putting you in charge." The last thing Hoover wanted was a penetrating review of the FBI's role in the intelligence community, and he certainly had no stomach to chair the committee himself. More important, he wanted to avoid the responsibility of acting as the chairman of anything. After all, if he did the job himself, who could he blame if things went wrong?

Hoover told me, "We're going to call a conference on the matter and I want you to sit in on it. The committee that I'm making you the acting chairman of will be made up of the nation's chiefs of intelligence."

When the conference was called, Hoover got up and said, "The president wants a historical study made of intelligence operations in the United States and the present security problems of the country." After Hoover's short statement there was a heavy silence until Huston, who was seated on Hoover's left spoke up. "I didn't hear the president say that we should prepare a historical document," Huston said. "I understood President Nixon to say that he was dissatisfied with present-day operations and what the president really wants to know is what the present-day problems are in the security and intelligence fields. Further, the president wants to know to what extent they are being solved and what we can do to elevate the quality of our intelligence operations."

You could hear a pin drop. Not one of the intelligence chiefs said a word until Admiral Gayler spoke up, "Yes, Mr. Hoover, that was also my understanding." Then the silence continued as Hoover became crimson. "Well," Hoover said, looking at me, "You're the one in charge of the working committee. Go ahead—do a study and prepare a report." That meeting increased Hoover's hatred of Huston.

I designated C. D. Brennan to sit on the subcommittee as the FBI's representative (as I was acting chairman, I couldn't speak for the FBI as well) and we met with representatives from the CIA, the NSA, the White House (Huston spoke for the president), and the armed forces intelligence agencies. It was like a mini U.S. Intelligence Board. Although, after the fact, most of our critics believed that the main thrust of our planning was directed toward antiwar and New Left dissidents, we were just as concerned with stepping up our programs against the Soviets and other foreign agents. In fact, our final recommendations relating to counterespionage—breaking into embassies, for instance, or opening mail from the USSR (operations that we had been conducting for years with some success)—outnumbered our recommendations relating to domestic intelligence.

As acting chairman my role was to set the agenda for our meetings, to help direct the discussion, and to see that we did our job as quickly, objectively, and as well as possible. The result of our meetings was the first draft of what later came to be called the Huston Plan.* The draft, submitted on 25 June, contained an assessment of the internal security threat and the "investigative restraints" under which we at the bureau were working.

In fact, the plan wasn't Huston's at all—it summed up the thinking of the subcommittee as a whole. Once the material was gathered from the different agencies and once the recommendations were agreed on, I turned the whole thing over to one of my men in the Domestic Intelligence Division to be written up, and I submitted his draft to the committee at large.

Word of the report spread fast within the FBI, and everyone who heard about it in my division was elated. They were as eager as I was to get back in business against the Soviet agents who were operating so freely within our borders.

Hoover was not as pleased with the draft as the men in my division were, however. He called me to his office when, as chairman, he received his copy. "That hippie is behind this," he began. "Well, they're not going to put the responsibility for these programs on me," he continued. "I've had this kind of responsibility for years, and I just won't take it any more. I'll only accept the recommendations outlined in this draft if the president orders me to. And I'll only carry them out if someone else—the president, the attorney general, anyone else—takes the responsibility."

Hoover then asked me for my "cold, objective" analysis of the thirty-six-page draft irrespective of my own views. I gave him just

*See Appendix A for Huston's memo on the project.

that, outlining its advantages and disadvantages, separating myself as much as humanly possible given the circumstances. This was our first discussion of the report; we would have three or four others before it was submitted in its final form to the White House. And although it was evident from the beginning that Mr. Hoover was opposed to the entire report, not once did he say to me that he was opposed to it because the programs it described were unlawful, unconstitutional, or in violation of civil liberties. In fact, during my thirty years with Hoover, I never once heard the director say that he was against any FBI program on constitutional grounds or because it would be illegal.

As Hoover was the only committee member who wanted to make substantial changes in the draft the subcommittee had prepared, I suggested that he register his objections in the form of footnotes to the report. This was the method I had always used when the FBI disagreed with policy at the U.S. Intelligence Board, and Hoover agreed to use it in this case also. "You prepare the footnotes, Sullivan," he told me.

To what parts of the draft did the director object? Actually, all the report amounted to, apart from an analysis of the intelligence problems facing us, was a recommendation to reinstitute the programs and policies which Hoover himself had initiated, encouraged, and approved years ago and which the FBI had carried out under his direction for so many years. It was the few secondary recommendations that upset Hoover. The provisions for better interagency coordination were anathema to him; he believed that he and the FBI operated best independently and unilaterally. "We've got enough damned coordination in government now, too much in fact," he said to me more than once. But the provision for periodic review of the work of the entire intelligence community, including the work of the FBI, was even a greater threat to Hoover. The thought of someone— or, even worse, of some committee—looking over Hoover's shoulder and checking his work was out of the question.

Once he'd agreed to the footnotes that I prepared, Hoover decided that he also wanted to change some of the wording of the final report itself. Even though these changes were minimal when taken in the context of the whole report, Hoover was in no position to make them. "Mr. Hoover," I told him, "this isn't an FBI report. We have no right to change it without the knowledge and approval of the rest of the committee."

"Take out what I told you to take out," Hoover said in a steely voice, "and change what I told you to change." He put me in a hell of a position. I couldn't change a word of the final report without the permission of the rest of the committee members. Perhaps a braver man than I could present a doctored report to Richard Helms, Tom Huston, Admiral Gayler of naval intelligence, and General Bennett of army intelligence and convince them that those were their own words written on that piece of paper, but I was not that man and never could be. On the other hand, I couldn't refuse to obey Hoover.

I did make the changes the director had ordered me to make, but before I presented the altered final draft to the committee, I spoke to them off the record and told them what I had done—and why. "You can go one of two ways on this," I told them. "You can ignore the changes or you can challenge Hoover." As the changes had really done nothing to soften the impact of the report, the other men were very understanding. "We know what you're faced with," Admiral Gayler said to me, and indeed he did, as did every other top-ranking intelligence official who was on the Inter-Agency Ad Hoc Committee. They'd all had their run-ins with Hoover. "It would be expedient to ignore the changes and deletions," the admiral concluded. No one wanted to challenge Hoover, not even these important men. Hoover had so much power that Helms and the rest automatically assumed they'd come out second best in any flap.

Once the committee approved Hoover's version of the report, all that remained was to call for one final brief meeting so that all the members could sign it. It was decided that the meeting would take place in the chairman's—Hoover's—office.

On the day of the meeting, all the members of the Inter-Agency Ad Hoc Committee and their aides were seated around the big table in Hoover's outer office (there were too many of us to fit around the oval table in Hoover's inner office) except Admiral Gayler, who was two or three minutes late. When the admiral did arrive, he quickly apologized (he had been held up in traffic) and took his seat. Hoover, who never missed a chance to put a man on the defensive, greeted him by saying, "We hope this is not characteristic of the navy."

I had promised everyone that the meeting would only take ten or fifteen minutes—after all, how long does it take to sign a piece of paper—but Hoover surprised everyone by reading the entire report, all sixty pages of it, aloud. We couldn't believe what we were hearing. These were busy men with full schedules. And at the end of every page, Hoover would look up and ask each man at the table whether he had any comments. "Mr. Helms do you have anything to add?" he'd ask, and when Helms did not, he went on to Admiral Gayler, General Bennett, the others, and finally to "Mr. Hutchinson," as he called Tom Huston. After Hoover read another page he'd go around the table again, asking each man if he had anything else to add and finally, as Hoover got to Huston, he'd ask, "Mr. Hoffman?" At one point, I saw Dick Helms, who was sitting on Hoover's right, lean back in his chair and wink behind the director's back at Tom Huston, who was sitting on Hoover's left. I had to bite my lip to keep from laughing. All in all, the meeting took an hour and a half.

Everyone there was disgusted with Hoover's revisions and he rubbed it in. Toward the end of the session, Hoover said to Helms, "We're not going to open Soviet mail anymore. Any objections, Mr. Helms?" Helms said, "No, sir." Everyone at the table knuckled under to Hoover and signed his draft.

I don't know if Hoover could have defeated the Ad Hoc Committee's plan by himself, but it never came to that. Hoover found he had a very powerful ally with his own reasons for wanting the plan to fail: Attorney General John Mitchell. Mitchell's distaste for Huston and for what came to be known as the Huston Plan began when the Ad Hoc Committee was originally formed. I don't know if it was a deliberate omission or merely an oversight, but Mitchell was never invited to join the committee. As it turned out, Mitchell, Hoover's nominal boss, had wanted to be a member of that committee in the worst way. In fact, Mitchell should not have been a member of the committee at all. In the late 1960s, after Nixon became president, a secret group called the Committee of Forty was set up to give final approval to clandestine intelligence operations all over the world. When I heard that the attorney general, John Mitchell, was going to be a member, I was so astonished I immediately called General Haig. "General," I

With former Attorney General John Mitchell in 1970. *United Press International Telephoto*

said, "I don't think that the attorney general of the United States, the highest-ranking law enforcement official in the nation, should be in any way involved in a body approving clandestine operations, dirty tricks, and other possible illegalities." Haig said to me, "I think you're

Tom Charles Huston, the
Nixon White House aide whom Hoover
called a "hippy." *Wide World Photos*

right. It is inappropriate." I said, "Why don't you take this up with
Dr. Kissinger, the head of the Committee of Forty, and let Mitchell
gracefully get out of this thing." Haig said he'd pursue the matter but
nothing came of it and Mitchell stayed on as a committee member.

Mitchell's alliance with John Dean also helped to bring about the
downfall of the Huston Plan and the end of Tom Charles Huston's
White House career. Huston and Dean, both ambitious young lawyers on the president's staff, were natural rivals. Dean had been
Mitchell's protégé during his pre-White House days at the Justice
Department. And as much as the attorney general liked Dean, he
disliked and mistrusted Tom Huston. I believe that consciously or un-
consciously Mitchell disliked Huston for the very reasons I admired
him: we both sensed that Huston was a man of integrity and character. Not John Mitchell's kind of man at all. Huston was grossly inexperienced when it came to the realities of getting things done in government though, and his failure to include Mitchell in the committee
was a fatal tactical error. Mitchell was diametrically opposed to the

Huston Plan before the report was ever written.

Thanks to Hoover's and Mitchell's opposition the Huston Plan died aborning. After the final report had been submitted to the White House, the orders just never came through to get the programs in motion. After a few weeks I had Brennan run a check, and he found out that it was being held up in the attorney general's office. I called Tom Huston to ask what the problem was. "The whole thing is dead," he told me sadly. Not long afterward, Tom called me to say that he had resigned and that he planned to resume his law practice in Indiana.

"I was willing to forget my law practice and give all my time and energy to the president. Now I'm thoroughly disillusioned with everything from the president on down. They just don't seem to have any backbone. There's no real leadership. I'm going back home."

Huston's failure to bring Hoover into line forced the White House to forget about the FBI and look elsewhere for men to do the kind of investigative work Nixon, Mitchell, Haldeman, Ehrlichman, Dean, and the others felt was necessary. As it turned out, they ended up forming their own group, which later became known as the Plumbers.

FOURTEEN

The Seventeen Wiretaps

ALTHOUGH THE SUBJECT of electronic surveillance never came up in FBI training courses, two months after I became a special agent, I found myself listening in on a Communist cell meeting as the first announcement of the Japanese attack on Pearl Harbor came over the radio. Our technology was laughably old-fashioned in those days; agents wearing earphones took down the information they overheard by hand on long yellow pads. During the war, very few FBI agents stopped to ask for official authorization before tapping the telephone of a possible Nazi spy. With the country's future at stake, getting approval from Washington seemed like an unnecessary legal technicality. Years later, the FBI was still listening in on other people's conversations without the authorization of the attorney general, but now it was because we were afraid that his knowledge of some of our programs could prove publicly embarrassing.

Public opinion was on the side of the FBI in the 1940s, however, when our agents were discovered in the act with their earphones and yellow pads eavesdropping on Harry Bridges, the Head of the long-shoreman's union on the West Coast. Bridges's men began pushing the agents around and they actually had to fight their way out of the room. The story got some play in the newspapers and then died a natural death. Today, agents caught in a similar situation would be hung sky high.

Hoover was a strong advocate of electronic surveillance until the late 1960s when the FBI's crime-fighting image was at an all-time low. Concerned about his own image, Hoover didn't want to be forced to publicly defend the FBI against charges of violating the constitutional rights of United States citizens, and he called a halt to illegal wiretaps. But when President Nixon and his security advisor Henry Kissinger asked Hoover to tap the phones of a number of government employees who were suspected of leaking highly classified information to the press, the director quickly agreed.

I knew nothing of Hoover's meetings with Nixon and Kissinger until Alexander Haig, then a colonel working on Kissinger's staff, came to my office on 10 May 1969. I had never met Haig. Without mentioning any names, and making sure that I understood that he was merely acting as a messenger in this affair, Colonel Haig told me that he had been instructed to convey a "White House request" on "the highest authority." Security leaks, Haig explained, with honest concern in his voice, had been plaguing the Nixon administration for some time. Members of the National Security Council could read about their secret meetings in the *New York Times* forty-eight hours after the meetings took place. Newspaper stories on the most sensitive aspects of our foreign policy were almost commonplace. These leaks, Haig told me, were incredibly damaging to our bargaining position at the Paris peace talks. Indeed, they were damaging to our foreign policy as a whole, and they had to be stopped. How? By tapping the telephones of the men the White House suspected of leaking the information to the press. Haig explained that the wiretap program would be short lived—I remember him saying that the whole thing would take "a few days"—and he requested that because of the sensitivity of the operation, no written record of the program ever be made.

Haig obviously knew nothing about how taps were handled, so I told him that it would be impossible for the FBI to implement a totally secret wiretap operation with no written records. A single tap, I told Haig, would involve a minimum of two men for installation alone. The head of the office involved would know about the "secret tap," as would the people needed to monitor the information coming in. If twenty-four-hour monitoring was required, at least four people would be involved at that end. At least one typist would have to prepare the transcripts. That added up to a *minimum* of eight people who would know about the simplest single tap. No tap could be kept completely secret within the bureau, but I did tell Haig that I would try to keep the paperwork involved to a minimum by meeting with him personally whenever there was anything to report instead of writing memos back and forth. Haig was a career army man, as familiar as I was with bureaucracy and red tape, and he accepted what I said without argument. Before he left, Haig gave me the names of four men. One of them was that of Morton Halperin, a member of the National Security Council.

As soon as Haig walked out of my office, I was on the phone to Hoover. He wasn't in the office (it was a Saturday), but Helen Gandy, his secretary, made a record of my call and of the fact that I wouldn't move on Haig's request until I'd gotten the director's approval. The next day I finally got through to Hoover and told him about Haig's request, which he approved. His justification, he told me, was national security. He also told me that Attorney General John Mitchell had already approved the taps. Later that day, I wrote a memo to the director advising that he handle the taps with extreme caution. I'd had a funny feeling about the wiretaps from the first. I sensed that this program could be dangerous and I wanted to alert Hoover to any possible danger.

Although Haig sincerely believed that the wiretap program would be short lived, it lasted for almost two years. During that time we tapped the telephones of four journalists, including Hedrick Smith and Tad Szulc of the *New York Times,* and of thirteen government employees, although not all seventeen wiretaps were operational at the same time.

Despite Haig's initial request for no paperwork, with so many taps in effect for so long, the logs (the tape transcripts), correspondence, and memos began to pile up. Hoover instructed me to keep this material *out* of the FBI files. This was not unusual; to my knowledge, particularly sensitive material had been kept out of the files since the 1940s. In this case, at least at first, the material was kept in Hoover's own office.

The paperwork started as soon as Hoover approved the White House request. I told the director that it was my judgment that these taps should be handled in the same manner as other wiretaps, that an individual letter should be prepared on each tap for his approval and for the approval of the attorney general. Hoover agreed, but he

warned me that when I directed agents from the Washington field office to implement the taps, they make no copies of the original transcripts and send the original logs to bureau headquarters. Hoover
himself contributed to the growing mountain of paperwork when he
insisted that a letter go out over his signature to Dr. Kissinger every
time there was something in the logs that deserved White House attention. Haig's plea for secrecy meant little to Hoover—he wasn't
about to give any information to the president without getting the
credit. As the material came in, the relevant data was summarized in
a letter and sent over to the White House by special courier.

I delegated the day-to-day paperwork on the taps to one of my
men, for I could not and never did handle such work in my position.
As I was responsible for eighty to ninety thousand criminal and security cases at the time, it would have been a physical impossibility. But
I couldn't get out of it (though I tried) when Hoover asked me to go to
France personally and discreetly arrange electronic surveillance on
Joseph Kraft while the columnist was in Paris covering the peace
talks. Although he never told me why I was chosen for the job, it must
have been because I had a good personal relationship with the French
security people. They certainly didn't want to tap the phone of an important visiting American, but they wouldn't say no to a request from
me and they went along with it.

I had my own objections to the assignment. Kraft wrote a good
column—I read it myself—and I had never heard anything about him
that made me suspicious of the man. "Mr. Hoover," I said to the
director when he told me about my proposed trip to France, "to
my knowledge, we've never heard any detrimental information
about Mr. Kraft."

"We've got to do it," Hoover explained, "because Kraft is over in
Paris talking to the Viet Cong, and then he plans to go to Russia."

"All the journalists talk to the Viet Cong," I pointed out, "and a
lot of them go to Russia. If we use Kraft's contacts and travel plans as a
yardstick, we'll be putting surveillances on all the reporters." My objections were in vain, however, and I went over to Paris, set the thing
up, and told our man in Paris to send the tapes to me in Washington
for transcription and translation.

In July 1969, I sent a top-secret memo to Hoover requesting that all the wiretaps be removed. Nothing much had come to light as a result of the taps. We overheard Daniel Ellsberg ("not further identified") and Morton Halperin talking about effects of some drugs, and we heard Mrs. Halperin boasting to an unidentified friend that her husband was so important that he had the use of Henry Kissinger's car. Alexander Haig later described Hoover's reports to Kissinger as "reflective of a sensibility we did not share." Besides, some of the men who were being tapped seemed to realize that their conversations were no longer private. Although I considered the wiretaps important, legal, and justified, I had more urgent problems to attend to and I needed the men who were assigned to work on the secret wiretaps to work on other cases instead. The taps could always be put back on if necessary after I solved my more pressing cases. Hoover called me after he read my memo, however, and disagreed. As the taps were a White House operation, Hoover told me, they would remain on until the White House requested they come off.

At first Hoover kept all the logs of the tapes in his own office and told me that I'd be in charge of the super-sensitive material from then on. At the time, I was assistant director in charge of the Domestic Intelligence Division. The case carried over to when I was promoted to number three man in the bureau. For all practical purposes I acted as Hoover's number two man because by 1970 Clyde Tolson was very ill, having suffered from strokes that left him physically disabled. Each morning as Hoover's automobile pulled up and parked inside the Justice Department Building's courtyard, two old and sick men would get out. Hoover would be the first to leave the car and he would walk as quickly as he could to the building. Behind him, shuffling along, was the pathetic figure of Clyde Tolson, no longer able to keep up with the other half of what we called the "unipersonality." Hoover himself was seventy-five and ailing. Each day he would nap for about four hours and he had a full-time medical staff that supplied him with the medicines needed to keep him going. I moved to a new office in the Department of Justice Building from my old office across the street in the Federal Triangle Building and I suggested to Hoover that the records of the wiretaps go into bureau files as I did not want to transfer the material to my new office. But Hoover ordered me to keep the logs and records in my possession.

In December of 1970 I again suggested to Hoover that the logs go into the bureau files. Again Hoover refused. And when I called him in February of 1971 to tell him that Haig had informed me that the White House had finally called off the taps, Hoover still wanted me to keep the logs in my office. I hated being responsible for such sensitive material. It was the only time in my career with the FBI that I had been saddled with such a job, though plenty of secret material had been kept out of our files in the past, especially for Lyndon Johnson.

The situation between myself and the director had been getting worse and worse during this period, and when I was forced to resign from the FBI in October 1971, I felt I couldn't leave Washington without doing something about the wiretap logs. I couldn't help thinking of the way Hoover had abused sensitive material in the past—with these logs in his possession he could blackmail Nixon *and* Kissinger and hang onto his job forever. Even though Haig had conveyed the original requests for the wiretaps, I didn't feel I knew him well enough to turn to him. The only man in the Nixon administration who I actually knew and held high in regard was Assistant Attorney General Robert C. Mardian.

I had never heard of Mr. Mardian until I read the newspaper stories about his appointment to the job of assistant attorney general in charge of the Internal Security Division of the Department of Justice. I wasn't really interested in the stories though—to my mind, men like Mardian came and went with the wind.

At first I had no direct dealings with Mardian. I was used to getting along without the cooperation of the Internal Security Division. Mardian's predecessor was a former FBI man who had worked briefly for me, but he had great difficulty preparing and prosecuting cases.

Sometime after Mr. Mardian took over the job, my men came to tell me that an intelligent, capable man now headed the Internal Security Division. Mardian, they said, was a real fireball: a hard-worker who went after results. He was getting rid of the deadheads and replacing them with bright, talented, industrious young lawyers. My

Robert Mardian, the former assistant attorney general. *Wide World Photos*

assistant, C. D. Brennan, told me, "Mardian is a breath of fresh air, the best thing that has happened to the Internal Security Division in my memory."

One of Mardian's innovations was his idea for periodic conferences for bureau officials and their Department of Justice counterparts. These conferences helped to break down the wall that had separated the FBI and the Justice Department for so many years. At last we could discuss our mutual problems, agree on common conclusions, and work more effectively toward common objectives. In other words, it was just the kind of arrangement Hoover hated. I knew the director wouldn't be pleased when I sent him a memo advising him of the first conference. As I expected, he went into a rage and told me not to cooperate. The director couldn't actually outlaw the conferences—that would look bad in the press if the story ever came out—

but he could and did limit the materials the FBI made available to Mardian.

Conditions between Hoover and Mardian continued to worsen, and I was caught in the middle—not an unfamiliar position during my thirty years with Hoover. The director accused me of giving too much material to Mardian, and he even sent me a letter of censure about it. "Mr. Hoover," I told him in my defense, "we have an obligation to the taxpayers to cooperate with other government departments."

"Mardian is a goddamned Armenian Jew," Hoover replied, "and I won't cooperate with any such person."

Because of Hoover's attitude, I was faced with making the decision either to cut off the flow of material to Mardian, which would have seriously damaged the quality of our work, or to give him what assistance could be given quietly and under the table. I decided on the second course of action. We did manage to do some good work, but it was no record to be proud of, particularly compared to what could have been accomplished under normal working conditions.

Mardian was aware of Hoover's feelings, of course, and once during one of our conferences he remarked that Hoover had promised him "two hundred percent cooperation" when they first met after Mardian's appointment. One of my men told me Mardian didn't understand what Hoover meant by two hundred percent cooperation: "What does he mean?" Mardian had asked, bewildered.

"When Mr. Hoover promises two hundred percent cooperation," my man replied, "he really means he won't attack you publicly."

Although Mardian and I developed a good working relationship, we never had any social relationship at all. He was never at my home and I was never in his. And after we had our first political argument— we had a lot to argue about, as I was a liberal Democrat and Mardian had campaigned for Goldwater—we never discussed politics again.

But Mardian's attitude toward me changed when my break with Hoover became public knowledge. He became openly hostile, and said that neither he nor anyone else in the administration would take my side in a fight with the director. I told him that I had not asked for and did not want assistance from anybody. For thirty years I had placed the country's needs above my personal interests. To me, Mardian was a Johnny-come-lately.

Because of Mardian's attitude, our relationship did not end on a cordial note when I left the FBI. On the other hand, there had never been an open break between us before I left, so when I felt my departure from the FBI and Washington was growing imminent, I decided to talk to Mardian about the wiretap logs. The decision to raise the question with Mardian was entirely on my own. I had never discussed it with anyone. I could have left the logs where they were, in a file in my office, but I desperately wanted to maintain their confidentiality within the Department of Justice where I assumed they would be retained. And Mardian already knew about the taps—he was the logical man to approach.

When I warned Mardian that my days with the FBI were numbered, he assured me that Hoover wouldn't force me out. "He wouldn't dare," Mardian said. I disagreed, and when I told him I suspected that Hoover would misuse the logs when I was gone, he grew concerned. "I don't have the authority to make this kind of decision," he told me, "but I'll talk to people who do." A few days later, Mardian told me that "on presidential request" and "on the authority of the attorney general" he would personally take possession of the logs and correspondence. In May 1973, I learned that after our first meeting Mardian had flown to San Clemente to discuss the future whereabouts of the logs with President Nixon. Mardian kept something else from me too: he never mentioned that the logs would not be kept in his office, as I assumed, but in the White House. In all fairness to Mardian, whose intelligence and ability I still respect, I don't think that the logs were moved to the White House to obstruct justice, but to maintain security. When I turned in my inventory before leaving the FBI for the last time, I listed the logs and told Mark Felt that I had left them in Mardian's possession.

After Mardian left the Department of Justice, I believed that the logs were still safe at the department until May 1973, when Henry Petersen, an assistant attorney general, called me and asked if the FBI had ever had a tap on Daniel Ellsberg. I told him that we hadn't, although Ellsberg could have been a "walk-in" (someone who called or was called by someone under FBI surveillance) on someone else's tap. Then Petersen asked me if I knew where the wiretap logs were.

"They are at the Department of Justice," I told him immediately, "probably in Mardian's old office."

"No, they aren't anywhere at the Department of Justice," Petersen said.

"I turned them over to Mardian when I left the FBI." I told Petersen. "He lives in Arizona now. Do you want me to call him?" I asked.

"Yes," Petersen replied, "I wish you would." When I called, Mardian told me with no hesitation or guile that he had turned the logs over to John Ehrlichman before leaving Washington. I called Petersen and gave him that information. The logs were found in Ehrlichman's safe. It never entered my mind that the White House would try to keep the tapes from Daniel Ellsberg and his lawyers. Had I wanted to the tapes kept at the White House, I would have handed them over to Haig in the first place.

When Petersen called me to ask about the logs, I had been away from the FBI for a year and a half and Hoover had been dead for a year. William Ruckelshaus, acting director of the FBI, mistakenly believed that the logs had been destroyed. When Petersen told him that they were in John Ehrlichman's safe, he went over to the White House, got the logs, and brought them to FBI headquarters. "Unfortunately," Ruckelshaus said in a public statement to the press on 14 May 1973, "the records were not located in time to respond to Judge Bryne's inquiries about the potential taint of evidence in the Ellsberg trial."

Why did Ruckelshaus have to make a public statement on the whereabouts of the top-secret wiretap logs? The existence of the logs never would have been known to the press if it hadn't been for some of my old enemies at the FBI. They thought by leaking the story of my involvement with the logs to the press (and, of course, by painting that involvement in the worst possible light) that they could block me from consideration for the job I wanted: a special "reorganization consultant" to the FBI which would have resulted in their dismissal. When the story broke, I knew that the uneasy feeling I'd had about the wiretaps the very first time Alexander Haig came to my office was justified. Those damned tapes haunted me from the beginning. I just knew they would cause trouble.

Had my former associates known how Bob Haldeman felt about me, however, they never would have bothered to leak the story in the first place. When Nixon was looking for a successor for Hoover in May 1972, just after the director died, Haldeman said "I am totally opposed to Sullivan being director. He is far too independent and may use the FBI against us." The remark was repeated to me, but I didn't understand then what Haldeman meant. I do now.

FIFTEEN

John Dean and the Plumbers

MEETING: The President, Haldeman, and Dean, Oval Office, March 13,
1973 (12:42–2:00 P.M.)

DEAN: Now the other thing, if we are going to use a package like this: Let's
say in the Gray hearings—where everything is cast that we are the political people and they are not—that Hoover was above reproach, which is
just not accurate, total (expletive omitted). *THE PERSON WHO
WOULD DESTROY HOOVER'S IMAGE IS GOING TO BE THIS
MAN BILL SULLIVAN.* Also it is going to tarnish quite severely . . .

PRESIDENT NIXON: Some of the FBI.

DEAN: . . . some of the FBI. And a former President. He is going to lay it
out, and just all hell is going to break loose once he does it. It is going to
change the atmosphere of the Gray hearings and it is going to change
the atmosphere of the whole Watergate hearings.

ALTHOUGH I had heard John Dean's name mentioned when he
was John Mitchell's protégé at the Justice Department, I
never met him while I was at the FBI. He did call me on
the phone one day when I was heading up the Domestic Intelligence
Division to ask me to "check out" through the FBI files the name of a
young woman he planned to date.

I was busy working on a hijacking case that day, and I didn't have
time—or the desire—to do what he asked, so when he called back a
few hours later, I was being evasive when I told him that I hadn't
found anything derogatory. It was the truth—I just didn't tell him
that I hadn't looked.

I first saw Dean at Tom Huston's going-away party, but we
weren't introduced and we didn't speak. As I was a friend of Huston's,
sorry to see him leaving Washington, the party was a sad occasion for
me. On the other hand, it was a moment of triumph for Dean. Tom

Huston had been a rival, and now that he was going back to Indiana Dean had a clear track to the president.

When John Dean and I were finally introduced in the fall of 1972 at a party in a Virginia suburb given by an official of the State Department, Dean was President Nixon's counsel and I had left the FBI and was director of the Office of National Narcotics Intelligence. Curiously, my first day at ONNI was 4 August 1972, thirty-one years to the day after I started working at the bureau. My title at ONNI had originally been assistant attorney general, but when I pointed out the fact that I was not a lawyer, it was changed to director.

Dean's job had changed too, but his reputation had not. I had heard that he was as much the fair-haired boy at the White House as he had been at the Department of Justice. Indeed, I had never heard anyone say anything bad about Dean, and I had no reason to distrust him in any way.

Robert Mardian had told me that Dean might be able to help C. D. Brennan, my former assistant in the Domestic Intelligence Division, to get his old job back. Brennan's career had taken a nose dive during our investigation of Daniel Ellsberg in 1971, and when Hoover forced me to leave the FBI he placed Brennan under custodial detention because he was "one of Sullivan's men." With me gone, Chip Brennan became Hoover's number one target. Even many of Brennan's old friends stopped all contact with him and many agents who knew Brennan would shun him on the street so that Hoover wouldn't get word that they were speaking with Brennan. He was transferred from headquarters to one of our offices in Virginia, where he was put in a tiny room and given no real work to do. None of his old friends who were still at the FBI dared to be seen with him. Since I felt that Mardian had done as much (or more) than anyone to destroy Brennan's career, I told him that he ought to do something about helping Chip. Mardian suggested that I take the matter up with John Dean.

By the time I met Dean, Chip Brennan had been taken off custodial detention, but he was still sitting out his career in Virginia, so I took advantage of my meeting with the president's counsel to bring up Brennan's problem.

Dean appeared interested in the case, and he said he would do what he could to get my old friend reinstated. After a month went by with no word from Dean, I called to remind him. "I'm working on it," he said, "but you must have confidence in me because it will take a little time." As far as I know, he's still working on it. We never discussed Brennan again.

Dean called me a few months later, however, in February of 1973, with a problem of his own. Russell Asch, who had worked for

John Dean, the former White House lawyer. *United Press International*

me at the FBI and who now worked for me as deputy director at ONNI, was sitting in my office when Dean called, and he heard everything I said to Dean.

Dean was evasive at first. "I'd like you to come to my office— there is something I'd like to discuss with you," he said. When I insisted that Dean tell me what he had in mind, he said that he wanted to discuss a story in *Time* magazine concerning the seventeen secret wiretaps the FBI had placed on the telephones of government officials and newspapermen. Orders for the taps had come from President Nixon and his national security advisor, Henry Kissinger.

It was the first time I knew that Dean had any interest in the taps. The whole operation had been extremely sensitive, so sensitive that I didn't want to talk about it with anyone who hadn't been directly involved. "This is an intelligence matter," I said to him, "and since your field is politics I'm not at liberty to discuss it with you."

Dean wouldn't take no for an answer, though, and he pulled rank. "I'm general counsel to the president," he told me, "and there is no area of activity I'm not entitled to discuss." Dean insisted I come "right over to his office." I began to get angry with Dean and hung up on him.

"You shouldn't have been so rough with him," Asch said, "after all, he is the president's lawyer."

"Well," I said to Asch, "that's the way I felt. But I guess I simply have to go over there."

At Dean's office, we continued haggling about his authority to talk to me about the taps. "I'm not at liberty to discuss this with you," I said as soon as I sat down. Dean got very annoyed, and he played his trump card: he told me that John Ehrlichman had told him to talk to me. I was outranked again. I had to give in and talk to him, but I decided in my own mind that I wasn't going to go all the way, that I wouldn't tell him any more than I had to.

He started by asking some innocuous questions about the mechanics of tapping a telephone. Then the questions got more serious. He told me that he wanted me to tell him why the taps had been ordered in the first place. I felt safe in answering that—I was sure if Dean knew anything at all about the taps, he would have to know that the president and his security advisor felt that the taps would help them to discover who had been leaking top- top-secret information on American foreign policy in Southeast Asia to the press. Then Dean asked who had approved the taps and who had actually put them on the telephones. Dean knew damned well who had approved those taps—it had been Nixon, Hoover, and Mitchell—and I wasn't about to give him the names of my men. "Some seasoned veterans handled it," I told him.

When he testified before the Senate Watergate Committee on 26

June 1973, Dean said that I'd left him with the "impression" that Hoover was not in favor of the taps. It would not have been possible for me to have left Mr. Dean with this impression because the subject of Hoover's feelings about the taps never came up. Had it been raised, I would have told him the facts: namely, that I had never heard Mr. Hoover object to the seventeen wiretaps in any way. In fact, he seemed to be doing everything he could do to expedite the order. I remember that all his memos on the subject of the taps were hand-delivered to the White House just minutes after he signed them.

These preliminaries dragged on a bit longer until Dean finally asked the question I felt he had been building up to all along.

"I'd like to know the names of the seventeen men who were being tapped," Dean said to me. I couldn't imagine why he wanted me to give him those names. If he's discussed this whole thing with Ehrlichman, I thought, he must know those names himself.

"I won't tell you any names at all," I told him, angry and puzzled about his motives. I found out when I read the transcripts of the Nixon White House tapes that Dean actually called me over to the White House that day because he thought I was the one who had leaked the story to *Time*. "I was calling to really determine whether he was a leak," Dean told President Nixon and his aide Bob Haldeman in a meeting in the Oval Office on 13 March 1973. The damn fool—did he think that I'd leak a story that would cause me trouble? As it turned out, Dean had already known all about those wiretaps four or five months before our meeting took place. He was just fishing. He just wanted to find out how much I knew and how much I'd tell. I think he had already begun to gather material to use in his own defense in case he was called on to testify. He started covering himself early.

When Dean found that I wouldn't tell him anything substantial about the taps, he started asking general questions about the Domestic Intelligence Division. I told him then, as I'd told many others, that in my opinion it was wrong for one organization to combine criminal investigation with intelligence operations, and that neither branch could be truly effective until the two were separated. Later, when I read the White House tape transcripts, I found out that Dean had interpreted my remarks to mean that I was proposing to form and head a new intelligence gathering agency for President Nixon. I think Dean always assumed that other people have ulterior motives for their ideas and behavior.

"Bill Sullivan's desire in life . . . is to set up a domestic national security intelligence system," Dean told Nixon and Haldeman in the same conversation. "He says we are deficient," Dean continued. "He says we have never been efficient, because Hoover lost his guts several years ago. If you recall," Dean reminded the president and his aide, "he and Tom Huston worked on it. Tom Huston had your instructions to go out and do it and the whole thing just crumbled."

"If we could only put him out studying it for a couple of years," Dean concluded, "if you could put him out in the CIA or someplace. . . ." If Dean offered me a job as a payoff, it would have been a violation of the law and I'd have taken steps to have him arrested. I didn't want a damn thing from them. I never asked Dean or anyone in the White House for anything for myself. But that was a point that they all overlooked.

"We will do it," President Nixon replied. "There is no problem with Sullivan. He is a valuable man."

My future thus decided, Dean went on to give his version of the rest of our conversation that day in his office. "Then, after going through with his own explanation of what had happened," Dean told the president, "he started volunteering this other thing."

"This other thing" referred to the political use of the FBI by presidents who had preceded Nixon, and I didn't bring it up, Dean did. He started by asking me if I thought Pat Gray would be confirmed as director of the FBI. Gray's Senate confirmation hearings were going on at that time, and Gray was coming under heavy fire for allowing the FBI to become engaged in partisan political activities. Poor Pat Gray—he got crucified, and in some ways it was his own fault. He picked the wrong men, men I had warned him against, to work as his closest aides, and he was doomed from the start.

I didn't know of any wrongdoing on Gray's part, but if he did allow the FBI to engage in political activity, he was certainly not the first FBI director who did. Hoover had set the precedent years ago, and I said so to Dean.

"I suppose the Kennedys did that kind of thing with Hoover,"

Dean said. I told him truthfully that the Kennedys had been so wary of Hoover that they never used the FBI at all if they could help it. Dean didn't look as if he believed me. "What about Johnson?" he asked quickly.

Once again I answered truthfully. "Compared to Lyndon Johnson," I told him, "the current administration is spartan in its use of the FBI." Dean's tongue was practically hanging out of his mouth as I talked. I couldn't tell him about every one of Johnson's illegal uses of the FBI—DeLoach was the one who could—but I could tell him enough. I told him about the FBI surveillance I'd helped to set up on Madame Chennault. I told him how Johnson had praised Hoover and the FBI for keeping tabs on Bobby Kennedy at the Democratic convention in Atlantic City by tapping Martin Luther King's phone. I told him about the behind-the-scenes wheeling and dealing done by LBJ, Abe Fortas, and Deke DeLoach after Walter Jenkins was arrested in Washington, and I told Dean that Johnson had asked the FBI to dig up derogatory information on Senator Fulbright and other Democratic senators who had attacked Johnson's policies. Of course, the FBI wasn't chartered to do that kind of work, but Hoover loved to help his friends—and those he wished were his friends.

Dean asked if I would write a confidential memo for "White House use only" detailing some examples of previous illegal political use of the FBI. He didn't tell me, and I certainly never guessed, that Dean would give the "confidential information I'd supplied to the Watergate prosecutors. I did realize, though, that I could be heading into stormy waters, so I told Dean I'd send the memo, but that I'd only write about events that I would be willing to testify to publicly. Dean readily agreed.

Then he sat back in his chair and said, "I'd like you to write a second memo after you've done that one. I'd like to pick your brains. You've been around Washington for years, and I'd like your opinion on how we should cope with the situation we have with the Plumbers."

The first time I ever heard the word "Plumber" was when I read about the Watergate break-in in the newspapers. If the FBI had had a real intelligence division, we would have known all about these people and we might have been able to stop them and prevent Watergate. The Plumbers were already in jail when Dean and I met, and I guess they were beginning to make threatening noises to the White House.

I reminded Dean that I was not a lawyer. "No, no, no," he said with a friendly smile, shaking his head, "I'm a lawyer myself. There are more than enough lawyers around here. What I want is a fresh viewpoint, some new ideas from a veteran of the Washington scene." Dean made it clear that he didn't want his name mentioned in either memo.

I said I'd write the memos just to get out of Dean's office, but when I got back to ONNI I decided to wait and see if Dean would forget about me. He called after three days. "Where are the memos?" he asked in an impatient voice. I promised to write them immediately. I wrote a draft which concluded that if the people involved in the break-in at the Democratic National Committee headquarters at the Watergate building were guilty, that they should confess and take the punishment. They were, I said in the memo, expendable in the interests of the country. I also suggested that the lawyer hired to defend the Plumbers be a prominent Democrat.* Then I wrote out the second memo, jotting down a few relatively tame illegal uses of the FBI on the part of past presidents—Johnson of course, but Roosevelt and Eisenhower too—and dictated both memos to my secretary to type up for Dean.

I thought I had given Dean what he wanted, but when I took the memos over to his office, Dean flushed with anger the minute he looked at them. "You've dictated these to your secretary," he said.

"I dictate all my correspondence," I replied.

"But I told you to type it up yourself," he said. "Do you trust your secretary?"

Ann Barniker had worked for me for eleven years at the FBI before she worked as my secretary at ONNI. It was Dean I didn't trust. "I'd trust her with my life," I told him.

He gave a disapproving glance and started to read my memo on the Plumbers. I watched him read the first page, then turn to the second, and then read about my advice that the guilty parties lay themselves before the country and my judgment that such people were ex-

* For the complete memo, see Appendix B.

pendable. He stopped reading at that point, put the memo down on his desk, thanked me, and said that my advice had been "helpful." Of course, I never dreamt that Dean himself was one of the culprits, or that anyone from the White House had been involved.

Dean moved on to my other memo, skimmed over it, and thanked me for coming. Before I left, however, I made sure Dean understood that the FBI operations I'd told him about, and the only FBI operations I'd ever tell him about, were FBI operations that I'd testify to publicly. I thought my testimony might help Pat Gray, and I wanted to set the record straight.

Besides, I was becoming wary of Dean. After being in this business for over thirty years, I tend to get hunches about people. I certainly didn't want to establish a clandestine relationship with John Dean, so when I got back to my office at ONNI, I wrote him a third memo summing up our meetings and reminding him that I would be willing to testify publicly to the information I had given him on political abuse of the FBI. I never saw or heard from him again.

SIXTEEN

Locks on the Door

MY FINAL BREAK WITH Hoover was an indirect result of the publication of the Pentagon Papers in June 1971, one year after I'd moved up to the number three job. There was no mystery who had leaked the top-secret papers to the *Washington Post*, the *New York Times*, and other newspapers—it was Daniel Ellsberg, and my assistant, C. D. Brennan, had been assigned to the case.

Everybody who could tell us anything at all about Ellsberg was being questioned by FBI agents, and I was amazed when Brennan told me that Ellsberg's father-in-law, Louis Marx, a wealthy and prominent toy manufacturer, had not been approached. I recommended that Marx be interviewed as soon as possible, but I cautioned Brennan to get permission from Hoover to conduct the interview before Marx was questioned. Marx used to send three or four hundred dollars worth of toys to Hoover every Christmas for the director to distribute to children on behalf of the bureau. Hoover enjoyed doing this, and he prized his connection with Marx.

Unfortunately there was a slip-up, and the order to interrogate Marx went out to the New York office before Brennan's request for Hoover's permission to do the interview got to the director. When it did Hoover denied the request, but it was too late. It was a hot case, and the New York office had sent agents out to talk to Marx as soon as Brennan's order came in.

Completely terrorized, Brennan called me when he realized that he had done something against Hoover's wishes. I advised him to forget the whole thing and pray that Hoover never found out. But Brennan was afraid that he would be in worse trouble if he were caught covering up, and he admitted his mistake to the director in an apologetic memo.

Hoover hit the ceiling. Just like that he ordered Brennan demoted from assistant director of the Intelligence Division to special agent in charge and transferred to Cincinnati. It was a gross injustice, and I was determined not to let the transfer go through without at least speaking up.

I went to see Robert Mardian, assistant attorney general, told him what had happened and begged him to stop the transfer. When he heard the story, Mardian was as angry as I was. He called Hoover every name under the sun. "You just can't do business with that man," I remember him saying. Mardian had been having trouble with Hoover ever since he'd started working under John Mitchell at the Justice Deparment.

Mardian talked to Mitchell about Brennan's transfer, and I think he must have talked to Ehrlichman too, because Ehrlichman told the Watergate Committee that Bill Sullivan had threatened to quit if the transfer went through. I don't remember threatening to quit, but I was so goddamned mad that I can understand Mardian thinking I had. Mitchell did ask Hoover to cancel Brennan's transfer, but not for the right reasons. Instead, Mitchell told Hoover that he needed Brennan in Washington because he was the most knowledgeable man the FBI had working on the Ellsberg case. Keeping Brennan in Washington was "in the best interests of the administration," Mitchell said.

Hoover, the old fox, saw his opening right away. He let Brennan stay in Washington, but demoted him to inspector and put him on the Ellsberg case full time. Working on the case took no more than two hours a day at most, and Brennan ended up spending most of his time reading books to keep busy. Only certain agents were allowed to talk to him, even on the telephone, and he only had access to the files which concerned the Ellsberg case. Men who had known Brennan for years would cross to the other side of the street when they saw him coming for fear that someone from the director's office would see them talking and tell Hoover. And that's the way he existed for months. It was so miserable that anyone else would have quit. But Brennan was tough.

Hoover's treatment of Brennan infuriated me, and it also infuriated John Mitchell and Robert Mardian, and brought to a head their long-felt desire to get rid of the Old Man. "Don't worry," Mardian told Brennan one morning later that summer, "you'll have your old job back in three days." Mardian called me that same morning and asked me to come to his office (we worked in the same building). When I got there, he pointed at the clock. It was a quarter to ten. "At ten o'clock," he said, "our problem with Hoover will be solved. It will be all over. The president has asked Hoover to see him at the White House at ten, and he's going to ask Hoover to resign."

I was delighted. Mardian said they had a man ready to move into the job. A year before, I had told Mardian that I would put off my retirement if a new director was named. I told him that I would stay on for another six to eight months to help Hoover's replacement learn how to run things and to help with the reorganization of the bureau. Mardian remembered my offer, and he said he would be taking me up on it.

But when Mardian called me that afternoon, I could tell by the sound of his voice that something was wrong. I went right to his office. When I got there, his face was dark with anger. "Goddamn," he swore. "Christ almighty, Nixon lost his guts. He had Hoover there in his office, he knew what he was supposed to tell him, but he got cold feet. He couldn't go through with it."

Hoover, it seemed, started talking from the moment he entered the Oval Office. It was his usual line of conversation, starring John Dillinger, Ma Barker, and a cast of thousands, and he kept talking until Nixon ended the interview. "So," Mardian concluded, "we're left with the same old problem." After this episode, I knew Nixon would never try to fire Hoover again. I was devastated.

After thirty years with the FBI, and with the last hope of getting rid of Hoover until 1976 (Nixon's second term would be over) gone, it was time to listen to my wife and children and retire. I decided to use what little time I had left to advantage and force a final confrontation with Hoover. Perhaps if our differences became known to the public, or at least to official Washington, some good could come of it for the bureau. I didn't want to write about Hoover then, or go on television, or talk to newspaper reporters, but I did want the intelligent people in government to take notice. Perhaps *then* Hoover would be forced to retire.

Over the next few weeks I discussed my plan with a group of twenty-two men, men I had come to know and respect during my years with the FBI. I spoke to two assistant directors, eleven special agents in charge, one inspector, three section chiefs, two supervisors, and two special agents in the field. Every man I talked to was as concerned as I was about the deteriorating conditions at the FBI, but their reactions to my proposed collision course with the director were mixed. Of the twenty-two men, fifteen agreed that subjecting myself to the unpleasantries ahead might accomplish some good in the long run. In substance, they thought it was worth doing. Two of the men were undecided, and five men contended that this course of action would be disastrous and would result in the sacrifice of my career for nothing. These men advised me to wait it out as they were doing, hoping that Hoover would die soon.

I decided to go with the judgment of the majority. During my last few weeks at the bureau, I argued with Hoover, but I always carried out his instructions. I disagreed with him, but I was never insubordinate. When the chips were down, I did my job just as I always had. But I did make my opposition to his policies clear. I publicly opposed Hoover's campaign to expand our offices abroad. Although my opposition angered Hoover, it had no practical effect, as Hoover sold Nixon a bill of goods and convinced him to approve the expansion of our liaison offices around the world. Richard Helms, the head of the CIA, was furious when he heard that Nixon had given in to Hoover again. Yet Helms wasn't the kind of man to fight Hoover directly. He was smooth and suave, and he didn't want to risk getting roughed up, outpointed, and perhaps even knocked out by a real champion. So he just fumed inwardly, speaking his true feelings only to a few trusted associates.

Hoover, on the other hand, made no secret of his feelings, especially when it came to me. He was angry that I had dared to disagree with him, and he would try to force me to resign before things got completely out of hand. He was making life very difficult for me at the bureau, harassing me whenever and however possible. Every time I left my office—to attend a meeting of the U.S. Intelligence Board, for instance, or to give a speech that had been set up by Hoover—I'd come back to an angry phone call from Clyde Tolson.

"You haven't initialed your mail," he would complain. The FBI had a rule that all memos and mail which had to be acted on or forwarded had to be taken care of within two hours. As my trips from the office took longer than that, sometimes all day, I couldn't possibly initial my mail on time.

"Mr. Tolson," I'd explain, "I was out of my office working on an assignment for the director."

"You know the rules," Tolson replied.

"How can I initial my mail if I'm not in my office?"

Tolson was implaccable. "You know the rules," he repeated.

Hoover, of course, was worried that our feud would lead to bad publicity for the bureau. "You're not going to cause me trouble, are you?" he asked me at one of our typically vitriolic meetings that August.

"That's *my* decision, Mr. Hoover," I answered. I didn't intend to allow anything or anyone, not even J. Edgar Hoover, to interfere with my freedom of thought and expression. I'd had enough. If I was going to leave the bureau before Hoover did, and it looked as if that was going to happen, I was going to go with a bang. I went into the office on a Saturday morning, determined to get it all down on paper.*

PERSONAL   Saturday A.M.
Dear Mr. Hoover: August 28, 1971
    It is regretted by me that this letter is necessary. What I will set forth below is being said for your own good and for the FBI as a whole of which I am very fond. The premise from which I write is this: from diverse sources I have received the impression that you consider me to be disloyal to you but not to the FBI. If this is correct it is a serious matter that ought to be discussed.

    First, I wish to direct your attention to my 30 year record in the FBI. It is well documented and I don't need to present it to you here with its letters of commendation and awards given by you. You have access to all this. If this record of three decades is not conclusive evidence of loyalty what is? You have said that I consistently put the work of this Bureau above personal con-

*The exchange of correspondence following this letter is found in Appendix C.

siderations. My family certainly will attest to this for they have year in and year out suffered from my neglect. This I now realize was a mistake on my part. Countless others have also put the Bureau above all other considerations.

Second, you and I recognized years ago that we do not possess the same philosophical view or the same approach to FBI operations. We have disagreed but we worked together and I have carried out your instructions even when I disagreed with them strongly. This is as it should be because any organization must have an authority capable of making the final decision and invested with the power to implement all such decisions.

Third, during the past year in particular you have made it evident to me that you do not want me to disagree with you on anything. As one official of the FBI has said you claim you do not want "yes men" but you become furious at any employee who says "no" to you. I think this observation has much truth in it. If you are going to equate loyalty with "yes men," "rubber stamps," "apple polishers," flatterers, self-promoters and timid, cringing, frightened sycophants you are not only departing from the meaning of loyalty you are in addition harming yourself and the organization. There is no substitute for incisive, independent, free, probing, original, creative thinking. I have brought up my children to believe and act upon this truth. They disagree with me regularly. But, they are not disloyal to me. In fact I think their loyalty is more deep, strong and lasting because of this kind of thinking.

Fourth, ever since I spoke before the UPI Conference on October 12, 1970 you have made it quite clear you are very displeased with me because, according to you, I downgraded the Communist Party, USA. My answer to the question raised was accurate, factual, truthful. As I pointed out later to Mr. Tolson in Executive Conference I would give the very same answer again and again if it was asked. You know as well as I do that the Communist Party, USA is not the cause and does not direct and control the unrest and violence in this Nation. The UPI was wholly accurate in reporting what I said. Some papers were incomplete in reporting my remarks and there may have been a headline here and there that was not entirely correct. However, I repeat what I said was correct and I cannot understand your hostile reaction to it which had continued to this day.

Fifth, you are incensed because I have disagreed with you on opening new foreign liaison offices around the world and adding more men to those already in existence. It seems to me you should welcome different viewpoints. On this subject I want to say this here. I grew up in a farming community where all people in a family had to literally work from the darkness of the morning to the darkness of the night in order to make a living and pay their taxes. It could be that this is what causes me to be so sensitive about how the taxpayers' money is spent. Hence, I want to say once more that I regard it to be a serious waste of taxpayers' money to keep increasing the number of these offices, to continue with all that we now have and to be adding more and more manpower to these offices. Our primary responsibility is within the United States and here is where we need to spend the taxpayers' dollar combating crime. And, as our own statistics show we are not doing too well at it here. Why, then, should we spread ourselves around the world unnecessarily? You keep telling me that President Nixon has ordered you to do it and therefore you must carry out his orders. I am positive that if President Nixon knew the limitations of our foreign liaison operations and was given all the facts relative to intelligence matters he would reverse these orders if such have been clearly given. A few liaison offices can be justified but this expansion program cannot be no matter what kind of "reports" your inspectors bring back to you. Do you think many (if any) will disagree with you? What would happen if they did?

Sixth, I would like to convince you (but I am almost certain to fail in this) that those of us who disagree with *you are trying to help you and not hurt you.* For example, you were opposed to the Shaw case. This man should have been allowed to resign without stigmatizing him with the phrase "dismissal with prejudice." This was wrong. It cost us $13,000 I am told. On August 28 in a memorandum from Mr. Tolson to you we have been instructed to have no conversation or give any answers to representatives of certain papers and two broadcasting companies. Mr. Hoover, this is wrong and also it will sooner or later hurt us. You cannot do this kind of thing in a free, democratic society. It matters not whether we like or dislike certain papers or broadcasting companies they are entitled to equal treatment. Again, your decision to keep Mr. Roy Moore in Philadelphia is in my judgment both wrong and unjust. This man has been there since April. He has done brilliant work. It is definitely not necessary to keep him there any longer. He should be sent back to his office and family. I wish you would change your mind in both of these cases. Again, I want to say those of us who disagree with you are trying to help you. May I suggest that we are more loyal than those who are constantly saying "yes, yes, yes" to you and behind your back talk about "the need to play the game" in order to get the paycheck regularly and not be demoted or transferred.

Seventh, you have refused to give Assistant Director C. D. Brennan and myself any more annual leave. The reason you give is not valid and you know it. All it amounts to is this: you dislike us and intend to use your absolute power in this manner as a form of "punishment." I am hardened to all this and can take it. But my family cannot. My oldest son is registering for college in New Hanpshire this coming Tuesday. Naturally he wanted me to be with him and is extremely disappointed that I cannot be. Of course, I want to be with him and find out what kind of a roommate he has, talk to his professors, etc. My wife, in addition to respiratory trouble is now ill with colitus and cannot handle the situation (if you doubt this I will submit to you the doctor bills for the past three years and will give you their names and you can send out one or two of your global circling inspectors to talk to them and this time they will have to bring back what the doctors say and not what you want to hear). But even more serious is this: My son who has been staying with me has not driven a car a great deal and is not a good driver. Yet, because you refuse to give me any leave I had to tell him he must drive all the way to northern New Hampshire (well over 600 miles) alone today. He left at 5:00 a.m. this morning. Mr. Hoover, I want to tell you very simply but with deadly seriousness that I am hoping and praying for all involved in this that my adolescent son makes this long and dangerous trip today without any harm coming to him. Surely, I don't need to explain to you why my wife and three children regard you, to put it mildly, as a very strange man.

Eight, what I have said here is not designed to irritate or anger you but it probably will. What I am trying to get across to you in my blunt, tactless way is that a number of your decisions this year have not been good ones; that you should take a good, cold, impartial inventory of your ideas, policies, etc. You will not believe this but it is true: I do not want to see your reputation built up over these many years destroyed by your own decisions and actions. When you elect to retire I want to see you go out in a blaze of glory with full recognition from all those concerned. I do not want to see this FBI organization which I have gladly given 30 years of my life to along with untold numbers of other men fall apart or become tainted in any manner. We have a fine group of men in the FBI and we need to think of every one of them also.

Ninth, as I have indicated this letter will probably anger you. When you are angered you can take some mighty drastic action. You have absolute power in the FBI (I hope the man who one day takes over your position will not have such absolute power for we humans are simply not saintly enough to possess and handle it properly in every instance). In view of your absolute power you can fire me, or do away with my position (as you once did) or transfer me or in some other way work out your displeasure with me. So be it. I am fond of the FBI and I have told you exactly what I think about certain matters affecting you and this Bureau and as you know I have always been willing to accept the consequences of my ideas and actions.

Respectfully submitted,

[signed]   Wm. C. Sullivan

I sent the letter to Hoover and a copy to Mitchell. I got a call from Mardian as soon as Mitchell read what I'd written. "You shouldn't have sent that letter," Mardian told me. "The attorney gen-

eral is very upset and he wants you to stop this dispute with Hoover."
I told Mardian to tell the attorney general the same thing I'd told
Hoover. It was *my* decision, and I felt that our "dispute" was in the
best interests of the FBI and of law enforcement in general.

Although they wanted Hoover out of the FBI as much as I did, I
wasn't surprised when Mitchell and Mardian failed to support my
campaign either publicly or privately. From a practical, political
viewpoint, supporting Hoover and opposing me was the only position
they could take. I was a minor figure, an unknown, and J. Edgar
Hoover was . . . well, he was J. Edgar Hoover, and he had been
building up his image at the cost of the taxpayer since 1924.

I never expected the administration to support me and condemn
Hoover. Besides, the timing was all wrong. Nixon and Mitchell had
just backed Hoover in his dispute with Representative Hale Boggs of
Louisiana. Boggs mistakenly accused Hoover of tapping his telephone
and the telephones of other congressmen and senators. But Boggs
never came up with any proof, and Hoover and his defenders grabbed
the ball Boggs fumbled and ran with it. The president and the attorney general showered Hoover with lavish praise in a public display of
support. After that, how could they turn around a few weeks later and
support William C. Sullivan?

Although I wasn't surprised or angered by Mitchell's lack of support, he couldn't believe that I was going to disobey his orders and
carry on my personal crusade against Hoover. I believe that Mitchell
actually hated me from that day on. Mardian and I discussed the letter again a few days later. He said I was "too aggressive" (Mardian was
one of the most aggressive men I have ever met) and that my letter
was "intemperate." It was too strongly worded, Mardian told me, so
strongly worded that I left Hoover no options.

"You miss the point," I told Mardian. I had never intended to
give Hoover any options. Either he had to leave the bureau or I did.
As a matter of fact, the first draft of my letter had been written in
softer language, and was mild compared to the one I eventually sent.
I wrote it three times in all, making the language stronger each time.
It was the most temperate "intemperate" letter I ever wrote. I really
believed that if I kept my mouth shut and retired quietly, no one

would ever know that a conflict existed within the FBI. "When you and Mitchell failed to get rid of Hoover," I said to Mardian, "I knew I'd have to try something on my own." After that discussion, Mardian, who had been very cordial, and with whom I'd had a good working relationship, became quite cool.

Hoover called me in to talk about the letter three days after I'd sent it to him. It was 30 September 1971, a little over thirty years since I had first joined the FBI.

When our shouting match was finished, Hoover said, "I want you to take your annual leave immediately and then retire—get out of the bureau."

"I might be able to take a week," I told Hoover, "but since you refused my request for leave when my son was entering college, I don't see why I should take more now."

"You have three weeks coming," Hoover insisted, "and I want you to take them all."

"That's *my* decision," I said again. I wasn't going to make it easy for him.

"If that's how you feel," he said slowly, almost reluctantly, "Attorney General Mitchell agrees with me that it is you who should be forced out."

It was just what I'd hoped would happen.

When I arrived at my office the next day, the locks had been changed. I was out—literally. The story made the front page of the *Washington Post*, and my experience became public knowledge without my talking to one reporter. I never made a single public statement about my differences with the director during those difficult times.

I left Washington about a week later, headed for New Hampshire to join my family, but on the way out of town I stopped at a Texaco station on New York Avenue to call Mardian. I wanted to say good-bye, and to say how disappointed I was that Hoover was still there running the bureau. "We came so close," I said, and I went on to tell Mardian that there seemed to be a lack of effective leadership in the Nixon administration. I thought Mardian would give me an argument, but instead there was a long moment of silence.

"Time may prove you right," Mardian finally replied, and that's all he would say.

Before I left for New Hampshire, though, a day or two after I found myself locked out of my office, a small conference was held in the White House. My break with Hoover was the main topic of conversation, and President Nixon, John Mitchell, Robert Mardian, John Ehrlichman, and Bob Haldeman were among the participants. They found the whole incident embarrassing, and in order to avoid possible future embarrassment, they decided to get rid of Hoover once and for all; he would be told firmly to retire after Nixon was reelected. But Hoover died in May 1972, six months before the election. If I knew the egomaniacal old rogue was going to die less than a year after our quarrel, I would not have allowed our differences to surface.

After Hoover died, there was some talk of my returning to the FBI in some capacity. Richard Kleindienst, who succeeded Mitchell as attorney general, asked me to come to Washington to discuss the reorganization of the bureau. I remember sitting in Kleindienst's office before he stepped into the attorney general's post. He was on the telephone with Hoover. Kleindienst listened politely to the director at first, but as Hoover began to ramble on and on as usual, Kleindienst held the receiver away from his ear, looked at me, and pointed to his head with his finger. When Hoover finally wound down and hung up, Kleindienst said to me, "That man has been out of his mind for three years."

"Well," I answered, trying to be discreet, "I would say that he is out of touch with reality."

"That's the definition of insanity," Kleindienst replied. "How much longer do we have to put up with him?" he asked.

"That's up to you folks," I said, "It's not up to me."

When I met with Kleindienst to help him plan the future of the FBI, I made it clear that I didn't care what my title would be, as long as I had the authority to make my recommendations and be a part of any team that was formed to reorganize the bureau. Once that was accomplished, I would rejoin Marion and my children.

I told Kleindienst that I didn't think my part of the reorganization would take longer than six months, and that I didn't plan to stay in Washington longer than a year under any circumstances. Kleindienst led me to believe that my timetable would be no problem. But nothing ever came of our talk, or of my desire to help reform the bureau.

Early on the day that Hoover died, a friend who still worked at headquarters called to give me the news. He told me that word of his death had spread throughout the building even before the newspapers were out. "You know," he said, "something strange just happened in my office, something almost impossible to believe. We had a stack of letters waiting to be sent to Hoover's office for his signature and one of the young agents started up there just now to get Hoover to sign them. I told him 'Hoover's dead. Where are you going with that mail?' He said, 'To Hoover's office for his signature.' I repeated, 'Hoover's dead, he died early this morning.' The strange thing was that the young agent didn't stop. He just kept on going upstairs to Hoover's office . . . to get his signature."

APPENDIX A

Huston's Memo

Analysis and Strategy

Memorandum for H. R. Haldeman
From: Tom Charles Huston
Subject: Domestic intelligence review

1. *Background.*   A working group consisting of the top domestic intelligence officials of the F.B.I., C.I.A., D.I.A., N.S.A. and each of the military services met regularly throughout June to discuss the problems outlined by the President and to draft the attached report. The discussions were frank and the quality of work first-rate. Cooperation was excellent, and all were delighted that an opportunity was finally at hand to address themselves jointly to the serious internal security threat which exists.

I participated in all meetings, but restricted my involvement to keeping the committee on the target the President established. My impression [was] that the report would be more accurate and the recommendations more helpful if the agencies were allowed wide latitude in expressing their opinions and working out arrangements which they felt met the President's requirements consistent with the resources and mission of the member agencies.

2. *Mr. Hoover.*   I went into this exercise fearful that C.I.A. would refuse to cooperate. In fact, Dick Helms (Director of Central Intelligence) was most cooperative and helpful, and the only stumbling block was Mr. Hoover. He attempted at the first meeting to divert the committee from operational problems and redirect its mandate to the preparation of another analysis of existing intelligence. I declined to acquiesce in this approach, and succeeded in getting the committee back on target.

When the working group completed its report, Mr. Hoover refused to go along with a single conclusion drawn or support a single recommendation made. His position was twofold: (1) Current operations are perfectly satisfactory and (2) No one has any business commenting on procedures he has established for the collection of intelligence by the F.B.I. He attempted to modify the body of the report, but I successfully opposed it on the grounds that the report was the conclusion of all the agencies, not merely the F.B.I. Mr. Hoover then entered his objections as footnotes to the report. Cumulatively, his footnotes suggest that he is perfectly satisfied with current procedures and is opposed to any changes whatsoever. As you will note from the report, his objections are generally inconsistent and frivolous—most express concern about possible embarrassment to the intelligence community (i.e., Hoover) from public disclosure of clandestine operations.

Admiral Gayler and General Bennett were greatly displeased by Mr. Hoover's attitude and his insistence on footnoting objections. They wished to raise a formal protest and sign the report only with the understanding that they opposed the footnotes. I prevailed upon them not to do so since it would only aggravate Mr. Hoover and further complicate our efforts. They graciously agreed to go along with my suggestion in order to avoid a nasty scene and jeopardize the possibility of positive action resulting from the report. I assured them that their opinion would be brought to the attention of the President.

3. *Threat Assessment.*   The first 23 pages of the report constitute an assessment of the existing internal security threat, our current intelligence coverage of this threat, and areas where our coverage is inadequate. All agencies concurred in this assessment, and it serves to explain the importance of expanded intelligence collection efforts.

4. *Restraints on Intelligence Collection.*   Part Two of the report discusses specific operational restraints which currently restrict the capability of the intelligence community to collect the types of information necessary to deal effectively with the internal security threat. The report explains the nature of the restraints and sets the arguments for and against modifying them. My concern was to afford the President the strongest arguments on both sides of the question so that he could make an informed decision as to the future course of action to be followed by the intelligence community.

I might point out that of all the individuals involved in the preparation and consideration of this report, only Mr. Hoover is satisfied with existing procedures.

Those individuals with the F.B.I. who have day-to-day responsibilities for domestic intelligence operations privately disagree with Mr. Hoover and believe that it is imperative that changes in operating procedures be initiated at once.

I am attaching to this memorandum my recommendations on the decision the President should make with regard to these operational restraints. Although the report sets forth the pros and cons on each issue, it may be helpful to add my specific recommendations and the reasons therefor in the event the President has some doubts on a specific course of action.

5. *Improvement in Inter-Agency Coordination.*   All members of the committee and its working group, with the exception of Mr. Hoover agree it

is imperative that a continuing mechanism be established to effectuate the coordination of domestic intelligence efforts and the evaluation of domestic intelligence data. In the past there has been no systematic effort to mobilize the full resources of the intelligence community in the internal security area and there has been no mechanism for preparing community-wide domestic intelligence estimates such as is done in the foreign intelligence area by the United States Intelligence Board. Domestic intelligence information coming into the White House has been fragmentary and unevaluated. We have not had, for example, a community-wide estimate of what we might expect short or long-term in the cities or on the campuses or within the military establishment.

Unlike most of the bureaucracy, the intelligence community welcomes direction and leadership from the White House. There appears to be agreement, with the exception of Mr. Hoover, that effective coordination within the community is possible only if there is direction from the White House. Moreover, the community is pleased that the White House is finally showing interest in their activities and an awareness of the threat which they so acutely recognize.

I believe that we will be making a major contribution to the security of the country if we can work out an arrangement which provides for institutionalized coordination with the intelligence community and effective leadership from the White House.

6. *Implementation of the President's decisions.*   If the President should decide to lift some of the current·restrictions and if he should decide to authorize a formalized domestic intelligence structure, I would recommend the following steps:

(A) Mr. Hoover should be called in privately for a stroking session at which the President explains the decision he has made, thanks Mr. Hoover for his candid advice and past cooperation, and indicates he is counting on Edgar's cooperation in implementing the new de-report, announce his decisions [*sic*].

(B) Following this Hoover session, the same individuals who were present at the initial session in the Oval Office should be invited back to meet with the President. At that time, the President should thank them for the report, announce his decisions, indicate his desires for future activity, and present each with an autographed copy of the photo of the first meeting which Ollie took.

(C) An official memorandum setting forth the precise decisions of the President should be prepared so that there can be no misunderstanding. We should also incorporate a review procedure which will enable us to ensure that the decisions are fully implemented.

I hate to suggest a further imposition on the President's time, but think these steps will be necessary to pave over some of the obvious problems which may arise if the President decides, as I hope he will, to overrule Mr. Hoover's objections to many of the proposals made in this report. Having seen the President in action with Mr. Hoover, I am confident that he can handle this situation in such a way that we can get what we want without putting Edgar's nose out of joint. At the same time, we can capitalize on the good will the President has built up with the other principals and minimize the risk that they may feel they are being forced to take a back seat to Mr. Hoover.

7. *Conclusion.* I am delighted with the substance of this report and believe it is a first-rate job. I have great respect for the integrity, loyalty, and competence of the men who are operationally responsible for internal security matters and believe that we are on the threshold of an unexcelled opportunity to cope with a very serious problem in its germinal stages when we can avoid the necessity for harsh measures by acting swift, discreetly, and decisively to deflect the threat before it reaches alarming proportions.

I might add, in conclusion, that it is my personal opinion that Mr. Hoover will not hesitate to accede to any decision which the President makes, and the President should not, therefore, be reluctant to overrule Mr. Hoover's objections. Mr. Hoover is set in his ways and can be bull-headed as hell, but he is a loyal trooper. Twenty years ago he would never have raised the type of objections he has here, but he's getting old and worried about his legend. He makes life tough in this area, but not impossible—for he'll respond to direction by the President and that is all we need to set the domestic intelligence house in order.

RECOMMENDATIONS

TOP SECRET

Handle via Comint Channels Only
Operational Restraints on Intelligence Collection

A. *Interpretive Restraints on Communications Intelligence.*

RECOMMENDATION: Present interpretation should be broadened to permit and program for coverage by N.S.A. of the communications of U.S. citizens using international facilities.

RATIONALE: The F.B.I. does not have the capability to monitor international communications. N.S.A. is currently doing so on a restricted basis, and the information is particularly useful to the White House and it would be

Abbreviations used here include: B.N.D.D. (Bureau of Narcotics and Dangerous Drugs); C.I.A. (Central Intelligence Agency); C.P.U.S.A. (Communist Party U.S.A.); D.I.A. (Defense Intelligence Agency); F.B.I. (Federal Bureau of Investigation); I. & R. (Intelligence and Research); I.R.S. (Internal Revenue Service); N.S.A. (National Security Agency).

to our disadvantage to allow the F.B.I. to determine what N.S.A. should do in this area without regard to our own requirements. No appreciable risk is involved in this course of action.

B. *Electronic Surveillance and Penetrations.*

RECOMMENDATIONS: Present procedures should be changed to permit intensification of coverage of individuals and groups in the United States who pose a major threat to the internal security.

Also, present procedures should be changed to permit intensification of coverage of foreign nationals and diplomatic establishments in the United States of interest to the intelligence community.

At the present time, less than [unclear] electronic penetrations are operative. This includes coverage of the C.P.U.S.A. and organized crime targets, with only a few authorized against subject of pressing internal security interest.

Mr. Hoover's statement that the F.B.I. would not oppose other agencies seeking approval for the operating electronic surveillances is gratuitous since no other agencies have the capability.

Everyone knowledgeable in the field, with the exception of Mr. Hoover concurs that existing coverage is grossly inadequate. C.I.A. and N.S.A. note that this is particularly true of diplomatic establishments, and we have learned at the White House that it is also true of new Left groups.

C. *Mail Coverage.*

RECOMMENDATION: Restrictions on legal coverage should be removed.

Also, present restrictions on covert coverage should be relaxed on selected targets of priority foreign intelligence and internal security interest.

RATIONALE: There is no valid argument against use of legal mail covers except Mr. Hoover's concern that the civil liberties people may become upset. This risk is surely an acceptable one and hardly serious enough to justify denying ourselves a valuable and legal intelligence tool.

Covert coverage is illegal and there are serious risks involved. However, the advantages to be derived from its use outweigh the risks. This technique is particularly valuable in identifying espionage agents and other contacts of foreign intelligence services.

D. *Surreptitious Entry.*

RECOMMENDATION: Present restrictions should be modified to permit procurement of vitally needed foreign cryptographic material.

Also, present restrictions should be modified to permit selective use of this technique against other urgent security targets.

RATIONALE; Use of this technique is clearly illegal: it amounts to burglary. It is also highly risky and could result in great embarrassment if exposed. However, it is also the most fruitful tool and can produce the type of intelligence which cannot be obtained in any other fashion.

The F.B.I., in Mr. Hoover's younger days, used to conduct such operations with great success and with no exposure. The information secured was invaluable.

N.S.A. has a particular interest since it is possible by this technique to secure material with which N.S.A. can break foreign cryptographic codes. We spend millions of dollars attempting to break these codes by machine. One successful surreptitious entry can do the job successfully at no dollar cost.

Surreptitious entry of facilities occupied by subversive elements can turn up information about identities, methods of operation, and other invaluable investigative information which is not otherwise obtainable. This technique would be particularly helpful if used against the Weathermen and Black Panthers.

The deployment of the executive protector force has increased the risk of surreptitious entry of diplomatic establishments. However, it is the belief of all except Mr. Hoover that the technique can still be successfully used on a selective basis.

E. *Development of Campus Sources.*

RECOMMENDATION: Present restrictions should be relaxed to permit expanded coverage of violence-prone campus and student-related groups.

Also, C.I.A. coverage of American students (and others) traveling or living abroad should be increased.

RATIONALE: The F.B.I. does not currently recruit any campus sources among individuals below 21 years of age. This dramatically reduces the pool from which sources may be drawn. Mr. Hoover is afraid of a young student surfacing in the press as an F.B.I. source, although the reaction in the past to such events has been minimal. After all, everyone assumes the F.B.I. has such sources.

The campus is the battleground of the revolutionary protest movement. It is impossible to gather effective intelligence about the movement unless we have campus sources. The risk of exposure is minimal, and where exposure occurs the adverse publicity is moderate and short-lived. It is a price we must be willing to pay for effective coverage of the campus scene. The intelligence community, with the exception of Mr. Hoover, feels strongly that it is imperative the [was unclear] increase the number of campus sources this fall in order to forestall widespread violence.

C.I.A. claims there are not existing restraints on its coverage of overseas activities of U.S. nationals. However, this coverage has been grossly inadequate since 1965 and an explicit directive to increase coverage is required.

F. *Use of Military Undercover Agents.*

RECOMMENDATION: Present restrictions should be retained.

RATIONALE: The intelligence community is agreed that the risks of lifting these restraints are greater than the value of any possible intelligence which would be acquired by doing so.

BUDGET AND MANPOWER RESTRICTIONS

RECOMMENDATION: Each agency should submit a detailed estimate as to projected manpower needs and other costs in the event the various investigative restraints herein are lifted.

RATIONALE: In the event that the above recommendations are concurred in, it will be necessary to modify existing budgets to provide the money and manpower necessary for their implementation. The intelligence community has been badly hit in the budget squeeze. (I suspect the foreign intelligence operations are in the same shape) and it may be/will be necessary to make some modifications. The projected figures should be reasonable, but will be subject to individual review if this recommendation is accepted.

MEASURES TO IMPROVE DOMESTIC INTELLIGENCE OPERATIONS

RECOMMENDATION: A permanent committee consisting of the F.B.I., C.I.A., N.S.A., D.I.A. and the military counterintelligence agencies should be appointed to provide evaluations of domestic intelligence estimates, and carry out the other objectives specified in the report.

RATIONALE: The need for increased coordination, joint estimates, and responsiveness to the White House is obvious to the intelligence community. There are a number of operational problems which need to be worked out since Mr. Hoover is fearful of any mechanism which might jeopardize his autonomy. C.I.A. would prefer an ad hoc committee to see how the system works, but other members believe that this would merely delay the establishment of effective coordination and joint operations. The value of lifting intelligence collection restraints is proportional to the availability of joint operations and evaluation, and the establishment of this interagency group is considered imperative.

[*Note:* The above texts were published 7 June 1970 by the *New York Times*, without attribution as to source.]

APPENDIX B

Sullivan's Memo to John Dean

March 1, 1973

SECRET

Re: The Watergate Problem

In accordance with your request I have given this problem some thought. While it is probably unnecessary I would like to say first, that the concept underlying this operation, to put it mildly, reflected atrocious judgment and the implementation of the concept was even worse in its lack of professionalism and competency.

If I had been asked about this when it happened I would have strongly recommended that the President immediately establish a non-partisan commission to look into the matter. By doing this, it would dispel most suspicion and at the same time would give you some control and some direction over the work of the commission. I think it is now too late to do this because of the plans already made by Senator Ervin. There is no longer any choice of a forum.

At this time I would suggest, for what little value they have, if any, the following:

(1) us take a look at the elements in the problem. We have: (1) the breaking and entering of the building; (2) the applications of technical surveillances; and (3) the financing. It is possible that the financing might turn out to be the most serious and harmful element in the problem. If so, then this should be given primary consideration in setting up a defense.

(2) If the assumption is valid, that the Senator Ervin inquiry will be limited and relatively brief and more of a partisan political exercise than a serious probe, then it might be well to "sit tight," issue denials where they are valid and let the storm blow over (in a manner similar to range cattle who turn their backs, stand firm and are undisturbed while the fury of the gale spends itself harmlessly!!!). However, if the contrary assumption is the valid one, and this is going to be a very real and exhaustive investigation, then "sitting tight" would be the wrong tactic and a different course of action should be taken.

(3) it is going to be a harmful, exhaustive investigation, then I think it

would be well to hire one of the best legal minds in the country. He should be a man known publicly to be of great integrity, ability and professionalism and preferably a Democrat but not one who has engaged in Democratic politics. He should not be put on a government payroll but given a retainer fee. Every effort should be made in dealing with him to show the public that he is not identified with the Administration but is acting in a dispassionate, professional manner, and that he has no ties of any kind with the Administration. I believe that this would completely eliminate the obvious disadvantages of having the lawyer enter the matter who is already on the government payroll and identified with the current administration.

(4) not this man have a privileged attorney–client relationship? If so, this could be an advantage.

(5) lawyer should not have to deal with a number of individuals but only one or two men in high authority ("too many cooks spoil the broth").

(6) It is suggested that another man also be engaged to assist this lawyer. He should be a person who is extremely knowledgeable concerning the United States Senate and its members and not unacquainted with the Washington "jungle."

(7) It is suggested that when Senator Ervin commences his probe that Ron Ziegler issue a very clear, forceful and carefully constructed statement in representing the President, condemning again the Watergate activities and saying that he has instructed all concerned in the government to give their complete and willing cooperation to Senator Ervin and his colleagues.

(8) It would seem best that no issues be avoided; that each one be faced openly, briefly and without equivocation; that all possible should be done to move the inquiry along just as rapidly as possible so that it can be fully terminated in a short period of time.

(9) Naturally there will be some efforts to link the Watergate affair with the highest authorities in the White House and even to the President. Therefore, I think the main thrust of the thought given to this problem and the major positions taken should have one main purpose, expressly, to protect the President and the Office from any machinations or aspersions which would be harmful to both and a gross injustice to our Executive Branch.

(10) If worse comes to worse, bearing in mind the main objectives stated above, those involved in the Watergate affair should be considered expendable in the best interests of the country. Their culpability should be set forth in its entirety thereby directing the attention of the probers and the attention of the reading public away from the White House and to the men themselves where the blame belongs. In the position that I once occupied there were some operations necessary to carry out wither to save lives or to protect national security which were highly risky in an official sense. Those of us who carried them out did so fully understanding that if something went wrong we were expendable because values and processes far more important

than we must not be damaged. I assume that the men engaged in the Watergate affair see their problem in the same prospective.

(11) One last thought—I alluded earlier to the financial element in this problem. I do not know enough about it to make any comments here. However, if it is as serious as I think it could be then those fully knowledgeable in this area should give the matter the most searching thought possible. Much more harm could be done here than in the area of the other two elements, namely breaking and entering and possessing and using electronic surveillance devices.

(12) Lastly, the above observations have been made without having read the results of the investigation. If you think I can be of any further assistance by reading in your office the investigation reports, in whole or in part, I will, of course, do so.

APPENDIX C

The Final Hoover–Sullivan Correspondence

FEDERAL BUREAU OF INVESTIGATION
UNITED STATES DEPARTMENT OF JUSTICE

REPORT OF PERFORMANCE RATING

Name of Employee: _____ WILLIAM C. SULLIVAN _____

Where Assigned: EXECUTIVE OFFICE _____
          (Division)   (Section, Unit)

Official Position Title and Grade: ASSISTANT TO THE DIRECTOR-INVESTIGATIVE

Rating Period: from APRIL 1, 1970 _____ to MARCH 31, 1971 _____

ADJECTIVE RATING: _____ OUTSTANDING _____ Employee's
          Outstanding, Excellent, Satisfactory, Unsatisfactory   Initials

Rated by: *Clyde a. Tolson* Associate Director 4/1/71
              Signature   Title   Date

Reviewed by: _____
              Signature   Title   Date

Rating Approved by: *J. Edgar Hoover* Director 4/1/71
              Signature   Title   Date

TYPE OF REPORT

[X] Official   ☐ Administrative
  [X] Annual   ☐ 60-Day
                        ☐ 90-Day
                        ☐ Transfer
                        ☐ Separation from Service
                        ☐ Special

OFFICE OF THE DIRECTOR

UNITED STATES DEPARTMENT OF JUSTICE

FEDERAL BUREAU OF INVESTIGATION

WASHINGTON, D.C. 20535

September 3, 1971

PERSONAL ATTENTION

Dear Mr. Sullivan:

      I have given, as you know, very careful attention to your letter of August 28, followed by a lengthy conference with you concerning it's contents.

      It has been apparent to me that your views concerning my administration and policies in the Bureau do not meet with your approval or satisfaction, and has brought about a situation which, though I regret, is intolerable for the best functioning of the Bureau.

      Therefore I suggest that you submit your application for retirement to take effect at the close of business after you have had such leave to which you are entitled.

Very truly yours,

J. Edgar Hoover

Mr. William C. Sullivan
Federal Bureau of Investigation
Washington, D. C.

September 9, 1971

Honorable John Edgar Hoover
Director
Federal Bureau of Investigation
Washington, D. C.

Dear Mr. Hoover:

Please refer to your letter to me of
September 8, 1971. Thank you very much for suggest-
ing that I take leave from September 13 through
October 1, 1971.

As I understand it, the rule is that I am
not to take annual leave while one of my Assistant
Directors is on leave, even though Mr. Rosen may be
here. I would not want to violate this rule, if it
can be avoided. Further, in this particular instance,
Assistant Director Rosen will also be on leave, from
September 13 through 15, 1971. Additionally, I think
it would be quite unfair to the Bureau for me to be
gone while Mr. Sterling Donahoe of this office is
away, at the same time Mr. Rosen and Mr. Conrad are
in leave status.

I certainly don't want to put my personal
considerations above the Bureau's interests. In
view of this, I will take the liberty of declining
your offer, and will commence the leave you suggested
on September 27th. I think you will agree that this
is the most responsible, just, and smoothest way
in which to handle the situation.

Sincerely,

William C Sullivan

*I would prefer to have
you take the leave as I
suggested - The next in
rank in the Investigative
Div can serve on your
desk. H*

UNITED STATES DEPARTMENT OF JUSTICE

FEDERAL BUREAU OF INVESTIGATION

WASHINGTON, D.C. 20535

September 30, 1971

PERSONAL ATTENTION

Mr. William C. Sullivan
Federal Bureau of Investigation
Washington, D. C.

Dear Mr. Sullivan:

Since you have not as yet responded to my
suggestion in my letter of September 3, 1971, you are
hereby being relieved of all duties as Assistant to the
Director at once and placed on annual leave pending
your submission of application for retirement.

I deeply regret the occasion to take action
such as this after so many years of close association,
but I believe it necessary in the public interest. Your
recently demonstrated and continuing unwillingness to
reconcile yourself to, and officially accept, final
administrative decision on problems concerning which
you and other Bureau officials so often present me with
a variety of conflicting views has resulted in an incom-
patability so fundamental that it is detrimental to the
harmonious and efficient performance of our public duties.

Very truly yours,

J. Edgar Hoover

John Edgar Hoover
Director

Mr. J. Edgar Hoover
4936 Thirtieth Place, N.W.
Washington, D.C.

2810 64th Avenue
Cheverly, Maryland
October 6, 1971

Dear Mr. Hoover:

Please refer to your letters to me of September 3 and September 30, 1971. You state that I have not replied to your letter of September 3. In the light of our conversations this letter did not require a reply. However, as long as you want a response I will give you one now even though it is after the fact. This letter I am sending to your home in order that you may hold it privately for as you are aware the Bureau has become a bit of a sieve and this letter if seen would be the subject of gossip which, I am sure, we both wish to avoid.

First, I wish to say this complete break with you has been truly an agonizing one for me. You well know how fond I am of the Bureau and its work. To some degree this is the paradox for it is over this fact the rupture has risen. By this I mean the damage you are doing the Bureau and its work has brought all this on, but more of this later. At this time I want to again thank you for the support you have given me in the past and in particular when I was quite ill in Arizona years ago from a respiratory ailment. In the years now gone we have enjoyed some good conversations and some hearty laughter. I think you will agree I have with enthusiasm always, as time mounted, accepted every special assignment, dangerous or non-dangerous given me by you and carried them out to the best of my ability. We have had a reasonably close relationship and this is why it is so tragic for it to have ended as it did. It is regretted changes could not have been made to prevent it.

I will now turn to your letter of September 30, 1971, in which you say you are, in substance, forcing me into retirement for the sake of "public interest." May I suggest this is one of your minor faults—overstatement and overkill. More relevant is your charge that I have been unwilling to accept "final administrative decisions." This is not true and you know it. You cannot cite one instance where I have refused to carry out your instructions even when I disagreed with them vigorously and wholly. But, this leads to larger issues which I wish to discuss with you.

Many times I have told you what I think is right and good about the FBI, but now I will set forth what I think is wrong about it hoping that something worthwhile will come out of it. I want to make it clear that I am not blaming all these faults upon you. All of us in high places around you must also bear our share of the blame. One might call it a collective responsibility.

No. 1   *Concealment of the Truth and All the Facts from the People of this Nation who have a Right to Know*

A very good and serious example of this is the Communist Party of the United States. In the mid-forties when the membership of the Party was about 80,000 and it had many front organizations you publicized this widely month in and month out. In fact it was far too widely publicized to the point where you caused a Communist scare in the Nation which was entirely unwarranted. You had your staff of writers in the Crime Records Division (a "front" of your own to conceal our huge public relations and propaganda operations which no government Bureau should have) turning out hundreds of articles on the great "dangers of" and "serious threat" of Communism to our national security. You never seemed to be that concerned with organized crime. I am just as much opposed to Communism as you but I knew then and I know now that it was not the danger you claimed it was and that it never warranted the huge amounts of the taxpayer's dollar spent upon it. I stand condemned for not making an issue of it at that time. What happened when the Communist Party went into a rapid decline? You kept the scare campaign going just the same for some years. However, when the membership figures kept dropping lower and lower you instructed us not to give them out to the public any more and not even to the Justice Department. I told you at one time we should publish the low figures and let the Bureau get credit for a job well done and point out how successfully Communism can be met in a democratic society but you would have none of it. At the time of my leaving the Bureau this week the membership figures of the Communist Party are down to an amazing 2800 in a nation of over 200 million people and you still conceal this from the people. Of the 2800 only about half are active and wholly ineffective. I think it is a terrible injustice to the citizens and an unethical thing for you to do to conceal this important truth from the public. You keep complaining that in my lectures I downgrade the Communist Party. Had I remained in the Bureau any longer I would, contrary to your instructions, have told the public about the tiny 2800 membership of the Communist Party. I stand condemned for not doing so before, despite your instructions not to do so. You will recall that on October 12, 1970, speaking before the conference of UPI Editors at Williamsburg I told them the Party was not the cause of and did not direct or control the racial and student unrest in the Nation. On my return to Headquarters you were furious and gave me hell for what you called "downgrading the Communist Party" and you raised with me how were you going to get appropriations wanted if I kept doing that. We do not need to get appropriations that way. Further, if there is no longer a Communist problem we should not spend money on it. In fact, I have for some years been taking men off Communist work in the field and here at Headquarters and putting them on some important work.

No. 2 *Communism and the Protestant Clergy*

While on this subject of Communism I want to take you to task for often implying that the Protestant clergy of this nation were infiltrated by the Communists. This is not true. You have harmed and treated most unjustly a fine body of loyal men. Granted that a handful in the past did have some Communist connections (most unwittingly) and others joined some Communist fronts when such fronts were new and people unfamiliar with them. But this does not constitute infiltration and compared to the total number of Protestant clergymen the number was insignificant. You never did highlight the outstanding Protestant clergymen who were among the most effective anti-Communist leaders in the country. As you know, on our "special list" relative to an emergency in this country we never did have more than about a dozen clergymen and none of these belonged to any of the major denominations. I think this is a remarkable tribute to the Protestant clergy. Granting the freedom of thought and action which is the essence of Protestantism one would think far more would have been misled by Communist propaganda but they were not. Instead of smearing them, all credit should go to them. I could never understand why you caused this trouble among the clergy, dividing one branch from another all over an issue that did not exist. The kind of misleading propaganda you gave out was picked up by Carl McIntyre and others like him to attack innocent members of the Protestant clergy who did not see theology as he did.

No. 3 *The National Council of Churches in Christ*

You never liked this fine organization and berated me on at least one occasion for defending it against absurd charges of pro-Communist sympathies and alleged Communist connections. It never had either. There never was a Communist on its staff as some wild allegations had it. You condemned Lou Cassel, then a religious editor with the UPI, because he said in my lectures I had defended the Council and clergy against false charges of Communism. You will recall your "blue ink" notation that he was "a dangerous man" and after that we did not think it even safe to maintain contact with him.

No. 4 *Senator Joseph McCarthy and Yourself*

More than one of us at the Bureau were disturbed when you identified yourself with Senator McCarthy and his irresponsible anti-Communist campaign. His method was not the method which should be used to combat Communism and he did grave damage to national security in the sense that reflective men said if this is anti-Communism I want none of it. Yet, you had us preparing material for him regularly, kept furnishing it to him while you denied publicly that we were helping him. And you have done the same thing with others. This is wrong and one day the "chickens may come home to roost."

No. 5   *Your book Masters of Deceit*

As you know I had a number of men working for many months writing this book for you. Contrary to what you have said it was not done on private time. It was done on public time, during the day at the taxpayers' expense. This is why I recommended to you that the profit from it be given to some heart or cancer research association. But it wasn't and not only until recently did I learn that you put some thousands of dollars in your own pocket and Tolson likewise got a share and some into the Fund. All of it should have gone to charity or medical research. Do you realize the amount of agent time that was spent not only in writing the book but on advertising and publicizing it all around the country. All our field offices were told to push it. They went to their contacts, local newspapers and the like to run the sales up. We even wrote reviews here at the Headquarters which were sent to the field to have printed by different papers. We had a joke about it of this nature: "If Hoover wrote or had written for him a book on calculus with this kind of promotion it, too, would be a best seller." And, of course, *Masters of Deceit* was. Another joke around the Bureau was: "Hoover not only did not write the book, he even did not read it." As I look back upon it now, it was a demoralizing experience. The same was true with the second book we wrote: *A Study of Communism.* In this case I recommended that the proceeds be given to George Washington University to set up a scholarship in your name. Again you were not interested in giving anything away even though, as in the past, I had a number of men work for months each day writing this book. This time the proceeds, as far as I know, went into the somewhat mysterious Fund, the inner workings of which were held with such security it was hard to learn anything about it.

No. 6   *The FBI and the Negro*

For good reason we used to be referred to as the "Lily White" FBI. We should have hired Negro agents and clerks many years ago but you absolutely refused. Years ago you told me yourself you were opposed to it adamantly, and the remark was attributed to you: "There will never be a Negro Special Agent as long as I am Director of the FBI." This is not only prejudice of the worst kind it is also poor leadership and impractical. You know well, especially in recent years, we could not properly discharge our responsibilities in Negro Communities, therefore, more than one federal crime over which we had jurisdiction went uninvestigated. It is no wonder that the average Negro does not like the FBI. He had no reason to. Police departments in the south had the good judgment to hire Negro police officers long before we did. I tried a test case years ago and tried to get the son (college graduate) of an elevator lady (colored) hired as a special agent. I failed. He was turned down. The Department of Justice had to push you into hiring

Negro agents. Your defense at the time was you had some Negro special agents, 4 or 5. Of course you did. They were your chauffeurs who were made special agents by you during the War so they would not be drafted. Then there were one or two you inherited when you became Director in 1924 but what kind of work did he do and how many times did he come to retraining? It was all a farce until you were forced reluctantly to hire blacks. On leaving this week we have well over 50 field offices and not one has a Negro as Special Agent in Charge, or Assistant Special Agent in Charge or one among the supervisors. It is the same at the Headquarters. Not a Negro is an Assistant Director, an Inspector, a Section Chief, etc. We have some 8000 men and, as I recall, still only 70 odd Negro special agents. This is one of the most shameful chapters in the history of the FBI. The same is true of our many foreign liaison offices around the world. Not a one had a Negro Legal Attaché or Assistant Legal Attaché.

No. 7   *FBI and the Police Departments*

As you must know, we are not at all well-liked by the police departments around the country with some exceptions. They complain that it is a one-way street. We take everything from them, and give nothing, that we steal credit from them, deliberately overshadow them, etc. If it was not for the excellent personal friendships built up by our field office special agents with the police, conditions would be far worse. When I say disliked, I mean the official policy of the FBI toward the police, our headquarters' attitude, not the special agent in the field. The FBI National Academy to train police is one of the finest things you have done, yet until recent years it was not regarded highly by police who came in from large departments. When I was single I roomed at the same place with many of them when they were in Washington. Almost without exception they had a low opinion as to its practical worth for them. I remember a man from Los Angeles saying they had a far better training school than the FBI Academy. But, he said he was satisfied to come here because the FBI diploma from our Academy was valuable to him and would help to promote him. He laughed and said he was certainly not going to let out the "secret" of its low quality instruction and hurt himself and fellow class members, who, according to him felt the same as he did. He pointed out that men from very small police departments might get some practical value from the course but not any person from medium sized departments up. With our new quarters and training facilities at Quantico this has all been corrected. But, why was the old inadequate situation allowed to prevail for so many years? It was the same with the few officers from foreign nations who attended. I talked to some of them. They complained no special courses were set up for them; that courses geared only to police needs in the United States had very limited use for them. This, too, recently has been corrected but more needs to be done here if we are to train any large numbers of them. Lastly, and the most important point, is this: the FBI should not try to dominate the police (as we were repeatedly told to do in our In-Training class) but should cooperate and treat them as equals and wherever possible let them take the credit and publicity for cases worked in common. We should stay in the background. Why do we need to grab the headlines? If we did this, we would find police departments all over the nation anxious to give us all possible help and our war against crime would be far more effective than it is now. One more point, the police never liked recovering stolen automobiles then having our men on your instructions go down to where the cars were, take down all the basic statistics, set a recovery value (the highest possible) then have you, at the end of the year, total all this and take claim for so many cars recovered that were stolen, and the total value of them. Here was the FBI taking credit for what the police had actually done.

No. 8   *FBI and Members of the Intelligence Community*

We all know our intelligence product is not too good and never has been. You want the FBI to have as little to do jointly as possible with other members of the community. It is suggested this be changed. We should pool our assets in behalf of national security.

No. 9   *FBI and CIA*

This is, of course, related to the above. You have always been hostile toward CIA despite the usual polite exchange of letters. We should work very closely together in every respect, pool assets, work cases jointly where the facts warrant, etc. Breaking direct liaison with CIA was not rational.

No. 10   *FBI and Illegal Agents in the United States*

This is one of our most serious and harmful security problems in the United States today. Yet you abolished our main programs designed to identify and neutralize the enemy agents. I just cannot understand this. It simply is not a rational thing to do. This is one of your acts that led me to take a strong stand against you for I am convinced you are seriously damaging our national security. You know the high number of illegal agents operating along the east coast alone. As of this week, the week I am leaving the FBI for good, we have not identified *even one of them.* These illegal agents, as you know, are engaged, among other things, in securing the secrets of our defense in the event of a military attack so that our defense will amount to nothing. Mr. Hoover are you thinking? Are you really capable of thinking this through? Don't you realize we are betraying our government and people by abolishing programs to protect them from enemy illegal agents? Now that I am gone you do not have to save face anymore by holding out against what I recommend. Please reconsider and start those programs again. I must say again I just cannot understand you. I do not know what is the matter with you that you should do such a thing.

No. 11 *FBI and Security Investigations*

I think we have been conducting far too many investigations called security which are actually political. This is our policy and it should be changed at once. What I mean is investigations mainly of students, professors, intellectuals and their organizations concerned with peace, anti-war, etc. We have no business doing this. Now, if there are definitely subversives (a word that always bothered me, hard to define) among them seeking to violate our laws, all well and good, investigate them as individuals but with great care so as not to smear the organization they are with. Just think of the time and money we have wasted on nothing but political investigations. Is it any wonder so many students and professors detest the FBI. I am not the only one who thinks this. Many, many field office agents think the same and some have resigned and commented about it.

No. 12 *FBI and Organized Crime*

Here is where we should concentrate more time, money and brains. It was not so many years ago we refused to admit the existence of the Mafia or Cosa Nostra. In fact, the Criminal Division said it did not exist in this country. You will remember the monograph which I had charge of preparing which definitely proved from our own files that it did exist. You will recall the big meeting of the nation's top hoodlums at Apalachin—over 30 in number. Was it not astonishing that we in the FBI had no idea they were to meet and did not know who they were? We had to then put on a big public relations show to indicate how much we did "know" and how much we had done in the field and how much we had helped the police to get convictions. It was accepted. Our public relations operations with all 50 odd field offices working with Headquarters has no equal anywhere. With all our mistakes and poor work we could never have survived without it. Incidently, remember the monograph on the Mafia that was sent to the Department before you really knew the dynamite that was in it? You then ordered that we get it back from the Department quickly before the higher officials knew about it. Also, do you recall it did not at first go to the field offices because you did not want the agents to know the unpleasant truth?

No. 13 *FBI and the Inbred Situation*

May I suggest we are much too inbred. We have been talking to ourselves and about ourselves and for ourselves for years and years. This is not good. It hinders progress and keeping abreast of things. There have been improvements of some importance in recent years but why did it take so long. We have no monopoly on brains. On hard unsolved problems let us use the best brains which are available to us both inside and outside of government. As I have said we have improved much in recent years but far more can be done.

No. 14   *FBI and our Statistics*

We all know they have never been either definitive or wholly reliable. More than one scholar has pointed this out down through the years and instead of appreciating their interest we looked upon them as enemies to be attacked. Why do we have such an attitude? Is it because long years ago you projected the image of infallibility and now you are stuck with it? No one is infallible and he who takes this position is doomed to be exposed and taken apart sooner or later. To return to our statistics, in many instances we came up with about any thing you wanted. The story has long been told in the FBI that one year when you were testifying you were asked the cost of crime in the United States and you replied 22 billion. According to the account, it was 11 billion based on our scanty statistics. The men said now what will we do for the Director is wrong. One enterprising young supervisor said we have no problem at all. Just multiply the 11 billion by two and you have established the correctness of the Director's figures. So 22 billion it was for years until some taxpayer wrote in and said he noted that for some years the cost of crime remained constant at 22 billion and how could that be? Needless to say it started to change and move up from that time on. What the new figures were based on I do not know. It is suggested that we get some of the most brilliant statisticians in the country on contract and set a real and useful statistical system.

No. 15   *FBI and Domestic Liaison*

The abrupt abolishment of our Liaison system is another example of a decision which was not rational. It is a badly needed Section. If the Liaison section is not necessary then it was poor administration on your part to keep it in existence all these years. If it is necessary then it is bad administration on your part to abolish it as you did. Think it over.

No. 16   *FBI and Foreign Liaison*

I have discussed this with you in my August letter and will say no more other than to stress the great waste of taxpayers' money in maintaining so many needless offices in foreign nations. We need Ottawa, Mexico City, London, Paris and possibly Hong Kong, but all the others could be gradually phased out. The few leads we need covered can be done by CIA and the State Department as they are done now in nations where we have no FBI offices. We could save a couple of million dollars at once and more later.

No. 17 *The FBI and Jewish Applicants*

You know well we have avoided hiring Jewish agents and this must stop. In over 8000 agents how many are Jewish? Very few, a relative handful. We have over 50 Special Agents in Charge and to my knowledge none are Jewish. We have the same number of Assistant Special Agents in Charge and to my knowledge none are Jewish. The only Legal Attaché abroad who is Jewish is the one in Israel. How many Jewish field office supervisors do we have? How many Jewish supervisors at Headquarters do we have out of the hundreds thereP It seems to be the unwritten policy. I recommended a Jewish youth some years ago for Special Agent and finally got him in. You have always had one Jewish official up front for people to see. Years ago it was a Mr. Nathan I am told. In my time it was Al Rosen. Let us take a look at the Headquarters officials. How many Assistants to the Director have been Jewish? In my time none until you moved up Al Rosen. How many Assistant Directors are Jewish? None to my knowledge. How many inspectors do we have who are Jewish? How many Section Chiefs do we have who are Jewish? Mr. Hoover, before it is too late, I suggest you change this situation. It is no use to ask the few Jewish employees about it for they will have to agree with whatever you want. Years ago a Jewish agent told me in the FBI you don't stress your Jewish origin in whole or in part. Again, you should correct this.

No. 18 *Free Services at Your Home*

Whether you know it or not there has always been critical comment about the free services year in and year out you receive at your home which the taxpayer pays for. For example, the building of the porch on your home, the care by the laboratory of all electrical appliances, etc. The expensive gifts you received, as you know, caused grumbling and, in fact, years ago I believe letters were sent to the press complaining. The furniture bought for Mr. Tolson came in for caustic comment though done years ago. Your $30,000 cars and your taking money for the books that the men wrote have all been criticized. I think you should stop all this for your own good. You have always told us: "It is not enough to be right. You must look right also."

No. 19 *FBI and the Budget*

Our budget goes up each year. Does it really need to? Why not take a good hard look at it. It could easily be reduced by 2 or 3 million dollars in one year. We are very, very wasteful in some ways. We have become accustomed to luxury. We should return to that which is necessary only.

No. 20 *FBI and TWA*

I could never understand your decision and other ones in these matters. They just did not make sense. Why do you do these things? It causes unnecessary turmoil and hurts us in getting the work done.

No. 21 *FBI and Infallibility*

I mentioned this once before briefly. Here I want to say this. Our effort (though you may deny it) to create the impression in the mind of the American people that we are infallible, perfect and sort of superhuman has over the years done us far more harm than good. Why can't we take a cold, factual, sensible position and set forth where necessary what we have done that is right and good, and also set forth our mistakes when we make them and what was wrong with our action. We would be respected far more. Often we have gone into long-winded explanations as to why we were not wrong when actually we were. Truth needs no lengthy explanation. We have wasted much time and money arguing and defending ourselves when a brief, simple statement of our error would have paid us richer dividends. Let us get away from infallibility and present ourselves as ordinary human beings trying to do the best job possible but not always succeeding.

No. 22 *The Half Truth*

Related to item 21 is our propaganda. Let us dispense with it. We tell the public with much flourish how many fugitives we catch in a given year but we do not tell them how many we failed to catch and remain to be caught. We tell about all cases we solve in a year but do we say anything about those we failed to solve? In short, we publish all our successes but say nothing about our failures. Any organization can look good with this system. True, some of our failures do get out but I am talking about the ones we say nothing about. Now there is nothing really sinister about this, it is simply the system which has grown up over the years and it is time to change. No one is really at fault. It is just something which slowly develops and remains until it is challenged, thought about and changed. The main point is the people of a country are entitled to the whole truth not just a part of it.

No. 23 *FBI, Public Relations, Propaganda*

Reference has been made in passing to the above. All I want to say here is this: no government Bureau should spend the vast sums of money on public relations and propaganda as we have done and still do. If we do outstanding work that is all which is necessary. It will speak for itself. It is only when work is mediocre that extensive public relations and propaganda are necessary. Everyone of 50 odd offices has its own program all linked to the central one here at Headquarters. Take the correspondence desk for example. Why should taxpayers' money be spent answering letters as how you like to have your steak done, or what is your favorite recipe for popovers, etc. Yet this has been done for years and years. I strongly urge all this be eliminated.

No. 24   *The Hoover Legend and Mythology*

As you know you have become a legend in your lifetime with a surrounding mythology linked to incredible power. This is not good for either you or the Bureau. It is not all your fault. I share a responsibility here and so do all other officials. We did all possible to build up your legend. We kept away from anything which would disturb you and kept flowing into your office what you wanted to hear. Let us face it—everyone knew of your ego. This type of thing had gone on I was told long before I entered the FBI in 1941. One official followed in the footsteps of the other and so it was year after year. Gifts, letters of great praise on your many anniversaries, your return from west coast and Florida trips, which you did not call vacations but inspection trips and annual physical examinations, and any other occasion which would justify a letter. You may not know this but I would get a call from some official and he would say "do you know that so and so has just written the Director a flowery letter on his appearance on the Hill." The word went out at once and then all officials would write you a similar letter. This was all part of the game but it got to be a deadly game that has accomplished no good. All we did was to help to put you out of touch with the real world and this could not help but have a bearing on your decisions as the years went by. This is why I say you are not to be blamed for all of this. All the officials around you like myself down through the years must share the blame.

No. 25   *Military Leave*

A few years ago I could see the beginning of the breakup of the FBI. At first I did not admit it even to myself. I made excuses. I rationalized. I turned aside from the obvious. At last I had to face up to reality. You had abolished vital programs, your decisions were fouling up other operations and I decided I could better serve my country in the army and I wrote to you and said I would like military leave to go to Vietnam. This was a time when many of our young soldiers were getting ambushed and killed because of a lack of good intelligence, I was told. You made it clear you did not want me to take military leave so I dropped the idea. I wonder how much different it all would have been if you said "yes go ahead." No use now of speculating about it.

No. 26   *Leaks of Sensitive Material*

Mr. Hoover, you have regularly told the public FBI files are secure, inviolate, almost sacred. Years ago when I first discovered this was not true at all I was stunned. But, we had created in time a certain atmosphere in the FBI difficult to describe and one learns to live with what one learns, both good and bad. We have leaked information improperly, as you know, on both persons and organizations. My first recollection was leaking information about Mrs. Eleanor Roosevelt whom you detested. And so it was year after year right up to our leaking the investigation on the killing of President John F. Kennedy and thereafter to the present. This should also stop.

No. 27 *FBI and Politics*

This topic I have saved until the last because it has done more than anything else to bring on my disillusionment with the FBI. Like so many young men before I entered the FBI I thought the FBI was the epitome of purity and that you were about as flawless a leader that can be found. I held on to this belief while I was in the field offices despite stories told me by old agents. I held on to it for a long time after I returned to Headquarters as a supervisor. This again despite stories circulated that the FBI was the most political agency in government and that you were completely immersed with politics with every administration. I do not have to go into detail. I saw example after example of how you willingly served any powerful figure in an influential office. While you are extremely conservative yourself I noticed it did not matter whether the political figure was liberal or conservative, if it served your cuds, you were eager to act. It did not matter whether it was a Republican or a Democrat or whether the Administration in power was Republican or Democrat. I saw clearly at last that the FBI always presented to the American public as non-political, as being outside, above and beyond politics, was just the contrary. It was immersed in politics and even went so far as to conduct purely political investigations and inquiries. At times, it seemed that when we were not asked to perform politically we sought opportunities to do so. I was so concerned about this under Mr. Johnson's administration that I wrote you a letter and expressed my concern and urged that the FBI not be used politically. Again, you are not the sole blame here. We who helped you inside the Bureau to carry out such activities must share the blame. And, the politicians who used the FBI must also share the blame.

Final Observation

Mr. Hoover, you know this was not an easy letter for me to write, both physically and psychologically. The first is true because as you can see I am no typist so please pardon the mistakes and organization. The second is true because we have been friends and worked together for years even though our views often differed. The hardest decision I have ever made in my lifetime was the decision in July to take a stand and break with you hoping that some good would come out of it for the Bureau, not for me because I would be leaving. It was a last resort. You know well I tried in every proper way to bring about the badly needed changes. You did away with vital programs. You falsely accused me of writing the two fine letters which Sam J. Papich, former liaison with CIA, had written trying to prevent you from further damaging the Bureau. I never wrote these letters but I would have been proud to have done so and had you listened to Mr. Papich, one of the finest and most able men this Bureau ever had, we would not be in the horrible condition we are in today and there would have been no need of my writing this letter to you. Like myself, Mr. Papich was most fond of the Bureau but he saw it was deteriorating and tried to prevent it. After the reception his two fine letters received he knew the cause was hopeless and retired. Perhaps I should have done the same thing at the time but I still clung to the hope that changes could be brought about orderly and quietly and once more the Bureau would be moving ahead and doing what the people thought it had been doing all along.

Once again I want to say, Mr. Hoover, we are not blaming you alone. We were all part of your staff for years. We all share the blame and responsibility. This is no time for anger, recriminations or vindictiveness. There is still time to bring about the progressive changes needed. I am gone now so you do not have me any longer as a "thorn in your flesh." Why don't you sit down quietly by yourself and think this all over and then get some of the men together and work out a plan to reform, reorganize and modernize the Bureau. If you do not give reality to what to some degree has become a bubble that bubble will burst and it will be bad for all. You can still do it if you will only see the situation as it actually is and then act. It is an internal situation and it need not even get into the press. Just handle it quietly in a professional manner. This is what I hope you will do.

Mr. Hoover, if for reasons of your own you cannot or will not do this may I gently suggest you retire for your good, that of the Bureau, the intelligence community and law enforcement. More than once I told you never to retire; to stay on to the last, that you would live longer being active. It looks now that I may have been wrong. For if you cannot do what is suggested above you really ought to retire and be given the recognition due you after such a long and remarkable career in government.

Sincerely yours,
[signed]   William C. Sullivan

Index